Changing Attitudes to Punishment

Changing Attitudes to Punishment

Public opinion, crime and justice

**Edited by Julian V. Roberts
and Mike Hough**

WILLAN
PUBLISHING

Published by

Willan Publishing
Culmcott House
Mill Street, Uffculme
Cullompton, Devon
EX15 3AT, UK
Tel: +44(0)1884 840337
Fax: +44(0)1884 840251
E-mail: info@willanpublishing.co.uk
Website: @www.willanpublishing.co.uk

Published simultaneously in the USA and Canada by

Willan Publishing
c/o ISBS, 5824 N.E. Hassalo St,
Portland, Oregon 97213-3644, USA
Tel: +001(0)503 287 3093
Fax: +001(0)503 280 8832
Website: www.isbs.com

First published 2002

ISBN 1-84392-002-6 (paper)
ISBN 1-84392-003-4 (cased)

British Library Cataloguing-in-Publication Data
A catalogue record for this book is available from the British Library

Typeset by TW Typesetting, Plymouth, Devon
Project Management by Deer Park Productions, Tavistock, Devon
Printed and bound by T J International Ltd, Trecerus Industrial Estate, Padstow, Cornwall

Contents

List of figures

List of tables

Acknowledgements

Most of the chapters in this volume originated in presentations made at a conference held at Southwark Cathedral on Friday, 7 December 2001. The conference was attended by about 50 individuals whose participation contributed to the subsequent chapters. The conference was funded by the Esmée Fairbairn Foundation. Finally, the event could not have been taken place without the contributions of Sîan Turner; we are accordingly most grateful for her assistance on that occasion and in the subsequent preparation of this volume.

Julian V. Roberts and Mike Hough
South Bank University, London
September 2002

About the authors

Rob Allen joined the Esmée Fairbairn Foundation in January 2001, directing 'Rethinking Crime and Punishment', a three-year project about public attitudes to imprisonment and other forms of punishment. Rob was previously director of Research and Development at Nacro where he was responsible for the organisation's work on crime reduction, youth justice and mental health as well as its fundraising department.

Brandon K. Applegate, PhD University of Cincinnati, is Associate Professor of Criminal Justice at the University of Central Florida. His research interests include public opinion about crime and punishment, the effectiveness of correctional treatment and decision-making among criminal justice professionals.

Francis T. Cullen, PhD Columbia University, is Distinguished Research Professor of Criminal Justice at the University of Cincinnati. His research interests include correctional policy, public opinion about rehabilitation, measuring sexual victimisation and building a social support theory of crime.

John Doble is founder of Doble Research Associates, a public interest consulting firm that explores public and leadership attitudes on crime and corrections and on other policy issues. Formerly vice president and research director at Public Agenda, Mr Doble is a political scientist with a Masters Degree from the University of Delaware. He has published widely, for example in *Foreign Affairs* (with Daniel Yankelovich), *Judicature* and *The Scientist*.

Bonnie S. Fisher, PhD Northwestern University, is Professor of Criminal Justice at the University of Cincinnati. Her research interests include public opinion about crime and punishment, crime prevention and the extent, sources and impact of the sexual victimisation of college women.

Mike Hough is Professor of Social Policy at South Bank University, London, where he set up the Criminal Policy Research Unit in 1994. He had extensive experience in quantitative research methods, especially large-scale sample surveys such as the British Crime Survey and the Policing for London Survey. He has published extensively on topics including attitudes to sentencing, crime prevention, policing, probation and drugs.

David Indermaur has worked at the Crime Research Centre at the University of Western Australia since 1993. Dr Indemaur teaches criminology, conducts a range of criminological research and publishes in the field of violent crime, crime policy and crime prevention. He also appears regularly on Australian media to comment on matters to do with crime and crime policy.

John van Kesteren is a Dutch national, and studied psychology at Leiden University. He has been responsible for the data management and standardisation of data analysis for the International Crime Victimisation Survey since 1990. Presently he is a statistical and methodological consultant at UNICRI in Turin.

André Kuhn is a Professor of Criminal Law and Criminology at the University of Lausanne Law Faculty. He is a former Examining Judge in the Canton (State) of Neuchâtel (Switzerland) and his main interests are sentencing and corrections.

Helmut Kury is Professor of Psychology at the University of Freiburg and Research Fellow at the Max Planck Institute for Foreign and International Criminal Law, Freiburg, Germany.

Pat Mayhew is currently on secondment to the Australian Institute of Criminology from the Research, Statistics and Development Directorate of the UK Home Office. She has done much in the field of crime surveys and has been involved with the International Crime Victimisation Survey since its inception. She has an OBE for services to criminology.

Catriona Mirrlees-Black is Programme Director, Offenders Research and Analysis, in the Home Office Research, Development and Statistics Directorate. She has conducted extensive research on public attitudes to crime, using the British Crime Survey and other data sources.

Rod Morgan is HM Chief Inspector of the Probation Service for England and Wales and Professor Emeritus, Bristol University, UK. In addition to his many books and articles on aspects of criminal justice he is co-editor of *The Oxford Handbook of Criminal Justice* (3rd edn, 2002, Oxford University Press).

Joachim Obergfell-Fuchs is a Lecturer at the University of Freiburg and Research Fellow at the Max Planck Institute for Foreign and International Criminal Law, Freiburg, Germany.

Alison Park is a Research Director at the National Centre for Social Research (previously SCPR). She heads the team responsible for the annual British Social Attitudes surveys and has been involved in three of the deliberative polls carried out thus far in Britain.

Jennifer A. Pealer is currently a PhD candidate at the University of Cincinnati. Her research interests include effective treatment interventions with offenders, correctional programme evaluation and life-course criminology.

Julian V. Roberts is Professor of Criminology at the University of Ottawa. Since 1992, he has served as editor of the *Canadian Journal of Criminology*. Recent publications include *Penal Populism and Public Opinion* (with L. Stalans, D. Indermaur and M. Hough; Oxford University Press) and *Public Opinion, Crime and Criminal Justice* (with L. Stalans; Westview Press).

Shannon A. Santana is currently a PhD Candidate at the University of Cincinnati. Her research interests include correctional rehabilitation, workplace violence and the impact of gender on victimisation.

Ursula Smartt is Senior Lecturer in Law and Criminology at Thames Valley University, London, and Visiting Professor at the Max Planck Institute for Foreign and International Criminal Law, Freiburg, Germany.

Loretta J. Stalans is Associate Professor of Criminal Justice at Loyola University, Chicago. She has co-authored numerous journal articles or book chapters on these topics, and co-authored a book with Julian

Roberts on *Public Opinion, Crime, and Criminal Justice.* She is on the editorial board of *Law and Human Behavior,* the *Canadian Journal of Criminology* and *Criminal Justice Review.*

Foreword by Rob Allen

The origins of this volume are in a symposium held in London, December 2001. The symposium was funded by the Esmée Fairbairn Foundation as part of its Rethinking Crime and Punishment programme (RCP). RCP is a three-year strategic grant-making initiative which aims to raise the level of public debate about the use of prison and alternatives in the UK. RCP is funding a wide range of work to improve public understanding, increase involvement and stimulate fresh thinking. Increasing awareness of and interest in alternatives to prison, including restorative justice and other non-custodial and intermediate sanctions is a particular priority.

RCP grew out of the Foundation's long history of funding voluntary sector projects to prevent crime and rehabilitate offenders in prison and the community. During the 1990s, translating the lessons from these projects into policy became problematic in large part because of the increasingly punitive political and media climate. The Foundation decided that an initiative focused on public attitudes, which injects facts and evidence into the debate and engages organisations and individuals not usually involved in thinking about criminal justice, offered a way of contributing to better policy-making. More information about the RCP initiative can be found on its website, http://www.rethinking.org.uk/.

RCP is keen to learn from rapidly developing criminological interest in public attitudes and policy formation. While its focus is the UK, there is much to learn too from experience in other countries where interactions between public attitudes and policy-making have in many cases led to disturbing rises in prison populations.

This book is a particularly welcome initiative. It is increasingly important to understand how public attitudes to justice are formed, and how they can influence and constrain penal policy. A comparative perspective is particularly valuable in developing this understanding, as the book so ably demonstrates.

Rob Allen
Director, Rethinking Crime and Punishment

Chapter 1

Public attitudes to punishment: the context

Julian V. Roberts and Mike Hough

The criminal justice systems of all western nations face a common problem: responding to public attitudes to punishment. Legislators, policy-makers, judges and other criminal justice professionals often cite public opinion when making and implementing policy (see Roberts et al., 2002). Although politicians may use opinion surveys to show that the public supports specific policies, little effort is invested in exploring the nature of public attitudes to punishment, and even less to improving the state of public knowledge in the area. Attempts to manage public opinion are often seen, but little effort is directed to informing or consulting the public in a rational way. The point of departure for this international collaboration is the recognition that in order to best respond to the views of the public, we need to understand the evolution of public opinion, the limitations of public knowledge, the limitations on various methods of sounding the views of the public, and the impediments to rational penal reform.

This book draws upon research that has accumulated over the past few decades in a number of jurisdictions, both common law and continental. The principal focus here is on attitudinal change. Readers interested in a more general discussion of public attitudes towards sentencing are directed to a number of published reviews (e.g. Hough and Roberts, 2002; Cullen, Fisher and Applegate, 2000; Kury and Ferdinand, 1999; Roberts and Stalans, 1997; Flanagan and Longmire, 1996; Roberts, 1992). The ambiguity in our title 'Changing public views of punishment' reflects our concern with the evolution of public attitudes towards punishment. It is clear that change has occurred over a long historical span. The public executions that were commonplace in the early nineteenth century represented mass entertainment as much as the ultimate expression of legal censure. Community sentiment slowly changed, with the last public execution in England taking place in 1848. More recently, we have witnessed a growing acceptance of alternatives to imprisonment. These punishments still fail to generate the same support from members of the public as imprisonment, and that is one of the issues addressed in this volume.

The second change to which we refer in our title involves the ways in which public opinion shifts – and can be shifted – in response to factors such as the amount (and nature) of information that is publicly available. Several contributing authors explore the changing nature of public opinion, and specifically the effects of providing information to the public. Much of the research in the field of public opinion has focused on the English-speaking world. In the present volume we have attempted to broaden the scope of inquiry to include continental Europe. While this represents an important step towards a truly international inquiry, we still need to explore these issues in other countries and other social contexts.

Surveys in which the public is asked to evaluate various criminal justice professionals routinely show that judges in western nations attract more negative ratings than any other profession (e.g. Hough and Roberts, 1998; Mattinson and Mirrlees-Black, 2000; Roberts, 2002). Much of the criticism of judges is based on the perception that they are out of touch with 'what ordinary people believe', which is shorthand for the view that they impose excessively lenient sentences. For example, the 1998 administration of the British Crime Survey found that almost half the sample (45 per cent) believed that judges were 'very out of touch' with what the ordinary person thinks (Hough and Roberts, 1998). Since there is no reason to believe that judges are doing a worse job than the police or members of the defence bar, we attribute this finding to the lack of awareness of the judicial function and lack of knowledge of the sentencing process, including sentencing patterns. Moreover, a number of analyses have demonstrated that people with the poorest knowledge of crime and justice also hold the most negative views of the justice system in general and sentencers in particular (Hough and Roberts, 1998).

Public opinion and political leadership

Public attitudes evolve naturally over time, as the literature on capital and corporal punishment has demonstrated.[1] However, we believe that politicians, policy-makers and indeed judges – when passing sentence – have a duty to lead public views, to inform people about the utility of certain sanctions and the disutility of others. This exercise of leadership should not degenerate into the delivery of propaganda, and we have attempted in our review of the literature to avoid studies or polls that manipulate the public (although a number of these exist). Our goal is to move towards a more informed public debate about the future of sentencing, not simply to undermine public support for imprisonment and to 'sell' community punishments to a sceptical public.

Clearly there is often a fine line between informing people – raising the level of debate – and browbeating or manipulating them. If there is to be a healthy political climate it is essential that those with the power to shape public attitudes remain on the right side of this line. At present, politicians from the mainstream political parties in late-industrialised societies do not command a great deal of public trust in the way they talk about social policy in general or penal policy in particular. Public sensitivity to political 'spin' is growing. Cynicism about politicians who place 'spin' on stories is a key factor underlying public disengagement from traditional politics. One of the reasons why politicians are viewed as unreliable sources of information about crime and justice is that the public see them as self-serving power-seekers. The credibility of academics could also be at risk – if the public regard the policies they advocate to be guided by ideology rather than evidence.

Crime and punishment are emotive issues. If public trust in the administration of justice is eroded further, there are risks to the political process itself. In several countries there have been signs recently that far-right (or simply extremist) political parties can successfully exploit public anger about crime to broaden their electoral appeal. To guard against these risks it is important to ensure that the public is accurately informed on these issues. There must be honesty and openness in any approach to improving public knowledge about the criminal process.

Responding to public opinion

Reality has not always matched these aspirations, of course. The recent history of penal policy in many developed countries, most notably the United States, has been marred by a form of penal populism in which tough talk on crime has been seen by politicians of all parties as a precondition to electoral success. Elsewhere we have traced how this process has distorted penal policy, imposing ineffective penal reforms at very high cost (Roberts et al., 2002). On occasion, this has resulted in the promulgation of policies the severity of which is inconsistent with public views. Much as one may decry this tendency, however, it would be equally wrong to suggest that penal politics should somehow be totally *disconnected* from public opinion. There needs to be *some* political and judicial response to public opinion, as Rod Morgan notes in the final chapter of this volume.

There is little question that public opinion is increasingly given more formal consideration in shaping sentencing policy. A good illustration can be found in the report of the Sentencing Review in England and Wales, published in 2001 (Home Office, 2001). That report placed the issue of public confidence at the forefront when it noted that 'Sentencing, and the framework within which it operates, need to earn and merit public confidence' (p. ii). The report also noted that its 'assessment of public views on how sentencing should operate has informed its recommendations for a new [sentencing] framework' (p. ii). In addition, the review conducted a major initiative with respect to exploring and changing public attitudes. Catriona Mirrlees-Black reports some of the findings of that research in the present volume.

Until fairly recently, public opinion with respect to sentencing has existed on two planes which seldom intersect. Criminal justice schol-ars, including many of the contributors to the present volume, have explored the nature and limits of public attitudes to sentencing. They have made distinctions between 'top of the head' and more reflective opinions. They have tried to reveal the dynamics of opinion formation. Policy-makers and politicians on the other hand, have too often embraced opinion polls as their own (and only) measure of public opinion. The nature of public knowledge is one issue that separates these two groups. Researchers have documented the limits on public knowledge, while politicians hardly ever acknowledge these limits or propose strategies to improve public understanding of crime and justice.

We do have an agenda in relation to penal policy, and it is worth making this explicit. We hope that this volume will help accelerate a movement towards the use of public opinion research in which attitudes to punishment (and other criminal justice issues) are meas-ured after respondents have been given sufficient information about the issue at hand. In doing this, it is essential to ensure that the information is factual and balanced. There is no merit in changing attitudes to punishment by manipulating the public. Our aim is not to drift into an evaluation of different forms of propaganda; nor are we attempting to brainwash the public by offering a utopian rainbow of sentencing alternatives to the unremittingly aversive and pointless prison. We simply aim to explore public reaction to ways in which offenders can be held accountable without necessitating their exclusion from society. In our view, these alternatives must satisfy consensual principles of proportionality and equity in sentencing, and must not inflict further suffering on crime victims.

Two roadblocks impede progress towards a more humane (and less expensive) response to crime. One of these is the well-documented reluctance of criminal justice professionals and politicians to reduce the use of incarceration as a sanction. This is reflected in the fact that, notwithstanding the existence of many legislative reforms, prison populations are stable or rising in many western nations. As this volume goes to press in the summer of 2002, the prison population in England and Wales has reached record levels. The second problem is resistance to alternative sanctions on the part of judges and members of the public. The prison retains its primacy as a penal option in the minds of many people for whom alternatives carry insufficient penal 'bite' (see Petersilia, 1997; Marinos, 2000).

To a degree, this resistance reflects lack of awareness of the alternatives. This has been convincingly demonstrated by research in a number of jurisdictions. Research over many years by John Doble and his associates has revealed that people think first of prison as a punishment, but after being informed of the alternatives, demonstrate considerable flexibility. This research is summarised in a later chapter of this volume.

The hegemony of imprisonment

There are several reasons why members of the public associate crime with punishment, and punishment with prison. First, prison is simply the most familiar punishment in the public mind. Imprisonment has a unique public visibility as a result of its history. Second, the public is encouraged to make an association between punishment and prison by the news media, populist politicians and some advocacy groups. But there is a second, more fundamental reason for the association, and that involves a deep-seated attachment to punishment as a response to wrongdoing. Central to this response is the principle that punishments should be modulated by a sense of proportionality; that legal punishments, like punishments in everyday life, should reflect the seriousness of the conduct for which they are imposed.

The public is unlikely soon to abandon the notion of punishment (or proportionality). Restorative (non-punitive) responses carry considerable appeal for the public, particularly for young, and non-violent offenders. However, people remain sceptical about restorative responses to serious crime, particularly those involving violations of personal integrity. This is a generalisation, and quite possibly one that is becoming less true over time. Nevertheless, there remains, we believe, much scope to transform public conceptions of the form that punishment can take. The reflexive invocation of imprisonment can be replaced by more creative, non-carceral alternatives. If this happens, it will be of benefit to all parties, including crime victims.

Greater clarity needs to be brought to community penalties. In England and Wales for example, a confusing array of community punishments exists. The proposals of the 2001 Sentencing Review in England and Wales may help disperse some of the public confusion surrounding these penalties. In Canada, judges also have a large number of community-based penalties to consider at sentencing, and a number of complex rules determine the specific dispositions that may be combined (see Edgar, 1999). (For further discussion of the future of community penalties, see Bottoms, Gelsthorpe and Rex, 2001.)

There is also a great necessity to invest more resources in the supervision of offenders serving sentences in the community. The experience in a number of jurisdictions has been that inadequate supervision has led to a decline in judicial (and public) confidence in community punishments, and eventually a decline in the use of these sanctions. More intensive supervision would have several salutary effects. First, it would provide offenders with more assistance to help them desist from further offending. Second, it would help to ensure that non-compliance with conditions does not occur regularly or without response. An important weakness of community penalties in terms of public opinion is the perception that supervision is minimal and non-compliance widespread. Third, if more rigorous supervision existed, members of the judiciary would be more likely to sentence offenders to these sanctions, confident in the knowledge that the conditions imposed by the court would be observed.

A good illustration of the importance of establishing and maintaining judicial confidence in the adequacy of offender supervision can be found in Canada. In 1996, Parliament created a new, community-based sanction for judges to use at sentencing. The conditional sentence of imprisonment is effectively a term of imprisonment served in the community (see chapter by Roberts in this volume). The offender is subject to a number of conditions, and violations of these conditions can result in committal to custody. However, it has become clear to many criminal justice professionals, including judges, that supervision is minimal. For this reason, some judges have refused to impose conditional sentences unless and until adequate supervision or electronic monitoring is available.

The origins of this book

This book was conceived at a symposium held in London in December 2001. The symposium was funded by the Esmée Fairbairn Foundation as part of its Rethinking Crime and Punishment programme, a three-year strategic grant-making initiative which aims to raise the level of public debate about the use of prison and alternatives in the UK.[2] A number of themes emerged from the conference and are reflected in many of the chapters of this book.

First, it is clear that the public respond to crime with a rich array of reactions, what Loretta Stalans refers to as a 'kaleidoscope of sentencing preferences'. It is impossible therefore, to capture the essence of public opinion in this area by simplistic summaries of where the public stands. People respond to crime in manifold ways and the nature of their responses is highly dependent on the information available about the offence and the offender. In this respect, as a number of contributors note, public reactions to crime mirror those held by the judiciary. Judges do not align themselves behind one particular sentencing goal, but rather pursue different goals in different cases. With respect to community sanctions, the public and the judiciary tend to have a clear vision of the kinds of offenders that are appropriate candidates for a community penalty.

This continuity between the public and the judiciary echoes the findings from research that has demonstrated a degree of concordance between public and professional sentencing preferences. The links between the two are newsworthy and should be brought to the attention of both parties. Judges may be reassured to learn that the public reacts in similar ways, and this reassurance may promote the use of community penalties. In addition, public criticism of the judiciary – strident in most western nations – might be more muted if people knew that judges consider the same kinds of purposes, principles and sentencing factors regarded as important by community members.

We see considerable merit in promoting communication between sentencers and the community. Although we do not advocate changing

7

judicial practice in response to the winds of public opinion, we feel that judges do need to know more about the nature of public reaction to crime. Judicial training seminars address all manner of issues relating to the sentencing process, but to our knowledge, public opinion has never been on the curriculum in the countries with which we are familiar.

Opening up communication between the courts and the community would benefit both. A number of precedents exist. The Sentencing Advisory Panel in England and Wales seems to be sensitive to the issue, and has commissioned two surveys of the public (Clarke, Moran-Ellis and Sleney, 2002; Russell and Morgan, 2001). In the US, the federal sentencing guidelines commission conducted a large-scale investigation into the 'fit' between the views of the public and the sentences prescribed by the guidelines (see Rossi and Berk, 1997), while the Canadian Sentencing Commission undertook a number of studies into the views of the public with respect to sentencing and parole (Canadian Sentencing Commission, 1987).

It also seems important to educate politicians and policy-makers about the nature of public attitudes to punishment. There is a small but growing body of research that demonstrates that political leaders do not have particularly accurate views about the depth and direction of public opinion in this area. This research goes back almost two decades to seminal articles by Riley and Rose (1980) and Gottfredson and Taylor (1984). Riley and Rose compared public opinion in the state of Washington with perceptions of public opinion held by decision-makers in that state. They found that the public was far less punitive and more receptive to liberal reforms than the decision-makers believed.

Gottfredson and Taylor (1984) explored the perceptions that policy-makers held of public opinion, and compared these perceptions to the results of public opinion surveys. They found that policy-makers in the state of Maryland underestimated the amount of public support that existed for reform strategies. Gottfredson and Taylor concluded that 'those concerned with correctional reform must have a more sophisticated understanding of the general public' (p. 201), a conclusion which can be applied to policy-makers in many jurisdictions today. Since this article was published, a number of other studies have demonstrated a gap between the actual views of the public and the views ascribed to them by policy-makers or politicians. Whitehead, Blankenship and Wright (1999), for example, found legislators in Tennessee tended to overestimate the extent to which the public in that state supported the death penalty (see also McGarrell and Sandys, 1996; Johnson and Huff, 1987; Riley and Rose, 1980; Smith and Lipsey, 1976).

Finally, Brandon Applegate's study conducted in Florida carries implications for many jurisdictions. One common populist approach to crime seen in a number of jurisdictions involves making prison conditions harsher. In Ontario, Canada, the government has argued that making prison conditions more austere will lower recidivism rates of prisoners in the prison system. Making life harsher for prisoners is also likely to appeal to the public who often believe that life in prison is too easy and subscribe to a number of misconceptions about conditions in custody. Indeed, some research in the US has suggested that public pressure has been a factor in reducing the level of services in prison (e.g. Johnson, Bennett and Flanagan, 1997). The study by Applegate found little support for making prison life more austere. Applegate presented respondents with a list of 26 prison programmes, services or privileges, and asked whether they believed that these programmes should be retained or eliminated. Applegate found that a majority of respondents supported the retention of most of the programmes.

People's opposition to prison construction in their community offers the most recent example of this phenomenon. It has generally been assumed that many people display the 'not in my backyard' syndrome and oppose the creation of prisons or halfway houses in their neighbourhoods. It appears that the extent of public opposition to such steps has been overstated. Martin (2000) found that residents were neutral or even somewhat positive about the possible creation of a prison in their midst. For example, four out of five respondents thought that crime rates would not increase following the construction of a prison in their community. This discrepancy between views held by the public and opinions ascribed to them by others should not be surprising; politicians derive their image of public opinion from a number of sources of information, principally public opinion polls and feedback from constituents. The former presents a simplified and sometimes highly misleading view of public reaction to crime, while the latter has considerable political impact but little scientific merit.

To the extent that public opinion has influenced the direction of sentencing (and other criminal justice) policies over the past few years it has done so through the conventional opinion poll. In our view, this state of affairs has to change. We agree with Mark Moore who argues that democratic theory requires opinion 'based on information, reflection and discussion', and that 'Raw public opinion has relatively little normative status as a guide to public action' (1997: 49).

For researchers, there remains the challenge of explaining the dramatic variation in public attitudes to punishment revealed in several chapters of this volume. The International Crime Victimisation Survey, for example (see chapter by Mayhew and van Kesteren) reveals considerable differences between countries in the extent to which the public support the incarceration of a specific offender. What is responsible for this variability? No clear explanation emerges, although a number of plausible hypotheses exist.

How are we to explain the lower levels of public support in the West for punitive sentencing preferences? One explanation may be the significant constituency of advocates for community penalties. All common law jurisdictions have had at least one major Commission of Inquiry that has urged judges to use more restraint with respect to the use of incarceration as a sanction. To the extent that these reports have permeated the public consciousness, they may have created a greater tolerance of community penalties and may have undermined support for incarceration. Legislative reforms that have codified the principle of restraint in sentencing may also have contributed to an ethos that is more sympathetic to alternative sanctions. The over-use of incarceration has been represented as an important criminal justice problem in the West, even if this has yet to result in reductions in the prison populations of most countries. Commissions of Inquiry and statutory reforms have not yet emerged in the developing nations where support for incarceration remains high. These countries clearly have more pressing social and penal problems to confront; the use of incarceration must perforce recede in importance. The wide variability in attitudes to punishment around the globe requires further research.

Outline of volume

The first substantive chapter of the book, by Loretta Stalans, explores the ways in which public attitudes are constructed. She examines the architecture of public opinion, and draws a number of important conclusions about influences on public attitudes to punishment.

In Chapter 3, Julian Roberts explores the critical issue of community punishments. He begins by summarising the research around the world into public knowledge and opinion with respect to these penalties, and then discusses ways in which the image and hence the acceptability of these sanctions can be improved.

The International Criminal Victimisation Survey (ICVS), conducted in 58 countries in its most recent administration, contains a question in which respondents are asked to impose a sentence in a case involving an offender convicted of burglary. The ICVS therefore represents a unique research tool with which to explore cross-national variation with respect to attitudes to punishment. Several contributors to the present volume draw upon findings from the survey. In Chapter 4, Pat Mayhew and John van Kesteren summarise trends from the most recent administration of this survey. These findings show considerable variation in attitudes to punishment, with much greater support for community penalties in Western Europe than in Asia or Africa.

Our attention turns, in the next two chapters, to public attitudes in continental Europe. Chapter 5, by Helmut Kury, Joachim Obergfell-Fuchs and Ursula Smartt, discusses the evolution of attitudes to punishment (including the death penalty) in a number of Western and Eastern European countries. Chapter 6 presents a summary of research into public attitudes to punishment in Switzerland, written by André Kuhn.

In Chapter 7, Francis Cullen, Jennifer Pealer, Bonnie Fisher, Brandon Applegate and Shannon Santana explore the evolution of public attitudes towards rehabilitation in the United States. They draw upon new polling data to demonstrate that the American public – sometimes decried for its punitiveness – nevertheless clings tenaciously to the rehabilitative ideal. This finding has important consequences for the future of community penalties.

The next three chapters describe findings from innovative attempts to evaluate the effects of providing information to people about sentencing. In Chapter 8, John Doble who has conducted more attitude change research than anyone else in America, continues the discussion of the evolution of public opinion and punishment. He describes some findings from his research in which attitudes are measured before and after respondents have been given information about alternative sanctions. This research demonstrates that support for incarceration diminishes considerably when people are sensitised to the range of alternative sanctions available.

Mike Hough and Alison Park explore (in Chapter 9) results from the first 'deliberative poll' on crime conducted in the United Kingdom. The deliberative poll represents a method of measuring, and also changing, public attitudes to punishment. Opinions are measured before and after participants attend a weekend of seminars on crime and punishment. The expense involved in mounting deliberative polls means that they will not be routinely employed to measure and change public opinion. Nevertheless, this form of polling reveals much about the nature of public opinion.

Chapter 10, by Catriona Mirrlees-Black, describes a more practical test of the impact of sentencing-related information on public attitudes.

Mirrlees-Black presents the findings from an innovative attitude change experiment conducted in the United Kingdom as part of the 2001 Home Office Sentencing Review. This study demonstrates that it is possible to inform the public about sentencing-related issues without necessitating the expense of a deliberative poll.

In Chapter 11 David Indermaur and Mike Hough outline and discuss a number of strategies to respond to public calls for harsher punishment.

Finally, in the concluding Chapter 12, Rod Morgan reflects upon the role of public opinion in the evolution of sentencing policy. He focuses specifically on two reports recently published in the United Kingdom and draws some general conclusions applicable to many countries.

Changing public attitudes towards punishment is no easy task. However, as many of the contributions to this volume demonstrate, it is far from impossible. If the public is given better information, and if politicians pay less attention to simple opinion polls, the result will be an improvement in public confidence in justice as well as more rational sentencing policy development.

Notes

1. While public support for capital punishment in general has been stable over the past few decades, there has been a decline in support for executing specific categories of offenders such as the mentally ill and juveniles. With respect to corporal punishment, the percentage of the public supporting this as a legal sanction or as a means of disciplining children has declined significantly.
2. Further information about the initiative, and about projects supported by it, are on its website http://www.rethinking.org.uk/

References

Applegate, B. (1997) 'Penal austerity: perceived utility, desert, and public attitudes toward prison amenities', *American Journal of Criminal Justice*, 25: 253–68.

Bottoms, A., Gelsthorpe, L. and Rex, S. (2001) *Community Penalties: Change and Challenges*. Cullompton: Willan Publishing.

Canadian Sentencing Commission (1987) *Sentencing Reform. A Canadian Approach*. Ottawa: Supply and Services Canada.

Clarke, A., Moran-Ellis, J. and Sleney, J. (2002) *Attitudes to Date Rape and Relationship Rape: A Qualitative Study*. London: Sentencing Advisory Panel.

Cullen, F., Fisher, B. and Applegate, B. (2000) 'Public opinion about punishment and corrections', in M. Tonry (ed.), *Crime and Justice: A Review of Research. Volume 27.* Chicago: University of Chicago Press.

Edgar, A. (1999) 'Sentencing options in Canada', in J. V. Roberts and D. Cole (eds), *Making Sense of Sentencing.* Toronto: University of Toronto Press.

Flanagan, T. and Longmire, D. (eds) (1996) *Americans View Crime and Justice. A National Public Opinion Survey.* Thousand Oaks, CA: Sage.

Gottfredson, S. and Taylor, R. (1984) 'Public policy and prison populations: measuring opinions about reform', *Judicature*, 68: 190–201.

Home Office (2001) *Making Punishments Work. Report of the Review of the Sentencing Framework for England and Wales.* London: Home Office.

Hough, M. and Roberts, J. V. (1998) *Attitudes to Punishment: Findings from the British Crime Survey*, Home Office Research Study No. 179. London: Home Office.

Hough, M. and Roberts, J. V. (2002) 'Public knowledge and public opinion of sentencing: findings from five jurisdictions', in N. Hutton and C. Tata (eds) *Sentencing and Society: International Perspectives.* Farnborough: Ashgate

Johnson, B. and Huff, C. (1987) 'Public opinion and criminal justice policy formation', *Criminal Justice Policy Review*, 2: 118–32.

Johnson, W., Bennett, K. and Flanagan, T. (1997) 'Getting tough on prisoners: results from the National Corrections Executive Survey', *Crime and Delinquency*, 43: 24–41.

Kury, H. and Ferdinand, T. (1999) 'Public opinion and punitivity', *International Journal of Law and Psychiatry*, 22: 373–92.

McGarrell, E. and Sandys, M. (1996) 'The misperception of public opinion toward capital punishment', *American Behavioral Scientist*, 39: 500–13.

Marinos, V. (2000) *The Multiple Dimensions of Punishment: 'Intermediate' Sanctions and Interchangeability with Imprisonment.* Toronto: Centre of Criminology, University of Toronto.

Martin, R. (2000) 'Community perceptions about prison construction: why not in my backyard?', *Prison Journal*, 80: 265–94.

Mattinson, J. and Mirrlees-Black, C. (2000) *Attitudes to Crime and Criminal Justice: Findings from the 1998 British Crime Survey. HORS 200.* London: Home Office.

Moore, M. (1997) 'The strategic management of intermediate sanctions', *Corrections Management Quarterly*, 1: 44–52.

Petersilia, J. (1997) 'Diverting nonviolent prisoners to intermediate sanctions: the impact on California prison admissions and corrections costs', *Corrections Management Quarterly*, 1: 1–15.

Riley, P. and Rose, V. (1980) 'Public vs. elite opinion on correctional reform: implications for social policy', *Journal of Criminal Justice*, 8: 345–56.

Roberts, J. V. (1992) 'Public opinion, crime and criminal justice', in M. Tonry (ed.), *Crime and Justice. A Review of Research. Volume 16.* Chicago: University of Chicago Press.

Roberts, J. V. (2002) *Exploring Public Perceptions of Criminal Justice Professionals: A Comparative Analysis.* Ottawa: Department of Justice Canada.

Roberts, J. V. and Stalans, L. (1997) *Public Opinion, Crime, and Criminal Justice.* Boulder, CO: Westview Press.

Roberts, J. V., Stalans, L. S., Indermaur, D. and Hough, M. (2002) *Penal Populism and Public Opinion. Findings from Five Countries.* New York: Oxford University Press.

Rossi, P. and Berk, R. (1997) *Just Punishment. Federal Guidelines and Public Views Compared.* New York: Aldine de Gruyter.

Russell, N. and Morgan, R. (2001) *Research Report – 1. Sentencing of Domestic Burglary.* Sentencing Advisory Panel (available at www.sentencing-advisory-panel.gov.uk).

Smith, D. and Lipsey, C. (1976) 'Public opinion and penal policy', *Criminology,* 14: 113–24.

Whitehead, J., Blankenship, M. and Wright, J. (1999) 'Elite versus citizen attitudes on capital punishment: incongruity between the public and policy makers', *Journal of Criminal Justice,* 27: 249–58.

Chapter 2

Measuring attitudes to sentencing

Loretta J. Stalans

Introduction

Two contrasting images of the public emerge from the literature on public attitudes toward punishment in the United States. On the one hand, several findings support the idea of a punitive public that demands long prison terms. According to national opinion polls around the globe, the public believes that, in general, courts are too lenient in their sentencing patterns (for a review see Roberts and Stalans, 1997). Surveys addressing specific issues indicate that the public supports life in prison without parole for offenders that have committed three violent felony crimes, and supports the death penalty for premeditated heinous murder (Applegate et al., 1996; Roberts and Stalans, 1997). The public also favours the imposition of prison for burglary and robbery offenders (Turner et al., 1997). The public also agrees with the United States federal sentencing guidelines on most offences, and wants longer prison terms than the guidelines allow for drug dealers who use violence (Rossi and Berk, 1997).

At the same time, an image of a merciful public that supports rehabilitation, community-based sentences and less severe sentences than the law allows has also emerged from the literature. Findings from studies that compare public and judicial or legislative sentencing practices and from the jury nullification literature portray the public as merciful, flexible decision-makers who support the system's attempts to rehabilitate offenders (for a review see Roberts et al., 2002). When public sentencing preferences are compared with judicial practice, the public generally provides more lenient sentences in cases involving drug addicts, muggers and burglars (Diamond and Stalans, 1989). The majority of the public, even those who believe the courts are too lenient, also prefer spending taxpayers' money on crime prevention programmes and community-based sanctions rather than on building more prisons (Doob, 2000). Several survey studies have also documented the public's support for early intervention and community-based correctional alternatives to prison (Cullen et al., 1998; Payne and Gainey, 1999). It is clear, then, that the American public has more complex attitudes toward the punishment of criminal offenders than either of these simplistic images portray. This picture is also consistent with findings from other industrialised countries.

How do two very contrasting images of the public emerge from the literature? First, researchers have measured attitudes in a variety of ways and the public's response often depends on the manner in which the question is asked and the context in which it is located. Second, researchers have often ignored how the public interprets, recalls and integrates information in coming to their attitudes toward punishment. An understanding of attitude measurement and information processing is therefore critical in designing studies that obtain reliable and valid attitudes from the public. Finally, researchers have yet to fully explore the depth of public attitudes toward sentencing. Although the public holds diverse and complex attitudes toward sentencing, research to date has primarily focused on the surface layer of these attitudes.

In order to understand how public attitudes to sentencing, including opinions with respect to community sanctions, change, it is important to know about the structure of attitudes in memory. A considerable body of research has explored this topic, and this chapter describes how attitudes about punishment are organised in memory and outlines ways to measure attitudes to reach public views that are more stable and valid. It also illustrates how by using designs that stimulate emotional or less considered responses previous research has failed to capture the public's true opinion. By exploring how the public considers and evaluates information, the chapter describes the critical issues that researchers must consider in order to design an informative study of changes in the public's attitude toward punishment. In this sense the chapter serves as a guide for future research so that a better sampling of the public's kaleidoscope of sentencing preferences can be obtained.

Attitude structure in memory

An attitude is an internal state that is 'expressed by evaluating a particular entity with some degree or favour or disfavour' (Eagly and

Figure 2.1 Illustrative concept map of attitude toward punishment of burglary.

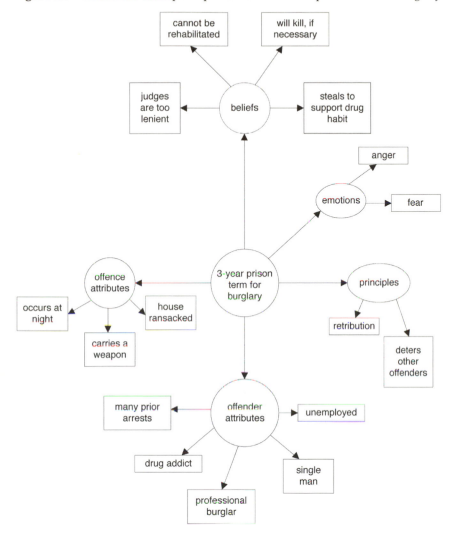

Chaiken, 1998: 269). Attitudes can be fleeting or can be quite enduring and resistant to persuasive appeals. Attitudes are not isolated in memory from other attitudes and beliefs; for example, a filing cabinet where each attitude is in a file is not an accurate representation of how people store and remember their attitudes. Instead, attitudes are stored in memory in an associative network (Fazio, 1989); a spider's web is a better analogy to describe how attitudes are stored in memory. The spider's web reveals that attitudes are embedded in other attitudes and are connected to images, beliefs, emotions and experiences.

Researchers have attempted to measure attitudes using a concept map so that values, beliefs, emotions and experiences that are connected to the attitude are also captured (Lord et al., 1994). Assume a person is asked a general question such as: 'What sentence would you impose on offenders who break into a home and steal the occupant's belongings?' The person answers, 'Three years in prison'. He or she is then shown how to complete a concept map to indicate what beliefs, emotions, images, experiences and values underlie his/her sentencing preference. Figure 2.1 illustrates the concept map of this hypothetical person's attitude about the punishment of burglars. The attitude is connected to an image of the burglar and burglary that is not representative of the burglary cases that come before the court. The attitude is also associated with emotions of anger and fear and a belief that the offender is a dangerous, professional burglar. The preference for three years in prison is also related to beliefs that the sentence is just and will deter other potential burglars. In this example, the person has carefully considered the sentencing of burglars, but some of the information associated with their attitude is unrepresentative of typical burglary cases.

Accessibility of attitudes

Another part of the structure of attitudes in memory is that some attitudes are more easily recalled (i.e. accessible) than others. Cognitive psychology suggests that it is helpful to think of people having at least two layers of attitudes in memory. The first layer contains 'surface' attitudes, and the second layer contains 'inner' attitudes. Surface attitudes are more accessible because they are more closely related to political or religious values and have been discussed or thought about more often. For example, conservative fundamentalists are more likely to support the death penalty, perceive a wide range of crimes to be equally morally wrong (Curry, 1996), and are more likely to support tough, mandatory sentencing laws (Grasmick et al., 1993). Fundamentalists also endorse more punitive sentences for criminals when responding to general questions (see Applegate et al., 2000). However, religion also can lead to support for merciful treatment of offenders. Religious people – for whom forgiveness is important – are more likely to support the rehabilitation of offenders (Applegate et al., 2000). Some of the common surface attitudes toward punishment are attitudes about the death penalty, the harshness or leniency of the court, the purposes of punishment and punishment for stereotypic groups of offenders such as murderers, burglars, robbers and drug dealers.

Inner attitudes are less accessible than surface attitudes. Inner attitudes, however, often represent the attitudes associated with the majority of cases in the criminal justice system. The flexibility, diversity and nuances of the public's kaleidoscope of sentencing preferences are discovered through measuring inner attitudes. Inner attitudes can be assessed through a more sophisticated survey methodology that employs detailed descriptions of criminal cases, through focus groups that discuss detailed vignettes of cases, and through experimental research that examines attitude change. One important implication for studies on attitude change is determining whether the attitude has actually changed or whether the study has just assessed surface attitudes in the pre-test and inner attitudes in the post-test. Studies that have demonstrated that the majority of proponents of the death penalty do not support the death penalty for more concrete and detailed cases have assessed inner attitudes when they introduced the detailed cases (for a review of death penalty attitudes see Roberts and Stalans, 1997).

In this way the public is selectively punitive and selectively merciful depending upon the specific conditions. Only through examining inner attitudes through a variety of methods can research begin to specify these conditions. For example, a considerable body of research indicates that violence – especially violence against strangers – evokes extremely punitive responses. The public consistently sees violent crime as more serious than property, white-collar or victimless crimes (see Roberts and Stalans, 1997). When the American public judged an array of vignettes, they imposed shorter prison sentences on drug dealers that did not carry weapons or use violence than on violent drug dealers (Rossi and Berk, 1997). Fear of crime, however, does not appear to drive public calls for harsher punishment (Cullen, Fisher and Applegate, 2000). Anger and a desire to denounce such offences are more likely motives (Lerner, Goldberg and Tetlock, 1998). From such research, it becomes clear that violence is a central concern of the public and the public favours long prison terms for recidivist violent offenders.

Strength of attitudes

The strength of an attitude refers to its persistence over time, its resistance to persuasive appeals, and its impact on behavior or the processing of information. It is clear that knowledge about the strength of public attitudes toward punishment is a central issue in changing public sentiment. There are several measures of attitude strength that can be obtained (for a more in-depth review see Petty and Krosnick, 1995). For example, it is possible and practical to include survey questions which cover some of the following:

- *Importance* (How important is this issue to you? How much do you care about this issue? How concerned are you about this issue?)

- *Accessibility* (Time taken to answer the question. How often have you thought about this issue? How often have you had conversations with others about this issue?)

- *Cognitive elaboration* (How easy is it for you to explain your views on this issue? How much effort did you put into evaluating this communication?)

- *Ambivalence* (Would you say that you are strongly on one side or the other on this issue or would you say your feelings are mixed?)

- *Value conflict* (How important is the goal of punishment in your sentencing decision? How important is the goal of rehabilitation in your sentencing decision? When punishment and rehabilitation are assigned the same importance, conflicting values underlie the attitude.)

How the public processes information

This brief review of attitude structure and measures of attitude strength reveals that studies on attitudes to punishment have barely scratched the surface of the public's real attitudes. To focus only on what the public wants creates a 'black hole' in the literature. Studies showing changes in sentencing preferences after more information is presented or alternative sentencing options are presented are unimpressive without information about what underlies the preference and how people integrated and interpreted the information. Before criminal justice professionals or researchers can effectively change attitudes, we must have an adequate understanding of how people interpret, remember, weigh and integrate information with their prior beliefs to form opinions about sentencing. By focusing on the processing of information, we can obtain a better sampling of the public's kaleidoscope of sentencing preferences rather than simply atypical and fragmented snapshots.

How does the public form sentencing preferences? This review provides a brief sketch of some of the most critical underlying processing strategies (for more information see Lurigio, Carroll and

Stalans, 1994; Stalans, 1994; Roberts and Stalans, 1997). There are two basic ways that people process information. *Systematic processing* is where people carefully evaluate, integrate and interpret all the information to form an opinion. *Heuristic processing*, on the other hand, is where people do not carefully attend to all the information but use shortcuts based on cues in the decision-making context to make a judgment (see Eagly and Chaiken, 1998; Petty, Haugtvedt, and Smith, 1995). For example, people may change their attitude based on the heuristic or template that the person is an expert and they like the expert instead of attending to the information. People are generally 'cognitive misers', relying on shortcuts to make decisions (and form attitudes) unless properly motivated to attend more carefully to the message. Research indicates that people engage in systematic processing when the messages are personally relevant, when they are accountable for their decisions, and they have the goal of making accurate or just decisions. Thus people can be considered pragmatic social thinkers who conserve energy for the most important tasks. The decision-making context can also influence whether systematic or heuristic processing is undertaken. People are more likely to engage in systematic processing when several sources present information from independent assessments, or when the messages violate people's expectations and induce surprise. In the following paragraphs, I review three strategies that people use to process information.

Discounting and counter-arguing

As Figure 2.1 demonstrated, some people may have a well-organised stock of information about specific crimes and criminals that support their attitudes. Research indicates that the public hold stereotypic conceptions of offenders. These stereotypes are often based on misinformation from the media, and can distort the public's preferences (see Roberts and Stalans, 1997). When people have well-formed attitude structures, they may carefully attend to the messages, but create counter-arguments or discount the value or credibility of information that is contrary to their attitude. Attitudes toward issues such as the death penalty or punishment for child molesters are more resistant to change and change very little when contrary information about cost or effectiveness is presented.

Representative heuristic

Most people are pragmatic thinkers who are interested in sentencing but conserve their 'cognitive' energy for the most difficult cases. When researchers ask the public to impose a sentence based on a detailed description of the offence and offender, people attempt to integrate the diverse information about the offender's criminal record, employment status, school achievement and level of intentionality among other factors. Recalled exemplars can be used to fill in missing information so that the story is more plausible as well as provide reasons for why the offender committed the crime, predictions about the likelihood that he/she will commit additional crimes, and inferences about the moral character of typical offenders and victims. In this sense, people are good 'story tellers' (and editors) using their knowledge, beliefs, experiences and attitudes from memory.

When asked to read a detailed description of an offender convicted of burglary, individuals may recall a recent media account of a burglar who was a gang member, carried a weapon, entered a house and stole over $10,000 worth of property. They may also recall that this burglar deserved to serve 15 years in prison. Using psychology students, Stalans (1988) tested whether the comparison of a current burglary case to the typical burglary case affected the length of assigned prison sentences. Consistent with Illinois sentencing statutes, students were instructed that the offender must be sentenced to prison for a period of time between four and 15 years. Students read either a description of a 'lenient' typical burglary case that contained mitigating factors suggesting a lenient sentence (e.g. the offender was employed, there was very little property stolen) or a description of a 'severe' typical burglary case that contained aggravating factors suggesting a severe sentence (carried a weapon, several prior arrests, etc.). Respondents then sentenced the typical burglary case. As expected, the 'lenient' case attracted an average sentence close to the four-year minimum and the 'severe' case received an average sentence close to the 15-year maximum sentence. After sentencing the typical case, students read a 'moderately severe' case that consisted of a mixture of mitigating and aggravating factors. Stalans predicted that, as pragmatic thinkers, the students would first judge whether the recalled exemplar is similar to the current 'moderately severe' case. This judgment of similarity is known as the representative heuristic. Students who read a moderately severe case that contained half of the features of the typical case gave a sentence closer to the sentence given to the typical case. This result is known as an 'assimilation effect', and is consistent with the anchoring heuristic.

Students who read a moderately severe case that did not contain features of their typical burglary case judged the case to be dissimilar from the typical burglar, and students who first read the 'lenient' typical burglary case compared to students who first read the 'severe' typical burglary case gave a more severe sentence to the same 'moderately severe' case. This displacement of the sentence away from the sentence given to the typical case is called a 'contrast effect'. The contrast effect occurs even when individuals attempt to suppress the influence of the recalled typical case.

The contrast effect also occurs when individuals hold strong attitudes about punishment. Lord and his colleagues (1994), after providing instructions on how to construct concept maps, asked undergraduate students to draw a concept map of their attitude toward the death penalty. Seven months after completing the concept maps, these students were asked to participate in a study on jury decision-making. Students gave individual sentences to two mass murderers ranging from death to five years in prison. One of the cases matched their perception of the typical murderer and the other case had only half of the characteristics of the typical murder. Proponents of the death penalty based their sentence on how similar the case was to their stereotype of the typical murder, and imposed less severe sentences than in the case that was atypical, suggesting that they used a representative heuristic. Opponents of the death penalty based their sentences on principles and values and gave similar sentences to typical and atypical murderers. This study demonstrates that how people process information depends on the structure of their attitude and the underlying beliefs that support the attitude. Indeed, individuals differ on whether they rely primarily on beliefs and information in forming their attitudes or whether they form attitudes based on emotions and values. Not everybody uses the representative heuristic; only individuals that rely on information about the offence/offender in forming their attitudes will make similarity judgments.[1]

Availability heuristic

Many national opinion polls ask general questions such as: 'Are judges too lenient, about right, or too harsh in sentencing criminal offenders?' These general questions trigger surface attitudes that are partly based on biased, stereotypic beliefs about offenders or unrepresentative, very serious cases from the media. Several survey studies indicate that when individuals are asked general questions about punishment, they rely on atypical images of criminals and demand more severe punishment (see Roberts and Stalans, 1997). In an experimental study, Stalans (1993) demonstrated that people rely on information that is most easily recalled to answer general questions about punishment.

This reliance on information that is most easily recalled is known as the 'availability heuristic', which often results in a biased sample of information (Tversky and Kahneman, 1982). Thus, when the public responds punitively to general questions, they actually want harsh punishment only for the extremely serious violent offenders.

The majority of the public believes that judges are too lenient in their sentencing of criminal offenders. Studies have demonstrated that people rely on extremely serious cases and unrepresentative, lenient sentences reported in the media to form this attitude. Stalans and Diamond (1991) conducted an experiment to see if attitudes about judicial leniency could be changed through changing people's images of the typical offender. Students responded to a number of questions, one of which asked them to state whether judges were too severe, too lenient or about right. Five weeks later, students participated in the main study with no apparent connection to the pre-testing. Students were randomly assigned to receive either a 'lenient' case that contained many characteristics of the burglar and burglary that suggested a less severe sentence (e.g. four prior misdemeanor offences, only small amount of property taken, did not ransack house, expresses sincere remorse) or a 'severe' case that contained many characteristics that suggested a severe sentence (e.g. carried a weapon, took a large amount of property, had seven previous property offences and was in prison three times).

Students were told that this case was the most frequently occurring case composition of offenders convicted of residential burglary in the state of Illinois. After reading the case, they sentenced the offender and indicated their opinion of judicial sentencing severity using the same question they had responded to in the first session five weeks earlier. Individuals who had read a lenient sentence changed their perception of judicial sentencing severity toward 'about right' whereas individuals who read a 'severe case' did not change their opinion. This study suggests that perceptions of judicial leniency are malleable and can be changed by informing the public about the typical features of cases that come before the court.

Does the public have real attitudes about punishment?

Based on the public's tendency to change their attitudes when presented with alternative sanctions or other information, some scholars have labelled the public's attitudes to sentencing as 'mushy' (e.g. Cullen et al., 2000). This term implies that there is little substance behind such views. I disagree. From an early age we are socialised to think about what is just or unjust punishment for violating rules. As we go about our daily lives, we have many opportunities to think about fairness in responding to those who fail to abide by the rules. Public attitudes toward sentencing only appear 'mushy' because much research has neglected the critical issue of how people form general attitudes, and how prior attitudes and beliefs about criminals affect sentencing preferences for detailed cases. I believe that people hold general attitudes toward sentencing and are appropriately motivated and able to make sentencing preferences in specific cases.

Three findings have often been used as evidence that the public does not have prior opinions about the sentencing of criminal offenders. I will show that processing strategies can also account for these findings. Moreover, I will provide evidence that similar findings are found with legal professionals, which supports the processing strategy interpretation and contradicts the interpretation that the public does not have pre-existing attitudes about sentencing.

First, public sentencing preferences for the same case are different on different occasions (Rossi, Berk and Campbell, 1997). This finding has been interpreted to mean that individuals are unreliable in sentencing the same case on two different occasions. But other research has demonstrated that legally trained sentencing judges also demonstrate the same lack of reliability across time when asked to sentence the same case on two different occasions (see Diamond, 1981). Thus, both lay persons and legally trained professionals fluctuate in their sentencing preferences for the same case when the decision-making environment changes. In these studies, the cases that preceded the duplicate case were different at the two points in time, and as a result different recalled exemplars may have been activated, producing different interpretations about the causes of the crime, the dangerousness of the offender or the seriousness of the offence. This instability cannot reflect merely ignorance or lack of prior opinions when judges' decisions are also unstable. Instead, it reflects the importance of the decision-making context.

Second, there is consensus among the public about the relative seriousness of different crimes: violent crimes are always seen as more serious and deserving of more severe punishment than property crime. However, there is considerable disagreement about the absolute severity of the sentence that should be imposed (see for a review Roberts and Stalans, 1997). Once again, similar results have been found with judges. There is much disagreement between judges on the appropriate sentence for the same case (e.g. Palys and Divorski, 1986). Research also indicates that juries and judges display similar levels of

25

inter-judge sentencing disparity (Smith and Stevens, 1984). This dis-agreement may be due to variations in the layperson's and judicial sentencing philosophies (e.g. Hogarth, 1971), in the exemplars that are recalled (Stalans, 1988) and in the importance assigned to different case information (Diamond, 1981).

Third, studies have asked respondents to sentence a range of briefly described offences. Respondents are then presented with cost informa-tion about sanctions or with information about alternative sanctions and a significant proportion shifts toward a less severe community-based sentencing alternative (e.g. Doble, 1987). Clearly, the public is ill-informed about the cost of sanctions, about alternative community-based sanctions and about other aspects of our criminal justice system. The respondents can easily guess the purpose of the second question-naire, and many comply with what they believe the researcher wants. Before the malleability of public attitudes can be determined, better designed studies that include a control group and a post-test only group and that measure the reasons behind their preferences before and after are needed.

Malleability, however, does not mean lack of substance or moti-vation. Judges and legislators also support community-based alterna-tives when given information about effectiveness, cost and public safety. Indeed, it would be an unreasonable person who did not change his or her attitudes in response to the arrival of relevant information. Some individuals, however, are more easily persuaded than others. Many judges and a substantial proportion of the public may place equal importance on punishing and rehabilitating criminal offenders; these individuals' attitudes are connected to values (rehabilitation and punishment) that often suggest different solutions. People that support conflicting values engage in less counter-arguing and discounting, and tend to have more moderate attitudes that are less resistant to change (Chaiken and Yates, 1985). Cost information may have forced people with high value conflict to place more importance on rehabilitation and justify punishment with community-based sanctions. Research further suggests that people that have conflicting values underlying their punishment attitudes do hold 'real' attitudes before the questions are posed. People with conflicting values compared with people who have chosen a value consistent with their punishment attitude are less influenced by changes in question wording or changes in the survey context, indicating that people with conflicting values have not made a top of the head response (Tourangeau et al., 1989a, 1989b).

Moreover, individuals that hold informed or personally important attitudes also are susceptible to influences from the decision-making context such as time pressure, distracting tasks and too much information, and may change their attitudes based on erroneous information. For example, importance does not provide a shield against question ordering effects and people with high importance are equally likely as people with low importance to give a different answer depending on the questions that preceded the target question. This persistence of question-ordering effects probably occurs because related attitudes activate a certain segment of information related to the target question and individuals base their answers on what is easily available (Bassili and Krosnick, 2000).

Creating enduring attitude change

How, then, can enduring attitude change be achieved? The social psychology studies on cognitive elaboration suggest ways to create enduring attitude change. Cognitive elaboration refers to how much thought people give to the topic of punishment and how much they considered and evaluated information that was presented on the topic. Research shows that people have more enduring attitude change if they think in a careful systematic way about the persuasive appeal while the speaker is presenting it (Petty, Haugtvedt and Smith, 1995). This finding has very important implications for research on changing punishment attitudes. Much of this research has been conducted using a focus group paradigm where individuals are asked their initial attitudes about sentencing certain types of offenders. After their initial attitudes are obtained, they are presented with community-based alternatives and asked to assign a sentence to the offender. The majority changed their initial attitude of preferring a prison sentence to preferring a community-based sentence (e.g. Doble, 1987). However, this focus group research has not assessed how well this change in attitude persists over time and how resistant it is to media and political appeals to get tough with criminals.

There are several ways to make people think in a more systematic and careful manner. Participants can be led to believe that they will be accountable for their attitude/decisions or will have to explain their decision to other people.[2] Research has demonstrated that individuals who believe that they are accountable for their attitude or will have to communicate their attitude to others think more about the information and become 'flexible, balanced thinkers who actively entertain counter-arguments from conflicting sides' (Lerner, Goldberg and Tetlock, 1998: 564).

Moreover, when people have an accountability motive, anger or other emotions are less likely to influence their judgments of blameworthiness and punishment. Research has demonstrated that respondents who were angry gave more severe punishment than respondents who were not angry, but accountability eliminated the influence of anger on punishment judgments (Lerner, Goldberg and Tetlock, 1998). Accountability also attenuated punitiveness among individuals with high authoritarianism. Thus, accountability leads to more systematic and careful processing of information rather than reliance on emotions or prior attitudes or values.

Another problem in the area of creating enduring attitude change is achieving attitude change when people hold strong personally important attitudes about punishment. Personally important attitudes are more resistant to change and are more stable across time, in part because they are often connected to a person's core values or self-image (e.g. Judd and Krosnick, 1989). People with personally important attitudes typically have more extreme positions, have more knowledge about the issue, are able to quickly recall their attitude and are able to recall more information about the issue (Judd and Krosnick, 1989). For example, research may demonstrate that the majority are strongly in favour of prison sentences for residential burglars, and believe that the punishment of residential burglars is a personally important topic. The criminal justice professionals in the jurisdiction may discover that most of the burglars are young men addicted to illicit drugs who learn more burglary skills while in prison. The professionals may want to try a community-based programme that focuses on eliminating the substance abuse problem, and requires community service that provides skills for eventual employment. How can the professionals 'sell' their programme to the public? One option suggested in the attitude change literature is to frame the argument of the programme to fit with the function that the attitude is serving. For example, the public may support prison because they believe residential burglary is a serious crime that requires meaningful punishment and that this will change the offender. To fit this function, professionals could 'frame' the programme as requiring burglars to work off their debt to society through meaningful work and to fight their drug addiction rather than to acquire more 'crime skills' in prison.

Conclusions

Members of the public are pragmatic reasoners. The representativeness and availability heuristics provide laypersons and judges with strategies to conserve cognitive energy for more difficult atypical cases. These processing strategies also suggest that there is considerable promise in changing misinformation about crimes, criminals and sentencing practices. In order to gauge the malleability of public attitudes toward punishment, future research needs to explore to a greater extent underlying attitudes. Questions such as the following need to be answered: (1) How connected are the attitudes to core religious or political values? (2) How consistent is the information and principles underlying the attitude? and (3) What functions does the attitude serve?

This review of the social psychology literature on attitude structure demonstrates that the structure of the attitude in memory determines the nature and direction of attitude change. The nature of the changes in punishment attitudes will also need further examination. Sometimes change results in further attitudinal specificity rather than change of the overarching general attitude. For example, does the new support for community alternatives apply to all burglars or only to youthful burglars with a drug addiction? Hopefully this chapter will stimulate researchers to determine the conditions under which the public is merciful or punitive, and to measure attitudes and attitude change in a more systematic and careful manner.

Notes

1. There are scales that have been developed that attitude researchers can use to determine individual differences in whether thinking versus feeling underlies attitudes (see Epstein et al., 1996).
2. An accountability motive may be induced in several ways: (a) through having the participants believe that they will have to communicate the persuasive message in their own words to another group; (b) that they will have to explain to newspaper reporters their attitude and the information that was presented on sentencing; (c) that legislators will consider their attitudes and listen to their account of the information presented; (d) that they are chosen representatives for their area and judges want to know what the public really wants and why.

References

Applegate, B. K., Cullen, F. T., Turner, M. G. and Sundt, J. L. (1996) 'Assessing public support for three-strikes-and-you're-out laws: global versus specific attitudes, *Crime and Delinquency*, 42(4): 517–34.

Applegate, B. K., Cullen, F. T., Fisher, B. S. and Vander Ven, T. (2000) 'Forgiveness and fundamentalism: reconsidering their relationship between correctional attitudes and religion', *Criminology*, 38(3): 719–53.

Bassili, J. N. and Krosnick, J. A. (2000) 'Do strength-related attitude properties determine susceptibility to response effects? New evidence from response latency, attitude extremity, and aggregate indices', *Political Psychology*, 21(1): 107–32.

Chaiken, S. and Yates, S. M. (1985) 'Attitude schematicity and thought-induced attitude polarization', *Journal of Personality and Social Psychology*, 49: 1470–81.

Cullen, F. T., Fisher, B. S. and Applegate, B. K. (2000) 'Public opinion about punishment and corrections', in M. Tonry (ed.), *Crime and Justice: A Review of the Research, Volume 27*. Chicago: University of Chicago Press.

Cullen, F. T., Wright, J. P., Brown, S., Moon, M. M., Blankenship, M. B. and Applegate, B. K. (1998) 'Public support for early intervention programs: implications for a progressive policy agenda', *Crime and Delinquency*, 44(2): 187–204.

Curry, T. R. (1996) 'Conservative Protestantism and the perceived wrongfulness of crimes: a research note', *Criminology*, 34(3): 453–64.

Diamond, S. S., (1981) 'Exploring patterns in sentencing disparity', in B. D. Sales (ed.), *Perspectives in Law and Psychology: Vol. II, The Trial Process*. New York: Plenum Press.

Diamond, S. S. and Stalans, L. J. (1989) 'The myth of judicial leniency in sentencing', *Behavioral Science and the Law, Special Issue on Sentencing*, 7(1): 73–89.

Doble, J. (1987) *Crime and Punishment: The Public's View*. New York: prepared by the Public Agenda Foundation for the Edna McConnell Clark Foundation.

Doob, A. N. (2000) 'Transforming the punishment? Environment: understanding public views of what should be accomplished in sentencing', *Canadian Journal of Criminology*, 42(3): 323–41.

Eagly, A. H. and Chaiken, S. (1998) 'Attitude structure and function', in Daniel T. Gilbert, Susan T. Fiske and Gardner Lindzey (eds), *The Handbook of Social Psychology*. New York: Oxford University Press, pp. 269–322.

Epstein, S., Pacini, R., Denes-Raj, V. and Heier, H. (1996) 'Individual differences in intuitive-experiential and analytical-rational thinking styles', *Journal of Personality and Social Psychology*, 71, 390–405.

Fazio, R. H. (1989) 'On the power and functionality of attitudes: the role of attitude accessibility', in A. R. Pratkanis, S. J. Breckler and A. G. Greenwald (eds), *Attitude Structure and Function*. Hillsdale, NJ: Erlbaum, pp. 153–79.

Grasmick, H. G., Cochran, J. K., Bursik, R. J. and Kimpel, M. (1993) 'Religion, punitive justice, and support for the death penalty', *Justice Quarterly*, 10: 289–314.

Hogarth, J. (1971) *Sentencing as a Human Pocess*. Toronto: University of Toronto Press.

Judd, C. M. and Krosnick, J. A. (1989) 'The structural bases of consistency among political attitudes: effects of political expertise and attitude importance, in Anthony R. Pratkanis, Steven J. Breckler and Anthony G. Greenwald (eds), *Attitude Structure and Function*. Hillsdale, NJ: Lawrence Erlbaum Associates, pp. 99–127.

Lerner, J. S., Goldberg, J. H. and Tetlock, P. E. (1998) 'Sober second thought: the effects of accountability, anger, and authoritarianism on attributions of responsibility', *Personality and Social Psychology Bulletin*, 24(6): 563–74.

Lord, C. G., Ross, L. and Lepper, M. R. (1979) 'Biased assimilation and attitude polarization: the effects of prior theories on subsequently considered evidence', *Journal of Personality and Social Psychology*, 37: 2098–109.

Lord, C. G., Desforges, D. M., Fein, S., Pugh, M. A. and Lepper, M. R. (1994) 'Typicality effects in attitudes toward social policies: a concept-mapping approach', *Journal of Personality and Social Psychology*, 66(4): 658–73.

Lurigio, A. J., Carroll, J. S., and Stalans, L. J. (1994) 'Understanding judges' sentencing decisions: attributions of responsibility and story construction', in Linda Heath, R. Scott Tindale, John Edwards, Emil J. Posavac, Fred B. Bryant, Eaaron Henderson-King, Yolanda Suarez-Balcazar and Judith Myers (eds), *Applications of Heuristics and Biases to Social Issues*. New York: Plenum Press, pp. 91–115.

Palys, T. and Divorski, S. (1986) 'Explaining sentencing disparity', *Canadian Journal of Criminology*, 28: 347–62.

Payne, B. K. and Gainey, R. R. (1999) 'Attitudes toward electronic monitoring among monitored offenders and criminal justice students', *Journal of Offender Rehabilitation*, 29(3/4): 195–208.

Petty, R. E. and Krosnick, J. A. (1995) *Attitude Strength: Antecedents and Consequences*. Mahwah, NJ: Lawrence Erlbaum Associates.

Petty, R., E., Haugtvedt, C. P. and Smith, S. M. (1995) 'Elaboration as a determinant of attitude strength: creating attitudes that are persistent, resistant, and predictive of behavior', in R. E. Petty and Jon A. Krosnick (eds), *Attitude Strength: Antecedents and Consequences*. Mahwah, NJ: Lawrence Erlbaum Associates, pp. 93–131.

Roberts, J. V. and Stalans, L. J. (1997) *Public Opinion, Crime, and Criminal Justice*. Boulder, CO: Westview Press.

Roberts, J. V., Stalans, L. J., Indemaur, D. and Hough, M. (2002) *Penal Populism and Public Opinion*. New York: Oxford University Press.

Rossi, P. H. and Berk, R. A. (1997) *Just Punishments: Federal Guidelines and Public Views Compared*. New York: Aldine De Gruyter.

Rossi, P. H., Berk, R. A. and Campbell, A. (1997) 'Just punishments: guideline sentences and normative consensus', *Journal of Quantitative Criminology*, 13(3): 267–90.

Smith, B. L. and Stevens, E. H. (1984) 'Sentence disparity and the judge-jury sentencing debate: an analysis of robbery sentences in six southern states', *Criminal Justice Review*, 4: 1–7.

Stalans, L. J. (1988) 'Sentencing in Ambiguous Cases: Prototypes, Perceived Similarity, and Anchoring', unpublished Masters Thesis. Chicago, IL: University of Illinois Chicago.

Stalans, L. J. (1993) 'Citizens' crime stereotypes, biased recall and punishment preferences in abstract cases: the educative role of interpersonal sources', *Law and Human Behaviour*, 17(4): 451–70.

Stalans, L. J. (1994) 'Lay evaluations of encounters with government officials: do expectations serve as filters and standards?', in Linda Heath, R. Scott Tindale, John Edwards, Emil J. Posavac, Fred B. Bryant, Eaaron Henderson-King, Yolanda Suarez-Balcazar and Judith Myers (eds), *Applications of Heuristics and Biases to Social Issues*. New York: Plenum Press, pp. 137–61.

Stalans, L. J. and Diamond, S. S. (1990) 'Formation and change in lay evaluations of criminal sentencing: misperception and discontent', *Law and Human Behavior*, 14(3): 199–214.

Sundt, J. L., Cullen, F. T., Applegate, B. K. and Turner, M. G. (1998) 'The tenacity of the rehabilitative ideal revisited: have attitudes toward offender treatment changed?', *Criminal Justice and Behavior*, 25(4): 426–42.

Tourangeau, R., Rasinski, K. A. and Bradburn, N. (1989a) 'Belief accessibility and context effects in attitude measurement', *Journal of Experimental Social Psychology*, 25: 401–21.

Tourangeau, R., Rasinski, K. A., Bradburn, N. and D'Andrade, R. (1989b) 'Carryover effects in attitude measurement', *Psychological Bulletin*, 103(3): 299–314.

Turner, M. G., Cullen, F. T., Sundt, J. L. and Applegate, B. K. (1997) 'Public tolerance for community-based sanctions', *Prison Journal*, 77(1): 6–26.

Tversky, A. and Kahneman, D. (1982) 'Availability: a heuristic for judging frequency and probability', in D. Kahneman, P. Slovic and A. Tversky (eds), *Judgment under Uncertainty: Heuristics and Biases*. New York: Cambridge University Press.

Chapter 3

Public opinion and the nature of community penalties: international findings[1]

Julian V. Roberts

Introduction

Most western countries have, over the past decade, adopted reforms to promote the use of community-based sanctions (see Bottoms et al., 2001, for a discussion). Part of the impetus for this movement towards greater use of alternatives can be explained by rising prison populations in several nations. As of 30 April 30 2002, the prison population in England and Wales hit a record 70,589 people (Home Office, 2002). New Zealand is the latest jurisdiction to pass legislation encouraging judges to use community penalties: legislation proclaimed into law in July 2002 creates a statutory statement of the purpose and principles of sentencing which notes that a sentencing court 'must have regard to the desirability of keeping offenders in the community'.[2] This chapter explores public reaction to community penalties, and then addresses a problem confronting all jurisdictions wishing to increase the use of community rather than custodial penalties: how to convince the public that these dispositions constitute a viable alternative to imprisonment, particularly for cases of intermediate seriousness?

Community support for these sanctions is an important consideration from a number of perspectives. First, the widespread use of any sanction that provokes public criticism of the sentencing process is clearly undesirable; some degree of acceptance by the public is necessary to avoid undermining public confidence in the administration of justice. The significant body of literature that has explored the concordance between judicial practice and public opinion attests to this (e.g. Gibbons, 1969; Hough and Mayhew, 1985; Diamond and Stalans,

1989; Rossi and Berk, 1997; Roberts, 2002; Roberts and Stalans, 1997: 209–11). Public opposition may lead to the elimination of the sanction. Indeed, as is well-known, public opposition to the execution of offenders convicted of minor larcenies was an important factor in the restriction of the death penalty to the most serious offences.

Although the literature is somewhat sparse, it is clear that in some cases, judges sentence offenders with one eye on the dock and the other on the reaction of the community. Indeed, judges will on occasion advert to the influence that the community has upon judicial sentencing practices. Surveys of the judiciary reveal that it is in the area of community penalties that judges are most likely to be apprehensive of public hostility (see discussion in Roberts, 2002). Finally, a larger body of literature has revealed the 'unseen hand' of public opinion at work in the formulation of sentencing policy (see Roberts et al., 2002). Simply put, politicians are reluctant to create, and judges slow to impose, community punishments if the general public is perceived to be hostile.

Perceived leniency of community penalties

Although all western nations have increased the number of alternative sanctions over the past few decades, a credibility gap still remains: most members of the public (and indeed, not a few judges) remain rather sceptical about the utility of these penalties for crimes of intermediate seriousness, on the basis that community penalties are not severe enough. This is true around the world. Petersilia notes that in America: 'A major obstacle to diverting prison-bound offenders to alternatives is the public perception that community sanctions are not punitive enough' (1997: 12). In England and Wales, the recent Home Office Review noted that 'Although the range of community sentences is wider than ever, and their intensity can be greater than before, they are still viewed by many as being insufficiently punitive' (Home Office, 2000: 38). This view is shared by many, including members of the judiciary. In fact, in a recent speech, the Lord Chief Justice lamented the 'regrettable fact that neither the public nor sentencers have confidence in the community alternative'.[3] Indeed, increasing public confidence in community punishments is identified as a core outcome of the government's criminal justice strategy (see Home Office, 2001: 8). The 1996 National Opinion Survey on Crime and Justice in the US found that over half the sample agreed that community sentences were evidence of leniency in the criminal justice system (Seiter, 1998). As for the judiciary, Mair writes that: 'A perennial complaint of sentencers is that the enforcement of community penalties is not strict enough, that this in turn makes sentencers lose confidence in such penalties and thus not use them as often as they might' (2001: 175). The credibility of community penalties in Ireland is also a problem (see Lockhart and Blair, 2002: 316). Judges in other jurisdictions such as Canada and Australia appear to share these sentiments.

Purpose of chapter

The purpose of this chapter is threefold: first, to summarise research on the extent of public knowledge of, and the nature of attitudes towards, community penalties; second, to explore the impact that information about these sanctions has upon public opinion with respect to this issue; and third, to identify ways in which these penalties may be made more acceptable to the community.

Community sentences: the context

Community penalties have traditionally assumed a subordinate position beneath imprisonment on a hierarchy of the perceived severity of sanctions. Part of the explanation for this is that the experience of imprisonment is sufficiently aversive as to distinguish it from alternative sanctions. Indeed, it is the very aversiveness (and subsequent consequences of imprisonment) that has inspired many attempts to reduce the use of incarceration as a sanction. Nothing punishes like prison, and the public are keenly aware of this fact.

Second, most jurisdictions provide judges with a wide array of community-based penalties from which to choose at sentencing. In Canada, as well as England and Wales, the number has increased in recent years. Legislators in western nations appear to have pursued a logic which suggests that simply increasing the number of alternatives available will change judicial behaviour, a strategy which has yet to result in the anticipated reduction in admissions to custody (see discussion in Doob, 1990; Cavadino and Dignan, 2002;[4] Brownlee, 1998). As well, the very diversity of community penalties makes each specific alternative less visible to the public, a problem noted by the recent Home Office Sentencing Review (Home Office, 2001).

Third, community penalties achieve the goals of sentencing by means of a complex set of arrangements. Sentences of imprisonment can be made more severe simply by being lengthened; the onerousness of the custodial term is a direct consequence of its duration. Community punishments, however, become more severe, and therefore encompass a greater range of criminal behaviour, by becoming more complex. A community penalty for a crime of intermediate seriousness will carry a number of conditions for the offender, some mandatory for all cases, some tailored to the needs of the specific individual. Reporting requirements will exist, and there will be mechanisms in place to detect violation of conditions, as well as back-up penalties and other possible judicial responses to violation.

In addition, any particular community penalty will in all likelihood be part of a package of dispositions imposed: probation may be accompanied by a community service order, as well as a restitution order, and possibly other autonomous sanctions, such as non-association orders. In contrast, a prison sentence has greater clarity, even allowing for the intervention of parole. Given their scepticism with respect to sentencing in general, the public may well believe that the compliance rate for conditions attached to a community-based sanction is quite low. The conditions of imprisonment can be monitored far more easily, and sanctions such as loss of privileges imposed expeditiously.

Finally, community penalties encompass a wide range of sanctions that are imposed singly or in combination to achieve a variety of sentencing goals. Some sanctions, such as probation, attempt to promote the rehabilitation of the offender, and punishment is a subordinate aim, if it is an aim at all (for example, see Hignett, 2000). Other community sanctions, particularly those which are designed to replace imprisonment, carry a clear punitive element. The conditional sentence in Canada, to be discussed later in this chapter, is an example of a sanction which if properly constructed, must contain a punitive and a restorative element, in order to fulfil its statutory objectives. Moreover, there is no clear consensus about the rationales underlying community penalties. As Kalmthout notes: 'the different rationales surrounding community sanctions undermine both their credibility and their application . . . consequently many judges who could impose [these penalties] have serious reservations about its punitive character' (2002: 589).

For these reasons, it is perhaps only to be expected that public reaction to community penalties will be complex (see Doob and Marinos, 1995), and in some cases characterised by considerable ambivalence. That said, public attitudes towards alternatives to imprisonment have clearly evolved. Twenty years ago, Fattah noted that 'Public attitudes to non-custodial dispositions range from habitual apathy and indifference to outright opposition and hostility' (1982: 371). Such a statement could hardly be made in 2002, as will be seen later in this chapter.

Public knowledge of community penalties

A necessary but not sufficient pre-condition for public acceptance of community penalties is public knowledge of their existence. This has been acknowledged in Australia (Freiberg, 2002), Canada (Canadian Sentencing Commission, 1987) and England and Wales (Home Office, 2001). Although a wealth of research has addressed public attitudes towards the use of alternative sanctions, few studies have examined the extent of public knowledge of these penalties. The limited literature on the topic suggests that most people are unfamiliar with the alternatives available to judges in their particular jurisdiction.

Canadian research conducted in the mid-1980s by the Canadian Sentencing Commission found that most respondents were able to identify the correct definition of community service, but otherwise they knew little about the other community sentences available (Roberts, 1988). In England and Wales, one sweep of the British Crime Survey contained a question in which respondents were asked to identify the sentencing alternatives other than imprisonment. Although over two-thirds of the sample identified community service, there was far less awareness of the other alternatives (Hough and Roberts, 1998). Approximately half the sample identified a fine, and even smaller percentages of respondents evinced awareness of the other alternatives (see Hough and Roberts, 1998).

A nationwide survey of Canadians reported by Sanders and Roberts (2000) explored the public's awareness of a specific community sanction (the conditional sentence) that had attracted widespread media coverage in the five years since its creation. Respondents were asked to select the correct definition from among three choices. Even with this simple question, more respondents were wrong than right; the sample performed at chance level (Sanders and Roberts, 2000). More than half the sample confused this community penalty with bail or parole.

Even probation, the most widely-used and oldest community sentence in most countries, is little known to large numbers of people. Hough and Roberts (1998) found that when the public were asked to identify community sentences, only approximately one-third of the BCS sample spontaneously identified probation. Woelinga (1990) explored public knowledge with respect to probation in Holland, and found that almost a quarter of adults aged 18–24[5] and one-fifth of all female respondents had not even heard of the probation service. Moreover, over half the respondents confused probation officers with prison officers (Woelinga, 1990). Taken together, these results make it clear that an important challenge for western criminal justice systems is to increase public knowledge of community-based alternatives to imprisonment.

Public support for community penalties

Although public knowledge of community penalties tends to be poor, there is considerable evidence that people support these sentences. Indeed, research around the globe has revealed widespread support for alternative sanctions, although this may have escaped the attention of politicians.[6] The degree of public support for community penalties is clear from many representative surveys published around the world in recent years. The findings from qualitative studies such as focus groups also reveal strong support for alternatives to imprisonment. Some of the polls pose general questions, others provide specific cases and ask the respondent to impose a sentence (e.g. Walker, Collins and Wilson, 1988). Regardless of the method, the results are generally the same.

A good example of the general approach can be found in a survey of Canadians in which people were simply asked whether they were for or against community sanctions. Almost nine out of ten respondents expressed support (Solicitor General Canada, 1998). In another poll, views were canvassed about future prison overcrowding. A sample of the public was asked to choose between building more prisons and making more use of 'sentences like probation or orders to perform community service'; over one half of the sample supported the latter, compared to one-third for prison construction (Environics Research Group, 1998). Britons, too, have long displayed support for certain community penalties. Over 20 years ago, a poll found that 85 per cent thought that it was good idea to make some offenders perform community service instead of going to prison (Shaw, 1982).

In the US, the 1999 American Bar Association survey asked respondents whether they agreed or disagreed with the statement that 'Alternative sentences, such as doing community service, should be used instead of sentencing people to prison'. The wording of this statement is noteworthy because most polls that have posed a general question about community-based sanctions have placed the issue squarely in the context of 'non-violent' offenders or offenders who do not pose a risk to society. The ABA poll, however, allowed people to consider alternatives without specifying such offenders. When most people consider sentencing questions, the image that comes to mind of offenders is of the more serious cases. The results from the ABA poll are therefore all the more impressive: the sample split in favour of alternatives in a two to one ratio (15 per cent neither agreed or disagreed; American Bar Association, 1999).

Research conducted by John Doble and his colleagues in several states also illustrates the point. In a survey conducted in New Hampshire (Doble Research Associates, 1998), respondents expressed considerable support for alternative sanctions for a wide array of offences, including crimes by recidivists (see Doble Research Associates, 1998, table 29). In addition, with respect to non-violent offenders, increasing the use of alternative sanctions is preferred by the public to building new prisons. Turner et al. (1997) conducted some innovative research which examined the sentences that people preferred as well as those that respondents were willing to tolerate. Participants were asked about cases of robbery and burglary. The results indicated that almost half the sample preferred to impose a community sanction, and almost three-quarters were willing to tolerate these sanctions. Similar findings emerge from qualitative research using focus groups (e.g. Angus Reid Group, 1997).

Strong public support for community penalties can also be found in continental European countries, as can be seen in findings from a survey of the German public. Boers and Sessar (1991) report that restitution was preferred to punishment[7] for a wide range of offences committed by a 30-year-old first offender. In Holland, a representative survey of the public found that there was widespread support for alternative sanctions. Moreover, consistent with research in other countries (see Roberts and Stalans, 1997, for a review), public support for community penalties increased when additional information was provided about the offence or the offender (Laan, 1993).

Findings from the International Crime Victimisation Survey

The International Crime Victimisation Survey provides insight into the relative levels of support for community sanctions around the world. Respondents were asked to sentence a 21-year-old offender convicted of burglary for the second time (for further discussion, see Mayhew and van Kesteren, this volume). Table 3.1 summarises public sentencing preferences from the most recent administration in a number of western nations. As can be seen, there was considerable support for alternatives, including fines, community service and suspended sentences.[8] Across all jurisdictions, support for alternative sanctions over prison ran two to one (see Table 3.1).[9] In only five countries did incarceration attract more than half the respondents.[10] In addition, it is

Table 3.1 Public sentencing preferences, community sanctions and imprisonment in western nations

Country	% of sample endorsing non-custodial sentence* for a repeat burglar	% endorsing prison
Austria	86	10
France	84	12
Catalonia	83	7
Finland	80	19
Denmark	76	20
Belgium	76	21
New Zealand	71	26
Portugal	70	26
Italy	66	22
Sweden	65	31
Australia	57	37
Netherlands	56	37
Canada	51	45
Malta	48	52
England and Wales	44	51
Scotland	44	52
Northern Ireland	43	54
United States	38	56
Average	*65*	*34*

*This total includes the small percentage (usually around 3 per cent) of respondents who chose 'other sentence' without specifying the nature of the sanction. I have included it in the alternatives percentage because I am assuming it refers to a community-based sanction other than imprisonment that is less punitive than prison, and not capital or corporal punishment.
Source: ICVS (adapted from Mayhew and van Kesteren, this volume; totals do not sum to 100% due to 'don't know' responses).

important to note that, as with other surveys in which the public are asked to sentence offenders (e.g. Hough, 1998), respondents to the ICVS were not permitted to impose multiple sanctions.

This restriction on respondents' freedom to choose sanctions is important and creates two problems. First, it means that the survey seriously underestimates the true extent of public support for community sentencing.[11] If people were able to assemble 'packages' of sanctions, fewer respondents would favour incarceration. A fine would be more attractive as a sentencing option to the public if it could have been combined with community service. Previous research has demonstrated that when given the opportunity, the public combine community sentences to achieve a satisfactory overall disposition for the case (e.g. Hough, 1996). Forcing subjects to choose a single sanction privileges the one penalty most able to stand alone as a sanction, namely imprisonment. Clearly then, respondents should be allowed to combine sentences for the same offender.

In addition, respondents were asked to identify 'the most appropriate' sentence. It is possible that some respondents may believe that prison is the most appropriate sanction, but may nevertheless find some alternative sanction quite acceptable. As will be seen during the course of this chapter, when people favouring imprisonment are asked whether an alternative sanction is nevertheless acceptable, a significant proportion of the sample responds affirmatively.

The second limitation created by this restriction on respondents' sentencing preferences is that it prevents us from making comparisons between public sentencing preferences and judicial practice, since judges combine sanctions in complex ways in order to generate a sentence which satisfies the multiple goals of sentencing. For example, even in Canada, a country with fewer community penalties than some jurisdictions such as England and Wales, on average judges imposed almost two sanctions per criminal charge. In half the cases of imprisonment, at least one other sanction was also imposed (Roberts, 1999).

However, these limitations do not undermine the central finding from the ICVS with respect to community punishments: consistent with responses from general questions, when confronted with a specific case, people display considerable support for the alternative punishments.[12]

Relative support for specific community penalties

Which community penalties are most popular? It is curious that this question has seldom been explored by researchers. The few studies that have addressed the issue find that the public tend to be most positive about community sanctions that have a compensatory element, either for the specific victim or the community in general. This is apparent from the ground-breaking work over 25 years ago by Gandy (1978), who found strong community support for restitution as a sanction (see also Wright, 1989). A 1997 survey conducted in Canada found that over 80 per cent of the public supported community service, and mandatory compensation for victims. A community penalty such as electronic monitoring received significantly less support from the public (Angus Reid Group, 1997).

In the United Kingdom, a survey conducted in 1994 found that almost three-quarters of the sample agreed that 'Most offenders who are not a big threat should be kept out of prison but made to spend a certain amount of time helping people in the community.' (Dowds, 1994). It is noteworthy that a significantly smaller proportion of the public supported an alternate statement to the effect that 'Most offenders who are not a big threat should be kept out of prison but made to report regularly to probation officers'. This suggests that for the public, periodic reporting to a probation officer is insufficient to constitute a sanction even for offenders who do not constitute a threat.

The same pattern emerges in the US. Research by John Doble, for example, in North Carolina found almost unanimous support for alternative sanctions for non-violent offenders: 98 per cent of the sample supported the use of restitution. Levels of support were significantly lower for non-compensatory community sanctions, such as house arrest or residential requirements involving halfway houses (Doble, 1995). Much of the attraction of community penalties derives from their ability to respond to victims' needs (Wright, 1989). This is confirmed by research in Holland by Junger-Tas and Terlouw (1991) who found that reparation was by far the most popular sentencing option. With respect to juveniles, reparation was supported by 84 per cent of the sample. Other community penalties attracted far less support: compulsory work was endorsed by only 46 per cent of the sample. For adult offenders, compensation was endorsed by 66 per cent, while non-compensatory alternatives such as electronic monitoring and intensive probation supervision were far less popular, attracting 7 per cent and 10 per cent of respondents respectively.

It is interesting to note that the public also regards compensatory community sanctions as being most effective at preventing crime. A national Gallup survey conducted in America in 1996 provided respondents with a list of alternatives, and then asked them to rate their effectiveness in terms of 'protecting citizens against crime'. Requiring offenders to work to pay compensation was perceived to be most effective; it was rated by almost half the sample as 'very effective'. Weekend jail sentences, home confinement and the more punitive alternatives to continuous custody were far less likely to be rated as being effective (Maguire and Pastore, 1998).

These findings demonstrate that an important source of the public's attraction to community penalties: they respond to the needs of crime victims. To date, many jurisdictions have stressed the (undoubted) financial benefits associated with the use of community rather than custodial penalties. However, it would appear that the issue of victim compensation is more attractive. This is confirmed by responses to a Canadian poll in which people were asked to respond to justifications for community sentences. Specifically, they were asked whether various arguments were strong or weak justifications for these penalties. Two-thirds of the sample believed that paying the victim back was a strong argument; significantly fewer respondents rated saving money as a strong argument for community penalties (Angus Reid Group, 1997). Another survey found that 69 per cent of the public backed community sentences because they allowed the offender to work and make reparation; fewer than 3 per cent supported these sanctions because they (a) enhance the prospects for rehabilitation; (b) teach the offender a lesson; or (c) reduce prison overcrowding (Focus Canada, 1998).

Effects of increasing public awareness of community sanctions

The absence of familiarity with community sanctions can be demonstrated by examining findings from research involving comparisons between sentencing preferences of people who are or are not provided with a 'menu' of sentencing alternatives. This kind of research has been conducted in different ways in a number of countries. When the community penalties are made salient, public support for these sanctions increases. The most compelling demonstrations of this finding come from research conducted by John Doble and his associates in the US (e.g., Doble, this volume; Doble and Klein, 1989; Doble, Immerwahr and Richardson, 1991). Members of the public were first asked to sentence offenders described in scenarios. Having responded, they were then given a list of the possible alternatives to imprisonment and again asked to sentence the offender. Simply making the subjects aware of the alternatives had the effect of changing their preference for the incarceration of the offender. For example, in one survey, when asked to sentence an offender convicted of armed burglary for the second time, 83 per cent of respondents favoured imprisonment. After learning about the alternative sanctions, the percentage endorsing custody dropped to 19 per cent (Doble and Klein, 1989: 37).

The deliberative poll conducted in Manchester, England in 1994, in which members of the public attended an educational weekend of presentations about criminal justice is another example (see Fishkin, 1995; Hough and Park, this volume). Although the presentations made to participants were not fully recorded and cannot therefore be evaluated with respect to their degree of 'balance', after attending the weekend sessions, participants showed an increased willingness to support alternative sanctions, both for juveniles and adults (Fishkin, 1995: 179; Hough and Park, this volume).

Figure 3.1 Percentage of respondents accepting an alternative to imprisonment for youth.

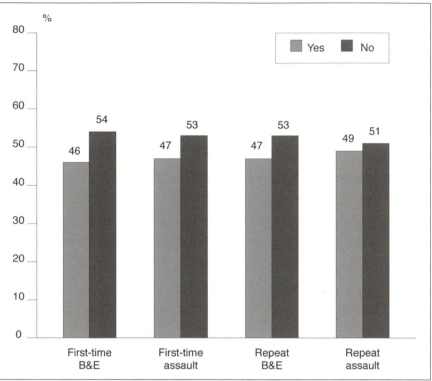

An alternative approach involves asking respondents who have already sentenced an offender to consider whether an alternative sanction would be acceptable. Doob and Roberts (1988) used this approach with a sample of Canadian respondents. After having expressed a preference for imprisoning an offender,[13] respondents were asked whether they would find an alternative, primarily reparative sanction acceptable as a substitute. Almost one-third responded 'yes, in all cases', and a further 31 per cent responded 'yes, in most cases' (Doob and Roberts, 1988, table 6.12). Most recently, Tufts and Roberts (2002) report that the majority of members of the public who expressed a preference to incarcerate juvenile offenders resiled from this position, and stated that they found an alternative acceptable as a sanction, even for a recidivist offenders convicted of a crime of violence. The results are presented in Figure 3.1.

It may be said that this methodology of asking participants for a sentence twice 'leads' the respondents and encourages them to move from supporting imprisonment to a community penalty. Critics of these studies may argue that the support for alternatives on the second occasion is therefore in part an artifact of the methodology. Two responses can be made to this criticism. First, the original sentencing decision made by the subjects is not necessarily the appropriate baseline to evaluate public support for incarceration, because subjects are not aware of all the available options. In this sense, the first sentencing decision taken by respondents may well underestimate the extent of public support for alternative sanctions. Second, this methodological problem (if problem it be) is overcome by studies in which two groups of people sentence offenders, one with information about alternative sanctions, and one without. (Equivalence between conditions is achieved through random assignment.) Several such studies using this 'between subjects' design have been conducted. In one of the earliest, Galaway found that subjects who had been given the option of restitution as a sentence were significantly less likely to support incarcerating the offender (Galaway, 1984)

More recently, Hough and Roberts (1998) divided the sample of respondents to the 1996 British Crime Survey in half, and provided a 'menu' of all sentencing alternatives to one group. The remaining participants were not provided with the list of possible sanctions. Both groups were then asked to sentence the same offender. Significantly less support for incarcerating the offender emerged from responses of the group who were provided with the list of all available sanctions, including the community penalties.

These quite significant shifts in subjects' sentencing preferences (away from imprisonment and towards community penalties) suggest that large proportions of the public support community-based alternatives but are simply unfamiliar with them. Even if members of the public are aware of alternatives in the sense of being able to recognise them if offered a list, this research shows that the 'top of the head' public reaction to many crimes involves imprisonment. An obvious step, then, in order to promote greater acceptability of alternatives is simply to increase public awareness of their existence, and to increase the profile of these sanctions. But it is insufficient to simply bring the existence of these penalties to the public's attention; they need to be better informed about the consequences of community penalties for the offender. Conveying this information also enhances the public image of community penalties in the public mind, and increases the degree to which they become acceptable.

Effects of providing information about nature of community penalties

The power of providing specific information about the conditions attached to community penalties (and hence their true consequences for the offender) can be seen in research on the community-based alternative to imprisonment in Canada: the conditional sentence of imprisonment. This sentencing option was created in 1996 and resembles the suspended term of imprisonment in England and Wales, and the First Offender Waiver found in certain American states (see Roberts, 1997).

The offender is first sentenced to a term of imprisonment, and then, if certain criteria are met, is allowed to spend the sentence in the community. Conditions will be imposed, and unjustified violation of these conditions may result in the committal of the offender to a correctional institution (for the remainder of the sentence). The sanction is called a 'conditional sentence of imprisonment', even though the offender remains at home, and if he abides by his conditions, will never enter a custodial facility. For this reason, I refer to a conditional sentence as a form of virtual imprisonment (Roberts, 1997; Roberts and Healy, 2001). Since the conditional sentence is designed specifically to replace imprisonment – indeed it can only be activated as a sanction once a term of custody has been imposed – this sanction represents a good test of the limits of public acceptance of community sanctions.

A nationwide public opinion study conducted in 2000 explored the nature of community reaction to the conditional sentence (see Sanders and Roberts, 2000 for further details). The hypothesis being tested was that the level of public awareness of the conditions imposed on the offender would determine the degree of community acceptance of this alternative to custody. It was predicted that public support for the conditional sentence would be greater if the conditions of the sentence were made salient. Respondents to a national survey were asked to impose sentence in a case of burglary committed by a repeat offender. They were given a choice between imposing a term of custody or a community-based conditional sentence. Respondents were assigned at random to one of two versions of the question.[14]

In version 'A', respondents were asked to consider a case in which 'An offender is to be sentenced for the crime of breaking into a hardware store and stealing $1,500. He has committed similar offences in the past.' Respondents were further told that 'The judge is trying to decide between a 6-month prison sentence, or 6 months to be served in the community as a conditional sentence of imprisonment.' The choice was simply six months in prison or six months under supervision in the community.

Table 3.2 Public support for conditional sentence vs. imprisonment

Experimental condition	% sample choosing prison	% sample choosing conditional sentence
Group A. Choice between: 6-month prison term or conditional sentence, conditions unspecified	72	28
Group B Choice between 6-month prison term or 6-month conditional sentence with conditions specified	35	65

Source: Sanders and Roberts (2000).

The second group of subjects were given this same choice, but the nature of the conditions imposed on the offender was specified. Specifically, respondents answering version 'B' of the question were told that 'If the offender receives the conditional sentence, he will have to remain at home every night after 7 p.m., and on weekends. As well, he will have to pay back the money he stole, perform some community work and report to authorities twice a week for 6 months.' Since it had already been established that most people did not know what a conditional sentence was (see above), all respondents had been provided with a general description of a conditional sentence of imprisonment (but one which did not identify the specific conditions).

As can be seen in Table 3.2, the results dramatically supported the experimental hypothesis. In the absence of specification of the conditions (version A), the public supported the imposition of a prison sentence over the conditional sentence by a ratio of almost 3:1 (72 per cent favoured incarceration, 28 per cent the conditional sentence). When the conditions of the order appeared in the description (version B), the pattern of results was a complete reversal: now only 35 per cent of respondents supported incarceration, 65 per cent the conditional sentence (see Table 3.2). My interpretation of the low level of public support in condition A is that the public image of probation – minimal conditions accompanied by minimal supervision – renders the community-based sanction unacceptable to most respondents. People appear to view the conditional sentence as being too similar to a term of probation – a recurrent image problem for the conditional sentence throughout its relatively brief existence. This study demonstrates that for this offence at least, a community-based sanction can, in the eyes of the public, compete against imprisonment.

Turner et al. (1997) report findings from a survey in Ohio which revealed considerable reluctance on the part of the public to support community sanctions that did not include close monitoring of the offender. If this condition was assured, support for this form of sanction rose substantially. Similarly, in the United Kingdom, Dowds (1994) reports that 59 per cent of the public agreed that offenders on probation should be subject to electronic tagging (monitoring). This is further evidence of the public's unease with a sanction in which occasional reporting is the only restriction placed on the offender. Completing a period of good behaviour alone simply fails to capture public conceptions of what constitutes an adequate punishment. As Cullen, Fisher and Applegate (2000) note: 'Citizens appear wary of "regular probation", a sanction that involves minimal contact with the offender. In contrast, they are willing to consider alternatives to incarceration if it appears that the community sanctions will involve some meaningful interventions' (Cullen et al., 2000: 37, emphasis added).

Summary

The discussion so far may leave the impression that public acceptance of community penalties can be achieved by (a) increasing public awareness of the existence of these sanctions, and (b) by dispelling some misconceptions about the penal value or impact of community penalties. In my view, however, it will require more than this before these sanctions collectively constitute a viable alternative to imprisonment. In fact, it will require some changes to the penalties themselves, and perhaps to the ambit of offences to which they are applied.

Changing the nature of community sanctions

The principal reason for the public scepticism with regard to community penalties is that they appear to have insufficient impact upon the lives of the offenders to constitute an adequate response to the more serious forms of offending, particularly crimes of violence. Probation well illustrates the problem. Most probationers in Canada face minimal conditions, and their low risk level, accompanied by excessive caseloads for most probation officers, means that violation of conditions frequently passes without detection.[15] And, even if violating a probation order constitutes a fresh criminal offence in many jurisdictions, the reaction of the court is fairly indulgent; the back-up sanction – a term of custody – is seldom imposed. Of course probation is not a substitute for imprisonment, and therefore should not carry the same penal value; nevertheless, the image of community penalties is clearly affected by perceptions (accurate and otherwise) of probation.

Many judges also subscribe to the view that community sentences lack sufficient impact. Evidence of this can be found in the reactions of judges interviewed as part of the demonstration projects in England designed to increase confidence in community penalties (see Hedderman, Ellis and Sugg, 1999). A significant number of judges expressed an interest in fusing a community sanction with a brief term of custody. Similarly, in Canada, judges have shown an interest in combining a period of 'straight' custody with a period of conditional imprisonment in the community. Split or blended sentences of this kind represent an attempt by the judiciary to ensure that a sentence with a community element also has impact on the offender. They also represent an attempt to mitigate the sentence: from the perspective of the offender, a blended sentence of one month in prison followed by 11 in the community is obviously preferable to a 12-month custodial term, subject only to the conditional release arrangements in effect.

The experience with the conditional sentence in Canada has demonstrated the dangers of creating an alternative form of imprisonment and then failing to treat offenders with sufficient rigour. Until the Supreme Court weighed in with a direction to the contrary,[16] many unjustified breaches of conditions resulted in modifications to the conditions imposed on the offender rather than committal to custody. Rather than holding the offender accountable for the breach, judges were accommodating the conditions to the recalcitrant offender. This seems to be a case of the tail wagging the dog. And of course the number of breaches resulting in a breach hearing was a small fraction of the total number of breaches committed.[17]

There is an argument to be made in favour of according sentencers some flexibility in response to breach of conditions, particularly with respect to drug-dependent offenders. The probability of relapse is generally high for these individuals, and in dealing with their dependence, people often take 'two steps forward and one back'. It would be self-defeating for the penal system to crack down on each and every incident of non-compliance. On the other hand, allowing non-compliance to pass without response from the court may encourage additional violations, and, if general enough, will undermine the sanction in the eyes of the public. As with many decisions relating to the imposition and enforcement of sentences, judges must tread a fine line.

Adopting a vigorous response to breach of any community sentence, whether probation, conditional sentence or a community service order, may appear to reflect mere punitiveness. But public confidence can only be assured if the public have confidence that the court order will be observed. Surveys of the public reveal considerable cynicism about the extent to which offenders comply with the conditions of a community sanction. People do not believe that community service orders are routinely fulfilled; they assume that the offender will complete some proportion of the hours, and be able to evade the remainder.

As with many aspects of community sentences, public and judicial confidence are linked. Judges who have little confidence that orders will be supervised adequately and that non-compliance will result in official action will be reluctant to impose the sanction. As one member of the judiciary in the United Kingdom noted: 'If an offender is not made to comply with a court order he will be contemptuous of both the order and the court, and that will encourage him to re-offend' (Calvert, 2000). Systematic research has demonstrated that the judicial faith in the administration of community sentences is essential if they are to be more widely used (e.g. Roberts, Doob and Marinos, 2000).

In its principal guideline judgment with respect to conditional sentencing, the Canadian Supreme Court directed judges to incarcerate offenders found to have breached conditions without justification, and for the remainder of the sentence. However, to some degree, the damage in terms of public and professional credibility had been done.[18] The conditional sentence had been (somewhat) unfairly caricatured by critics and the news media, and most people believed that offenders serving conditional sentences of imprisonment were no more harshly treated than offenders on probation. Indeed, this perception has been confirmed in the public mind by well-publicised statements made by high-profile offenders. For example, John Sharpe became one of Canada's most notorious offenders after having been convicted of possession of pornographic images involving children. His appeal to the Supreme Court attracted nationwide media coverage. He was eventually sentenced to a conditional sentence. When interviewed after sentencing, a beaming Sharpe responded that the sentence would 'have a minimal impact on his life'. He added, somewhat unhelpfully for the image of conditional sentence in Canada, 'I do not regard the sentence as very onerous compared to going to jail.'[19]

Community penalties will for the foreseeable future, remain restricted to crimes of low and intermediate seriousness, unless there are clear mitigating factors and these are transmitted to the community somehow. The imposition of a community-based sentence on an offender convicted of a serious personal injury offence is likely to provoke public opposition. But there is a more general negative consequence; the public are likely to be hostile towards the entire regime of community penalties if, when they are designed to replace imprisonment, they are applied in this way.

This is one of the lessons of the conditional sentencing experience to date, in Canada at least. A sanction which could prove most useful to judges was undermined by the statutory framework which created a very broad ambit of application. As long as the other statutory requirements were met, any sentence of imprisonment up to two years less a day can be made conditional. This means that almost all sentences of imprisonment fall within the range of the conditional sentence.[20] The alternative would have been to set a lower 'ceiling' of possibly six months. Had this been done, the loss of efficacy resulting from the fact that fewer cases would be eligible would have been minimal. On the other hand, the restricted ambit would have prevented judges from imposing conditional sentences in the most serious cases involving violence.[21] It is these cases that have attracted the most media coverage and commentary, and subsequently the greatest degree of public opprobrium.

Although we do not have hard evidence for this, it seems likely that public frustration with lax supervision of community penalties stems at least in part from the lack of transparency in the enforcement process. One option is to establish clear enforcement standards, as has been done in Britain, and to ensure that these standards are properly and regularly audited (cf. Hedderman and Hearnden, 2001). Another option is to replace administrative with judicial review of community penalties. This would place the onus more on sentencers and less on probation officers to determine responses to non-compliance – as is done in Drug Treatment Courts in the US and Canada, the Drug Court in Victoria (see Freiberg, 2002) and the Drug Treatment and Testing Orders in Britain (cf. Turnbull et al., 2000).

Community sentencing and victims

In 2002, it is hard to discuss sentencing without addressing in some respect the views of crime victims. In recent years, most jurisdictions have enacted reforms to increase the voice of the victim in sentencing. These reforms attract considerable public support.[22] The link to public opinion is that the public are very attentive to representatives of victim groups, and if these groups oppose the use of community sentences, this will only fuel public opposition. A Canadian survey asked the public how believable they found various spokespersons to be when it came to crime and justice issues. Victims' groups headed the list: two-thirds of the public rated these groups as always or usually believable. Ratings of academics were significantly less positive, and government officials were seen as the least believable of all: less than one-third of the public rated them as always or usually believable (Environics Research Group, 1998).

What implications does this have for the issue of public attitudes towards community punishments? One obvious consequence is that the utility of community penalties with respect to victims should be emphasised. While desirous of seeing a greater voice for victims in the sentencing process, the public probably fail to appreciate that imprisoning the offender may not always serve the interests of the victim. The compensatory elements of community-based sanctions therefore need to be brought home to the public. This is clear in light of the findings from a national survey which asked members of the public to identify the best reasons for supporting community sanctions.

The option 'to allow the offender to pay back the victim was by far the most often-cited justification, supported by 69 per cent of the sample. In contrast, only 33 per cent say 'allowing the offender to maintain community ties' and a paltry 3 per cent saw 'increasing the chances of rehabilitation' as reasons for using community-based sentences (Angus Reid Group, 1997). The public has a clear idea of the benefits of community penalties, and they lie in the direction of victim compensation and not crime prevention. The British Crime Survey is once again instructive in this regard. Respondents were asked about the relative effectiveness of various crime prevention strategies, and 'Increasing the use of community based sentences' attracted the support of only 2 per cent of respondents (Hough and Roberts, 1998).

The importance of compensation as a sanction (or condition of another sanction), should not be underestimated. Opinion surveys in many countries have shown that compensation appeals to members of the public as well as to victims. This observation is supported by findings from several sweeps of the British Crime Survey. For example, when asked to state their sentencing preference in a case of burglary committed by a recidivist, compensation attracted more support than prison (56 per cent vs. 52 per cent: see Mattinson and Mirrlees-Black, 2000; Hough and Roberts, 1998). Burglary victims were no more likely to support custody.

Similarly, in America, John Doble and his associates (this volume) report high levels of support for restitution as a sanction. Perhaps the most compelling evidence to support the importance of restitution comes from a survey of victims conducted by Klaus Sessar (1995) using a sample of German respondents. Sessar found that almost half his sample of victims were willing to disregard the punishment of the offender in their case in the event that the offender was willing to make restitution. In light of their considerable sympathy with crime victims, members of the public are likely to find this to be a very convincing argument in favour of community penalties.

The public may be more supportive of community penalties if they know that victims support the sanctions or at least are no more opposed to them than members of the general public. The findings from the 1998 British Crime Survey reveal that victims of violent crimes are not necessarily very punitive. Indeed, only 9 per cent of victims of violence favoured the incarceration of the offender.[24] This finding is consistent with other research which finds that in general, victims are no more punitive than non-victims.

In the latest comparison of sentencing patterns from victims and non-victims, Tufts and Roberts (2002) note that 'Results of the logistic regression illustrate that when all other factors are held constant, victimisation experience did not prove to be a significant factor in respondents' preference for prison' (p. 57). Among the victimised respondents to the BCS, there was far more support for compensation (see Table 3.3). As this table shows, there was little support for community service, curfews or tagging orders, a finding which

Table 3.3 Sentencing preferences of violent crime victims (British Crime Survey)

Disposition	Percentage of victims choosing disposition
Caution or discharge	26
Compensation	25
No action	14
Prison	9
Community service	8
Fine	4
Probation or suspended sentence	4
Curfew	3
Apology	3

Source: Adapted from Mattinson and Mirrlees-Black (2000).

probably reflects, as the authors note, lack of awareness of these sanctions (Mattinson and Mirrlees-Black, 2000). Although it only addresses the sentencing of one kind of offender, the ICVS also supports this conclusion. As Mayhew and van Kesteren note in their contribution to this volume, there was substantial support for community penalties and victims were no less supportive than non-victims.

Finally, when community penalties replace imprisonment they should carry a clear punitive element. This means the imposition of conditions which constitute a meaningful restriction on the offender's liberty. To the extent that offenders serving community-based sanctions lead lives comparable to those of the general public, these sanctions will suffer from an image problem. I am not arguing for a toughening of conditions imposed on offenders serving terms of probation, as these include low-risk individuals convicted of relatively minor criminal acts. But in order for community penalties to be imposed on offenders convicted of more serious crimes, or with more extensive criminal records, the public will need to know that such offenders are indeed incurring serious consequences as a result of their offending. To the extent that these consequences include compensation for the victim, and promote the rehabilitation of the offender, so much the better.

Understanding the penal significance of imprisonment

More research is needed to better understand the nature of public reactions to different penalties. A generally held assumption has been that public opposition to alternatives in cases of violence is that the sanctions are simply not severe enough to replace custody. Were this the case, multiplying and combining various community sanctions should result in greater public acceptability of alternative sanctions. While perceived severity must explain a great deal of variance in public reactions, it appears that the issue is not so straightforward. Although there is not much research on the issue, some researchers have demonstrated that community sanctions carry a different meaning for people, and that the distinction between prison and the alternatives does not hinge solely on the dimension of perceived severity. Doob (1990) reports that the considerations that judges saw as relevant to imprisonment were quite different from those considered when sentencing an offender to a community penalty.

Doob and Marinos (1995) and Marinos (2000), following Morris and Tonry (1990), suggest that there are sentencing goals that the prison is seen to be singularly best at advancing. Doob and Marinos (1995) found that 'even when respondents could set a fine of any size, they were generally unwilling to substitute a fine for imprisonment for minor violent offenses' (p. 431). This suggests that penalties were not distinguished on the basis of severity alone. Imprisonment held a particular significance for the subjects in the study. Marinos (2000) found that prison held a special appeal to members of the public. Why is this the case? Did participants believe that the offender would be unable or unwilling to pay a fine of sufficient magnitude to achieve the goals of sentencing? If mere severity fails to distinguish between prison and alternative sanctions, why is imprisonment seen to hold this power to denounce? Is it intrinsic to the nature of penal sequestration, or can this goal be captured by some form of seclusion in the community under house arrest or the use of strict curfews? Is it possible that the special status of imprisonment as a sanction can be explained by mere familiarity, and that as the more rigorous forms of community penalties become more prevalent, and more familiar, they will also become more acceptable to the public?

Conclusions

Community penalties have undoubtedly grown in stature over the past 20 years (in western nations at least).[24] Sanctions that would have seemed unacceptable decades ago are now commonplace for a wide range of offences and offenders. However, before further progress can be made, a number of steps will have to be taken. The public require more (and better) information about community sanctions, which need to be seen within the context of the alternative: the prison. As well, the public have to be encouraged to move away from a view of offenders as a relatively small, easily identifiable group for whom social exclusion and penal confinement is the only appropriate response. But education alone will be insufficient.

This review of the literature has made it clear that in order for community penalties in more serious cases to be acceptable for the public, they need to carry compensatory and punitive elements. Community penalties also need to deliver more than they have in the past in terms of penal utility. Saving the costs of incarceration and sparing the offender the pains of imprisonment alone are insufficient justification for the widespread implementation of community sanctions. Offenders serving community-based forms of imprisonment, or community penalties designed to replace custody, need to be monitored in a manner which more closely approximates the surveillance of offenders in prison. If this occurs, the public is going to be far more likely to accept community sentencing as an appropriate response to crime.

At the present, members of the public respond to crime by considering how much imprisonment is appropriate, and, latterly, whether a community-based sanction could possibly accomplish the goals of sentencing. As the chapter in this volume by Catriona Mirrlees-Black demonstrates, prison is generally seen by the public to be more effective at achieving a number of sentencing aims. If major inroads are to be made with regard to the use of custody as a sanction, this logic needs to be reversed. The public need to be encouraged to consider which community sanction, or a combination of community sanctions, is appropriate, and whether incarceration is at all necessary. This will only come about as a result of a combination of steps, some of which have been suggested in this chapter.

Notes

1. I am grateful to Mike Hough, Voula Marinos and Pat Mayhew for comments on an earlier draft of this chapter.
2. Sentencing and Parole Reform Bill, Section 14(1). Full text is available at: www.justice.govt.nz/pubs/reports/2001/sentence_reform/.
3. In a speech at the annual Prison Service Conference, 5 February 2002.
4. Cavadino and Dignan summarise the situation in England and Wales by noting that 'the policy of widening the sentencers' repertoire of noncustodial sanctions had notably failed to alleviate the prison numbers crisis' (2002, p. 153).
5. Woelinga (1990) notes that this age category constitutes the largest group of potential clients for the probation service.
6. Immarigeon (1986) found that criminal justice decision-makers in Michigan substantially underestimated the extent of public support for alternative sanctions. Tonry (2002) notes that: 'A wide range of opinion surveys shows the public to be more willing to support the use of community penalties in place of prison terms than most elected officials realise or are willing to acknowledge' (p. 55).
7. The nature of the alternative to restitution is a little unclear from this research. The punishment alternative to restitution was described in the following terms: 'The offender should be punished.' Some respondents may have had considered punitive alternatives to custody, and if this is the case the trends are even more striking.
8. Of the various alternative sanctions considered by respondents, community service was by far the most popular (see Mayhew and van Kesteren, this volume).

9. These statistics also underestimate the degree of public support for alternatives, as they do not include people who responded 'don't know'.

10. Although it will not be pursued here, it is interesting to note that the countries with the highest rates of incarceration also have the highest levels of public support for imprisonment as a sanction.

11. It would also be preferable to ask the sentencing question before people have been asked to recount the details of their own criminal victimisation, as this may influence sentencing preferences.

12. Comparisons between responses to the ICVS in 1996 and 2000 reveal a statistically significant increase in support for prison as a sanction in seven countries (Besserer, 2002). However, comparisons are only possible in a small number of countries, so it is hard to know if this is part of a general trend.

13. The crime scenario involved an offender convicted of burglary for the first time.

14. A third condition was also employed to test a hypothesis unrelated to the subject of this chapter (see Sanders and Roberts, 2000).

15. Recent research by the Home Office (May and Wadwell, 2001) demonstrates another reason for ensuring that community penalties such as the conditional sentence are adequately enforced. They demonstrated that when enforcement action was taken, the result was a reduction in the rate of reconviction.

16. In 2000, see Roberts and Healy (2001).

17. One reason for this is that prosecutors were reluctant to consume court time initiating a breach hearing unless the breach occurred early in the sentence. A breach occurring seven months into a 12-month order would not be worth the time to pursue.

18. The Supreme Court judgment appeared four years after the conditional sentence had been created.

19. *Globe and Mail*, Friday, 3 May 2002.

20. It is interesting to note that in a number of American jurisdictions, sentencing guidelines are careful to restrict their equivalent sanction to the least serious offences committed. Although this arrangement encroaches upon the exercise of judicial discretion, it has the benefit of preventing the imposition of a conditional sentence for the most serious forms of violent crime, such as manslaughter.

21. For example, conditional sentences were imposed in a number of cases of manslaughter, sexual assault and impaired driving causing death involving multiple victims. Each decision attracted a storm of adverse media coverage and commentary.

22. For example, in one of the few public opinion surveys which explored this issue, members of the Canadian public were asked whether they 'somewhat agreed', 'strongly agreed', 'somewhat disagreed' or 'strongly disagreed' that victims should be allowed to submit a Victim Impact Statement (VIS). The results revealed considerable support for VIS: 90 per

cent agreed with the concept, and two-thirds 'strongly agreed' (Department of Justice Canada, 1988).

23. It is important to consider the relative seriousness of the incidents; most were fights between friends or acquaintances and involved minor or no injuries.

24. As can be seen in Table A4.2 of Mayhew and van Kesteren (this volume), support for imprisoning the offender was much higher in Asia and Africa than in Western Europe.

References

American Bar Association (1999) *Perceptions of the U.S. Justice System*. Chicago: America Bar Association.

Angus Reid Group (1997) *Attitudes to Crime*. Ottawa: Angus Reid Group.

Besserer, S. (2002) 'Criminal victimization: an international perspective', *Juristat*, 22(4).

Boers, K. and Sessar, K. (1991) 'Do people really want punishment? On the relationship between acceptance of restitution, needs for punishment, and fear of crime', in K. Sessar and H. Kerner (eds), *Developments in Crime and Crime Control Research*. New York: Springer-Verlag.

Bottoms, A., Gelsthorpe, L. and Rex, S. (2001) *Community Penalities: Changes and Challenges*. Cullompton: Willan Publishing.

Brownlee, I. (1998) *Community Punishment. A Critical Introduction*. London: Longman.

Calvert, M. (2000) 'Community sentences – a sentencer's view', *Criminal Justice Matters*, 39: 20–1.

Canadian Sentencing Commission (1987) *Sentencing Reform. A Canadian Approach*. Ottawa: Supply and Services Canada.

Cavadino, M. and Dignan, J. (2002) *The Penal System*, 3rd edn. London: Sage.

Cullen, F., Fisher, B. and Applegate, B. (2000) 'Public opinion about punishment and corrections', in M. Tonry (ed.), *Crime and Justice. A Review of Research, Volume 27*. Chicago: University of Chicago Press.

Diamond, S. and Stalans, L. (1989) 'The myth of judicial leniency in sentencing', *Behavioral Sciences and the Law*, 7: 73–89.

Doble, J. (1995) *Crime and Corrections: The Views of the People of North Carolina*. Englewood Cliffs, NJ: John Doble Research Associates Inc.

Doble, J. (2002) 'Attitudes to punishment in the US – punitive and liberal opinion' (this volume).

Doble, J. and Klein, J. (1989) *Punishing Criminals. The Public's View*. New York: Edna McConnell Clark Foundation.

Doble, J., Immerwahr, S. and Richardson, A. (1991) *Punishing Criminals*. New York: Edna McConnell Clark Foundation.

Doble Research Associates (1998) *Crime and Corrections: The Views of the People of New Hampshire*. Englewood Cliffs, NJ: Doble Research Associates.

Doob, A. N. (1990) 'Community sanctions and imprisonment: hoping for a miracle but not bothering even to pray for it', *Canadian Journal of Criminology*, 32: 415–28.

Doob, A. N. and Marinos, V. (1995) 'Reconceptualizing punishment: understanding the limitations on the use of intermediate punishments', *University of Chicago Law School Roundtable*, 2: 413–33.

Doob, A. N. and Roberts, J. V. (1988) 'Public punitiveness and public knowledge of the facts: some Canadian surveys', in N. Walker and M. Hough (eds), *Public Attitudes to Sentencing*. Cambridge Studies in Criminology, LIX. Aldershot: Gower.

Dowds, L. (1994) *The Long-eyed View of Law and Order: A Decade of British Social Attitudes Survey Results*. London: Home Office.

Environics Research Group (1998) *Environics Focus on Crime and Justice*, National Opinion Survey. Ottawa: Environics Research Group.

Fattah, E. (1982) 'Public opposition to prison alternatives and community corrections: a strategy for action', *Canadian Journal of Criminology*, 24: 371–85.

Fishkin, J. (1995) *The Voice of the People. Public Opinion and Democracy*. New Haven, CT: Yale University Press.

Focus Canada (1998) *Focus on Crime and Justice*. Ottawa: Focus Canada.

Freiberg, A. (2002) *Sentencing Review*. Melbourne: Department of Justice.

Galaway, B. (1984) 'Survey of public acceptance of restitution as an alternative to imprisonment for property offenders', *Australian and New Zealand Journal of Criminology*, 17: 108–17.

Gandy, J. (1978) 'Attitudes toward the use of restitution', in B. Galaway and J. Hudson (eds), *Offender Restitution in Theory and Action*. Lexington, MA: Lexington Books.

Gibbons, D. (1969) 'Crime and punishment: a study in social attitudes', *Social Forces*, 47: 391–7.

Hedderman, C. and Hearnden, I. (2001) *Setting Standards for Enforcement: the Third ACOP Audit*. London: ACOP (available at: www.sbu.ac.uk/cpru).

Hedderman, C., Ellis, T. and Sugg, D. (1999) *Increasing Confidence in Community Sentences: the Results of Two Demonstration Projects*, Home Office Research Study 194. London: Home Office.

Hignett, C. (2000) 'Punish and rehabilitate – do they mean us?', *Probation Journal*, 47: 51–2.

Home Office (2000) *Protecting the Public. The Correctional Policy Framework*. London: Home Office.

Home Office (2001) *Making Punishments Work. Report of a Review of the Sentencing Framework for England and Wales*. London: Home Office.

Home Office (2002) *Occupation of Prisons, Remand Centres, Young Offender Institutions and Police Cells, April 30, 2002*. London: Home Office.

Hough, M. (1996) 'People talking about punishment', *Howard Journal of Criminal Justice*, 35: 191–214.

Hough, M. (1998) *Attitudes to Punishment: Findings from the 1992 British Crime Survey*, Social Science Research Paper No. 7. London: South Bank University.

Hough, M. and Mayhew, P. (1985) *Taking Account of Crime: Key Findings from the Second British Crime Survey*, Home Office Research Study No. 85. London: HMSO.

Hough, M. and Park, A. (2002) 'How malleable are attitudes to crime and punishment? The results of the British deliberative poll' (in this volume).

Hough, M. and Roberts, J. V. (1998) *Attitudes to Punishment: Findings from the British Crime Survey*, Home Office Research Study No. 179. London: Home Office.

Hough, M. and Roberts, J. V. (1999) 'Sentencing trends in Britain: public knowledge and public opinion', *Punishment and Society*, 1: 7–22.

Immarigeon, R. (1986) 'Surveys reveal broad support for alternative sentencing', *Journal of the National Prison Project*, 9: 1–4.

Junger-Tas, J. and Terlouw, G. (1991) 'The Dutch public and the crime problem', *Dutch Penal Law and Policy, Bulletin*, 05 12 1991.

Kalmthout, A. (2002) 'From community service to community sanctions. Comparative Perspectives', in H. Albrecht and A. Kalmthout (eds), *Community Sanctions and Measures in Europe and North America*. Freiberg: Edition Inscrim.

Laan, P. (1993) 'Het publiek en de taakstraf. Een maatschappelijk draagvlak voor de taakstraf', *Justitiele Verkenningen*, 19: 89–110.

Lockhart, B. and Blair, C. (2002) 'Community sanctions and measures in Ireland', in H. Albrecht and A. Kalmthout (eds), *Community Sanctions and Measures in Europe and North America*. Freiberg: Edition Inscrim.

Maguire, K. and Pastore, A. (1998) *Sourcebook of Criminal Justice Statistics – 1997*. Washington, DC: Bureau of Justice Statistics.

Mair, G. (2001) 'Technology and the future of community penalties', in A. Bottoms, L. Gelsthorpe and S. Rex (eds), *Community Penalties. Change and Challenges*. Cullompton: Willan Publishing.

Marinos, V. (2000) *The Multiple Dimensions of Punishment: 'Intermediate' Sanctions and Interchangeability with Imprisonment*. Toronto: Centre of Criminology, University of Toronto.

Mattinson, J. and Mirrlees-Black, C. (2000) *Attitudes to Crime and Criminal Justice: Findings from the 1998 British Crime Survey. HORS 200*. London: Home Office.

May, C. and Wadwell, J. (2001) *Enforcing Community Penalties: The Relationship between Enforcement and Reconviction*. London: Home Office.

Mayhew, P. and van Kesteren, J. (2002) 'Cross-national attitudes to punishment (this volume).

Morris, N. and Tonry, M. (1990) *Between Prison and Probation: Intermediate Punishments in a Rational Sentencing System*. Oxford: Oxford University Press.

Petersilia, J. (1997) 'Diverting nonviolent prisoners to intermediate sanctions: the impact on California prison admissions and corrections costs', *Corrections Management Quarterly*, 1: 1–15.

Roberts, J. V. (1988) *Public Opinion and Sentencing: Surveys by the Canadian Sentencing Commission. Research Reports of the Canadian Sentencing Commission*. Ottawa: Department of Justice Canada.

Roberts, J. V. (1997) 'Conditional sentencing: sword of Damocles or Pandora's box?', *Canadian Criminal Law Review*, 2: 183–206.

Roberts, J. V. (1999) 'Sentencing trends and sentencing disparitya, in J. V. Roberts and D. Cole (eds), *Making Sense of Sentencing*. Toronto: University of Toronto Press.

Roberts, J. V. (2002) 'Public opinion and sentencing policy', in S. Rex and M. Tonry (eds), *Reform and Punishment: The Future of Sentencing*. Cullompton: Willan Publishing.

Roberts, J. V. and Healy, P. (2001) 'Recent developments in conditional sentencing', *Canadian Bar Review*, 1035–9.

Roberts, J. V. and Stalans, L. (1997) *Public Opinion, Crime, and Criminal Justice*. Boulder, Colorado, CO: Westview Press.

Roberts, J. V., Doob, A. N. and Marinos, V. (2000) *Judicial Attitudes Towards Conditional Sentences of Imprisonment: Results of a National Survey*. Ottawa: Department of Justice Canada.

Roberts, J. V., Stalans, L. S., Indermaur, D. and Hough, M . (2002) *Penal Populism and Public Opinion. Lessons from Five Countries*. Oxford: Oxford University Press.

Rossi, P. and Berk, R. (1997) *Just Punishments. Federal Guidelines and Public Views Compared*. New York: Aldine de Gruyter.

Sanders, T. and Roberts, J. V. (2000) 'Public attitudes toward conditional sentencing: results of a national survey', *Canadian Journal of Behavioural Science*, 32: 199–207.

Seiter, R. (1998) 'Public safety and community supervision: an oxymoron?', *Correctional Management Quarterly*, 2: iv–v.

Sessar, K. (1995) 'Restitution or punishment. an empirical study on attitudes of the public and the justice system in Hamburg', *Eurocriminology*, 8: 199–214.

Shaw, S. (1982) *The People's Justice: A Major Poll of Public Attitudes on Crime and Punishment*. London: Prison Reform Trust.

Solicitor General Canada (1998) *Canadians on Crime*. Ottawa: Communications Group, Solicitor General Canada.

Tonry, M. (2002) 'Community penalties in the US', in H. Albrecht and A. Kalmthout (eds), *Community Sanctions and Measures in Europe and North America*. Freiberg: Edition Inscrim.

Tufts, J. and Roberts J. V. (2002) 'Sentencing juvenile offenders: public preferences and judicial practice', *Criminal Justice Policy Review*, 13: 46–64.

Turnbull, P., McSweeney, T., Webster, R., Edmunds, M. and Hough, M. (2000) *Drug Treatment and Testing Orders: Evaluation Report*. Home Office Research Study No. 212. London: Home Office.

Turner, M., Cullen, F., Sundt, J. and Applegate, B. (1997) 'Public tolerance for community-based sanctions', *Prison Journal*, 77: 6–26.

Walker, J., Collins, M. and Wilson, P. (1988) 'How the public sees sentencing: an Australian survey', in N. Walker and M. Hough (eds), *Public Attitudes to Sentencing. Surveys from Five Countries*. Aldershot: Gower.

Woelinga, D. (1990) 'Probation Service and public opinion in the Netherlands', *Howard Journal*, 29: 246–60.

Wright, M. (1989) 'What the public wants', in M. Wright and B. Galway (eds), *Mediation and Criminal Justice*. London: Sage.

Chapter 4

Cross-national attitudes to punishment

Pat Mayhew and John van Kesteren

Introduction

Despite the fact that opinion polls have explored public attitudes to punishment for over 50 years now, surprisingly little is known about international differences. The reason for this is that – with a few exceptions – researchers have explored public opinion within, rather than across, jurisdictions. However, international comparisons are now possible thanks to the International Crime Victimisation Survey. Analyses of responses to this survey permits us to explore variation across national boundaries as well as to test some hypotheses about public attitudes to punishment, using a truly international rather than simply a national sample.

This chapter takes the latest and most complete results from a question in the International Crime Victimisation Survey (ICVS) that asked respondents about the sentence they would recommend for a recidivist burglar. One strength of the data is the breadth of countries covered – 58 in this analysis, representing all world regions. Another is that results come via a standardised exercise in which the same questionnaire is used in all countries, similar survey procedures are adopted and data analysis coordinated. A third strength is the ability to link attitudes to sentencing – at the individual, country and global region level – to other measures in the ICVS, victimisation being a principal one. Lynch (1993) described the ICVS as a 'quantum leap in international statistics on crime and justice issues'.

Large-scale comparative analyses of social attitudes in different countries are relatively uncommon, in part reflecting the logistical difficulties of mounting standardised surveys in different jurisdictions. By far the two most developed exercises are the International Social

Survey Programme (ISSP) (http://www.issp.org/info.html) and the World Values Survey (http://wvs.isr.umich.edu/index.html). Neither of these, however, takes up attitudes to criminal justice issues. As regards these, there has of course been a multitude of 'local' surveys looking at what people know and think about sentencing, and what sentences they recommend for different types of offenders (see Roberts (1992) and Roberts and Stalans (1997) for reviews). Outside the context of the ICVS, however, comparative analyses have been sparse. Even attitudes to the death penalty – the focus of a particularly large number of local studies – have not been examined cross-culturally (Hood, 1996). A little work has been done comparing levels of victimisation and fear of crime – though the number of countries involved has been relatively small. Some studies have taken results from independently organised surveys so comparability is far from assured (Maxfield, 1987; Block, 1987). A few studies have fielded companion surveys in a handful of countries (e.g. Schwarzenegger, 1989).

A different body of research has involved comparisons of how the public ranks the seriousness of different offences (Newman, 1976; Lenke, 1974; Scott and Thakeb, 1977; Sanders and Hamilton, 1992). This research has revealed a broader consensus than might be imagined, although the number of countries examined has again been relatively limited. Newman (1976), for instance, looked at six countries and found broad agreement about more serious offences like murder and high-value theft, although developed countries were more tolerant of minor crimes. A study in 1974 was closer to the theme of this chapter. Scott and Thakeb (1977) interviewed 2,000 respondents in the USA, Great Britain, the Netherlands, Finland, Sweden, Norway and Denmark. Respondents were given vignettes of 24 offences and asked to recommend penalties from which Scott and Thakeb calculated a so-called 'moral indignation score'. This indicated both the perceived relative seriousness of different crimes (showing the same international consistency as other work), as well as relative degrees of punitiveness. For virtually every crime, Kuwaitis were the least tolerant, followed by the US, then Great Britain and then the Netherlands.

The ICVS has also contributed to the issue of perceptions of crime seriousness through assessments made by victims about the serious-ness of 'their' offences (see, for example, van Kesteren et al. (2000) for the industrialised countries, and van Dijk (1999) for world regions). Victim assessments were made on a simple three-point scale, indica-ting very serious (3), somewhat serious (2) and not very serious (1). Mean seriousness scores for all crimes covered by the ICVS were computed per country, and the crime types were rank ordered on the basis of mean scores. For some purposes, an overall mean score was computed for all crime types taken together (giving each crime type equal weight). The consistency of assessments in industrialised countries and – more surprisingly – across the global regions was notable. For one, overall mean scores did not differ much by country, suggesting the people everywhere have similar attitudinal thresholds about the seriousness of different crimes. Moreover, the relative ranking of the seriousness of different types of victimisation was largely consistent, again indicating a high degree of consensus about the impact of conventional crimes.

For instance, with the 2000 results for 17 industrialised countries, car theft was rated by victims as the most serious in eight out of 16 countries, and second or third most serious in all the rest (with the exception of Denmark). Sexual assault and robbery with a weapon came next, with burglary with entry and assaults with force around the middle of the rankings. Rank orders were similar looking at global regions (van Dijk, 1999): for instance, car theft was rated as the most serious in four of the six regions, and second in Western Europe. Van Dijk correlated each country's ranking with the overall 'world' ranking: the correlations were all very high. The lowest was for victims in Tanzania. The highest (all more than 0.9) were for Costa Rica, Finland and the Ukraine – each in a different world region. The worldwide consensus about the seriousness of these conventional crimes suggests that they involve similar elements everywhere, and have a similar impact. For present purposes, then, differences in views about punishing a burglar will more likely reflect real differences in punitiveness than disagreement about the seriousness of burglary.

The ICVS

The ICVS was set up to provide an alternative measure of crime to police statistics. For comparative purposes, these are problematic because of differences in the way the police define, record and count crime, and because the police in some countries may have more crimes to record simply as a result of higher reporting levels by victims. The essence of victimisation (or 'crime') surveys is that they ask representative samples of the general public about selected offences they have experienced recently, whether or not they reported the crime to the police. For the offences they cover, then, victimisation surveys potentially provide a 'truer' picture of how many people are affected by crime than the more filtered count derived from police statistics.

Comparisons of independently organised surveys offered limited value, however. The number of countries with appropriate surveys is fairly small, and comparability is compromised by differences in survey design, the construction of questions and administration. The standardisation of the ICVS, therefore, is a unique feature.

The ICVS has now been conducted in just over 60 countries (58 of which are used here). Surveys were conducted in 1989, 1993, 1996 and 2000 in just over 20 industrialised countries in Western Europe and what we call here the 'New World' (Canada, United States, Australia and New Zealand), with more than one sweep in many of them. The ICVS has been organised by an International Working Group, drawing in additional national coordinators who have been responsible for the conduct of fieldwork, and where necessary for ensuring sound translation of the questionnaire.[1] Around the time of the second main sweep, UNICRI (United Nations Interregional Criminal Justice Research Institute) started developing similar surveys in non-industrialised countries.[2] For the most part, these surveys were at city level because sampling frames for other areas were often inadequate and fieldwork more difficult. By now city surveys have been done in 19 East and Central European countries (for key results see Zvekic (1998) and Alvazzi del Frate and van Kesteren (forthcoming)), and just over 20 developing countries (see Alvazzi del Frate, 1998).

In the industrialised countries, interviews were mainly done by telephone, partly for cost reasons, partly for better standardisation. Elsewhere, personal interviews are used. Early methodological work on the ICVS offered no strong evidence that mode of interview made much difference to victimisation estimates. Whether it would for attitudinal questions remains open to question. Response rates have been variable (and not always high), but again technical work has not shown that variable response bias results in any substantial way. In industrialised countries, samples of 2,000 people aged 16 or more are the norm, although in less developed countries they are usually about 1,000. The questionnaire is mainly devoted to people's experience of household and personal crimes, but there are a few attitudinal items. The question addressing recommended punishment for a burglar is one of them. We take it as measuring punitiveness and this term is used throughout to describe those who opted for imprisonment.

The punishment question

People were asked about the case of a 21-year-old young man who had stolen a colour television and is found guilty of burglary for a second time.[3] Respondents were invited to state what sentence they felt would be most appropriate, with the choice read out as: fine, prison, community service, suspended sentence or another sentence. Those who opted for imprisonment were asked how long they felt the sentence should be. Community service was intended to denote a sentence that involved the offender performing specific tasks or working for a certain number of hours in the community. A suspended sentence was meant to be one not put into immediate effect, but that could be activated in the event of further offending.

A number of limitations need to be outlined. First, attitudes are being tapped essentially by a single question. There is no way of knowing whether the differences in attitudes observed across countries would hold for offences other than burglary. Second, the original and replacement value of a colour TV will differ according to the development status of the country, and this may influence punitiveness. There is little to be done about this. Third, some respondents may simply give a 'top of the head' response which may not reflect their true opinion. Again, this remains open, although Roberts (1992) argues that people tend to have firm opinions about sentencing that are relatively stable over time. Fourth, the details given in the hypothetical burglary scenario were fairly limited. There was enough information to guide a lay opinion, but probably not enough for a professional sentencer to be able to decide on the appropriate sanction. Fifth, it is possible that as respondents were only allowed one sentencing choice, this may have skewed response rather more to imprisonment than would have been the case if someone could impose a package – say, a fine as well as community service. Finally, preference for imprisonment (the main focus of this chapter) may in part reflect understanding of the other sentencing options (and indeed whether other options exist much at all). Kuhn (1993) argues, for instance, that people in countries where community service is rare may interpret it as hard labour and consider it 'tough'. The best defence here is that more or less everyone will understand the same thing about imprisonment, and will choose this if they feel it appropriate and will not otherwise. This also justifies the emphasis on imprisonment in this chapter.

There have been some previous analyses of the punishment question by Shinkai and Zvekic (1999), Kuhn (1993) and Besserer (2001). However, the results presented here reflect the fullest analysis to date.

The data

As noted, the analysis reported below covers 58 countries, grouped into six global regions: West Europe (14 countries), the New World (4),

East and Central Europe (ECE, 19), Asia (8), Latin America (6) and Africa (7) – where there is better coverage of southern Africa than the north. Table A4.1 in the appendix to this chapter shows the countries included, the type of survey (city or national), the date of the results being used, and the sample size involved (all told, results here are based on 90,000 respondents).[4] All samples are large enough for attitudinal measurement – and indeed cope with this task better than measuring victimisation. There are four cities with samples between 500 and 700. The median sample size was 1,500; it was lowest (approximately 1,000) in Africa and Latin America, and highest in Western Europe (2,000) and the New World (approximately 2,000). (All averages and medians used here and henceforth give each country equal weight to avoid results being biased in the direction of countries with larger samples.)

We were conscious that covering city areas only in some countries might create a source of bias – although findings as regards urbanisation and punitiveness are somewhat mixed, with urban dwellers in higher crime areas sometimes more punitive, but those in rural areas sometimes more so, at least as regards some kinds of offences (Walker and Hough, 1988). Possible bias was tested for all countries where there was appropriate data by comparing attitudes among respondents living in cities with more than 100,000 population against those in smaller localities. Results indicated no strong pattern. In most countries there was little difference, and in a few there were marked differences, but they worked in both directions.

Results from countries who participated only in the 1989 sweep are omitted to ensure timeliness (Spain, Norway, West Germany). Otherwise, data from the latest sweep in each country is used. There are seven countries where attitudes were measured in 1992, 18 in 1996/7, and 33 in 2000/1. In each country, those aged 16 or more were interviewed. To improve representativeness, results here are weighted by age and gender, and for the national surveys also by region within the country. Of course, country totals ignore within-country differences between people as regards their attitudes, although these are given some attention later.

Three measures of punitiveness are used below. The first is simply the percentage of respondents who chose imprisonment – the 'percentage prison measure'. (Those who could not recommend a sentence ('don't knows') are included in the base throughout. Overall, 4 per cent fell into this category, with the regional figures similar except in Africa, where few respondents did not have an opinion. The second measure – the 'punitiveness score' – takes account of the length of sentence

Figure 4.1 Support for imprisonment and community service, by global region.

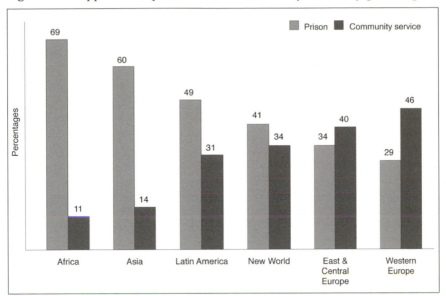

recommended by those who opted for imprisonment. A mean number of months in prison is calculated on the basis of the sample as a whole; this, then, reflects both the level of support for imprisonment, as well as the severity of the term. (Those who could not specify a sentence length were set to the mean of those who could.) The third measure - the 'sentence length measure' – is the mean number of months in prison calculated only for those who opted for imprisonment. Table A4.2 in the appendix to this chapter gives the full range of results.

Attitudes to imprisonment

Just over four in ten of all respondents chose imprisonment as the most appropriate sentence for the young recidivist burglar. Regionally, the figure was 69 per cent in Africa, 60 per cent in Asia and about 50 per cent in Latin America (Figure 4.1). Support was lowest in Western Europe (just over a quarter opted for imprisonment). There is a clear divide, then, between developing countries and others. The features of the punishment question mentioned earlier may contribute in part to this, but would not plausibly explain all of it.

There were country differences within each region, and the range of opinion was most marked in Western Europe and Asia. In the New

Table 4.1 Support for imprisonment, by regions (based on % opting for imprisonment)

	Quartile 4 (most punitive)	Quartile 3	Quartile 2	Quartile 1 (least punitive)
Western Europe	N. Ireland	Scotland, Malta, Eng. & Wales	Netherlands, Sweden	Portugal, Italy, Belgium, Denmark, Finland, France, Austria, Catalonia
New World	USA	Canada	Australia	New Zealand
East and Central Europe		Romania, Latvia, Albania, Belarus, Yugoslavia	Macedonia, Bulgaria, Russia, Slovakia, Ukraine, Slovenia, Estonia, Hungary, Kyrgyzstan	Czech Republic, Lithuania, Croatia, Poland, Georgia
Asia	China, Philippines, Indonesia, India, Cambodia	Japan	Mongolia	Azerbaijan
Africa	Uganda, Zimbabwe, Tanzania, South Africa, Egypt, Botswana, Tunisia			
Latin America	Paraguay	Argentina, Costa Rica, Colombia, Brazil	Bolivia	

World, those in the USA and Canada were more punitive than those in Australia and New Zealand. In the former, support for imprisonment was strongest in the UK and Malta (with just over half opting for prison); it was weakest in France, Austria and Catalonia. In the New World, those in the USA and Canada were more punitive than Australia or New Zealand. In East and Central Europe (ECE), the most punitive were in Romania, Latvia and Albania, and the least in Poland and Georgia (where fines got above average support). In Asia, people in China and the Philippines supported imprisonment most (eight out of ten did so); there were lower values in Mongolia and Azerbaijan. In Africa there was uniformly strong support for imprisonment, but Uganda and Zimbabwe stood out most. There was comparatively less variation in Latin American countries, where between four and six out of ten opted for prison. Table 4.1 summarises the country positions by dividing the range of values (percentage recommending imprisonment) into quartiles, and grouping them by region. For instance, the most punitive respondents in Western Europe were those in Northern Ireland; the very least punitive were in Catalonia.

As one would expect, results on the basis of the sample punitiveness score were fairly similar to the percentage prison measure (the correlation between the two was 0.738; $p < 0.001$). However, there was a tendency for the rank order of countries in Western Europe and the New World to be lower on the sample punitiveness score, reflecting a greater preference for shorter prison sentences among respondents from these countries. (The same applied to Japan.) The converse held in ECE. Here, several countries that opted for imprisonment wanted comparatively long sentences, and thus ranked higher on the punitiveness score measure than they did on the percentage prison measure.

Table 4.2 shows some details of the average length of imprisonment (in months) recommended by those who opted for imprisonment. The range on the values is to be noted. On this measure, the most punitive respondents were in Botswana, Tanzania and Cambodia where a sentence of seven years or more was the average recommended.

Fines and suspended sentences

Fines, and even more so a suspended sentence, generally attracted little support (Tables 4.3 and A4.2). At the regional level, there was no marked variation in support for a fine, with 10 per cent of all respondents opting for this. At the country level, there was more variation, with strongest support in Azerbaijan (36 per cent chose a fine), Albania (31 per cent), and Georgia (25 per cent). Overall, 5 per

71

Table 4.2 Average length of sentence recommended (those who opted for imprisonment)

	Average length of sentence recommended (months)	Standard deviation (months)	Highest values	Lowest values
Africa	69	36	Botswana (123) Tanzania (117)	Egypt (44) Tunisia (34)
Asia	43	25	Cambodia (87) China (62)	Philippines (31) Japan (19)
Latin America	38	11	Costa Rica (49) Paraguay (48)	Colombia (27) Brazil (26)
East and Central Europe	36	14	Romania (75) Ukraine (54)	Macedonia (22) Estonia (7)
New World	21	7	USA (30) Canada (22)	New Zealand (16) Australia (15)
Western Europe	17	7	Italy (30) Eng. & Wales (24)	Finland (8) Denmark (7)

cent opted for a suspended sentence, with the highest level in ECE and the lowest in Africa.

Community service order

The most evident polarisation was between support for imprisonment on the one hand and support for community service on the other (the correlation between them was −0.89). Community service was the most favoured sentencing option overall in Western Europe and ECE (see Figure 4.1). It attracted particularly strong support in France, Catalonia and Austria – where about two out of three respondents chose it in preference to any other sentence. About half made the same choice in six of the other West Europe countries. Support was surprisingly high in Latin America – although there is possibly some question as to the interpretation of the sanction.

Relationship between public support for imprisonment and national imprisonment rates

Some previous analyses of ICVS results for industrialised countries have shown some correspondence between public attitudes to the

Table 4.3 Percentage opting for a fine or suspended sentence (percentages)

	Average	Standard deviation	Highest values	Lowest values
% opting for a fine				
Africa	9	4	Tunisia (17)	Egypt (6) Tanzania (6)
Asia	13	11	Azerbaijan (36)	China (3) Indonesia (2)
Latin America	7	4	Colombia (11)	Brazil (0)
East and Central Europe	11	7	Albania (31) Georgia (25)	Yugoslavia (5) Slovakia (6)
New World	9	1	New Zealand (10)	Australia (8)
Western Europe	10	3	Catalonia (15) Finland (15)	Eng. & Wales (7)
% opting for suspended sentence				
Africa	1	1	South Africa (3)	Botswana (0)
Asia	5	4	Azerbaijan (12)	Philippines (1) Japan (1)
Latin America	5	6	Bolivia (16)	Brazil (0)
East and Central Europe	7	4	Kyrgyzstan (21) Georgia (14)	Belarus (1) Albania (0)
New World	5	4	Australia (10)	USA (1)
Western Europe	6	4	Finland (16) Denmark (13)	Catalonia (1) Portugal (1)

sentencing of a burglar and actual use of imprisonment (e.g. Mayhew and van Dijk, 1997; Besserer, 2001). The interpretation of this, of course, is equivocal. Public attitudes may mirror judicial practice, or alternatively judicial practice may simply reflect dominant public attitudes.

In any event, though, with the current range of countries and timing of results, there is no evident relationship between current imprisonment rates and either the ICVS percentage prison measure ($r = 0.028$) or the overall punitive score ($r = 0.105$). (Walmsley's (2002) figures are taken as the best guide to comparative imprisonment rates, although they are inevitably vulnerable to different practices in different countries – for instance, as regards whether pre-trial detainees and juveniles are held under the authority of the prison administration.) Even taking the Western European and New World countries, which have featured most in previous analysis, the relationship was relatively weak on the current data (Spearman's $r = 0.245$; $n = 18$; ns). For the ECE, it was negligible (Spearman's $r = 0.153$; $n = 19$; ns). On the face of it, then, this suggests that incarceration rates are independent of public punitiveness. Data limitations, though, may be an issue.

Trends

A number of countries have taken part in more than one sweep of the ICVS. One can look, then, at whether the most punitive countries tend to stay the most punitive, as well as whether support for imprisonment has increased or decreased over time within a single jurisdiction). Among the industrialised countries looked at by van Kesteren et al. (2000), there was considerable consistency in relative ranking for countries with repeat measures. For instance, of ten countries with measures for both 1989 and 2000, rank order positions on support for imprisonment were nearly identical.

For ECE countries with multiple administrations of the survey (there are 15 with more than one), there is the same general consistency, although among the six countries with measures for 1992 and 2000, the relative position of Georgia, and the Czech Republic changed most – with fewer in favour of imprisonment at the later date. For the 15 countries with measures for 1996/7 and 2000, country positions did not shift much either (Spearman's $r = 0.80$; $n = 15$; $p < 0.05$).

Leaving aside changes in relative levels of support for imprisonment, there are distinct differences by region as regards changes in attitudes. Taking Western Europe and the New World together, support for imprisonment has generally increased (at the expense of a decline in the popularity of community service). Figure 4.2 shows the average percentage in favour of imprisonment in the four countries that took part in all four sweeps of the ICVS, in six countries for which there are measures for 1989 and 2000, and in Sweden with measures for 1992 and 2000. Support increased in each country over these periods with the exception of France (no significant difference) and Belgium, where there was a fall in support between 1989 and 1992 but then an increase by 2000. The most marked increase in support since 1989 has been in Canada, the UK and the Netherlands

In contrast, the proportion of respondents choosing imprisonment for the burglar generally fell in the ECE countries, and in three Asian countries with two measures (Mongolia, Indonesia and the Philippines). Of 15 ECE countries with measures in 1996/7 and 2000, support fell in ten, remained on much of a par in three (Bulgaria, Latvia and

Figure 4.2 Changes in support for imprisonment, selected West European and New World countries (percentage supporting imprisonment for the burglar).

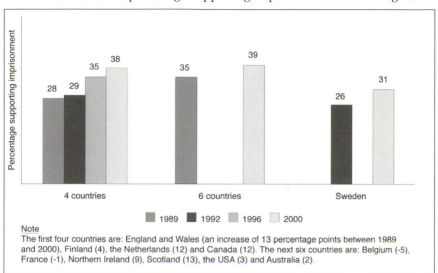

Note
The first four countries are: England and Wales (an increase of 13 percentage points between 1989 and 2000), Finland (4), the Netherlands (12) and Canada (12). The next six countries are: Belgium (-5), France (-1), Northern Ireland (9), Scotland (13), the USA (3) and Australia (2).

Belarus), and rose in Poland and Croatia. The most marked declines were in Georgia, Lithuania and Albania, where the number in support of imprisonment fell by 15 percentage points or more. Figure 4.3 summarises the overall picture. In Asia, the biggest fall was in Indonesia (1992–96).

This change over what is a relatively short time span is notable. Some variability in the figures might be expected because of sample sizes, although of the 13 ECE and Asian countries with falls, the change was statistically significant in eleven (10 per cent level, two-tail test). Social and political change over the last decade cannot be ruled out. There was no particular upward shift in the countries' rankings in terms of the UN Human Development Indicator, which is strongly associated with national-level support for imprisonment, as will be seen. Nonetheless, the change in views is consistent with social development having some part to play in liberalising attitudes.

It is also broadly consistent with falls in imprisonment. Of the 13 ECE countries for which data are available, national imprisonment rates fell in eight of them roughly between the middle and late 1990s. There was no clear correspondence between the extent of the falls in imprisonment and those in preferences for prison (for instance, imprisonment rates fell more in Latvia where preference for prison did not change much, than in the Czech Republic where it dropped markedly). However, the background fall in the use of imprisonment

Figure 4.3 Changes in support for imprisonment, selected East and Central European countries (percentage supporting imprisonment for the burglar).

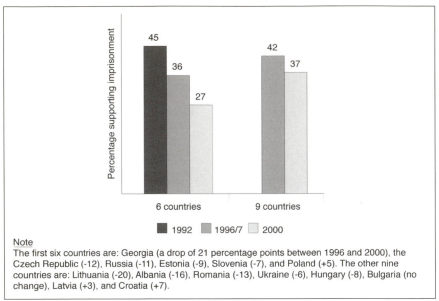

Note

The first six countries are: Georgia (a drop of 21 percentage points between 1996 and 2000), the Czech Republic (-12), Russia (-11), Estonia (-9), Slovenia (-7), and Poland (+5). The other nine countries are: Lithuania (-20), Albania (-16), Romania (-13), Ukraine (-6), Hungary (-8), Bulgaria (no change), Latvia (+3), and Croatia (+7).

alongside a general softening of attitudes in ECE countries is an interesting coincidence, and all the more so as it contrasts with the situation in Western Europe and North America. Here, the prison population rose in all countries where public support for imprisonment increased, with the exception of Finland and Northern Ireland, where special circumstances applied. (There was no sound data for the three Asian countries regarding change in imprisonment rates.)

Correlates of punitiveness

We now turn to the question of which types of people most favour imprisonment, and how invariant the picture is across different countries. Results from the ICVS have so far focused mainly on industrialised countries, albeit with a wider range than in other studies. One of the firmest findings is that the less educated hold more punitive views. Many studies also indicate that the elderly have more repressive views, but not all studies do, including ICVS analyses (e.g. Kuhn, 1993; Besserer, 2001). Men are usually found to be more punitive than women, and indeed this was the only consistent correlate in

Besserer's examination of 1996 and 2000 ICVS results for ten indus-trialised countries. There is no consistent evidence that experience of victimisation increases punitiveness. Walker and Hough (1988) suggest that this may be because few respondents have suffered crimes with long and serious effects, and that many victims realise from personal experience that what happens is not overly serious, whereas non-victims may instead exaggerate the consequences.

Since burglary is generally seen as a particularly upsetting offence, one might suppose this explanation holds up less well. In fact, though, ICVS analyses have not produced a clear picture even relating burglary victimisation specifically to punitiveness. There are also mixed results as regards fear of crime and punitiveness – though different measures of each may be an issue. A recent study by Sprott and Doob (1997), using the large sample in Canada's 1993 General Social Survey, found the more fearful to be markedly more punitive, holding age and gender constant. (They measured fear through questions of feeling safe at home and on the streets, and punitiveness by whether the courts were too lenient or not.) With regard to the ICVS, Besserer (2001) also found some relationship between punitiveness and fear in ten industrialised countries taking account of other factors. Kuhn (1993), however, presented more equivocal results, perhaps because he included in his model a 'country effect', which Skogan (1993) showed was itself related to fear independent of other things.

Some underlying attitudinal disposition linked to authoritarian or disciplinarian views seems a key factor in preferring repressive crime control – indeed more so than demographic characteristics. Most of the local studies have measured such a disposition at individual level. Although the ICVS included no such personal measure, it allows the possibility of testing whether a dominant socio-legal tradition – subsumed by the global regional variable – is a major factor in shaping attitudes.

The 58 countries here, then, provide an opportunity to look at the correlates of punitiveness across a very broad span. As a first step, we compared people who chose imprisonment as the sanction for the burglar to others in relation to a number of the key variables discussed above. Table 4.4 summarises the results by showing the number of countries in which results went in the dominant direction, and the number in which they did not. A significance level of 10 per cent was taken to assess this. The most consistent effect was in relation to gender (with men more punitive in 40 out of 58 countries). Other relationships were rather less consistent although the overall message was that punitiveness was higher for younger people, the less well-educated, those who had been

Table 4.4 Bivariate relationships between punitiveness and key variables

More punitive	Dominant direction	Other direction	No difference	N countries[1]
Men	40	0	18	58
Young (16–39 vs. 40 +)	20	12	25	57
Married	12	6	39	57
Lower education[2]	26	3	28	57
Lower income[2]	13	7	37	57
Burglary victim (5 years)	15	2	41	58
Feel unsafe after dark	21	3	33	57
Thinks burglary likely	21	3	34	58
Dissatisfied with the police	20	5	32	57

Notes
1. Some information missing for Estonia.
2. Education and income measures are dichotomised for each country so do not constitute an international measure.

victimised by burglary in the last five years, and who felt fearful either out of the streets at night or because they felt burglary was likely in the next year. There were deviations from the dominant pattern in all regions, but rather more so in Asia, Africa, and Latin America.

We next developed multivariate models using log linear analysis to assess differences in punitiveness taking account of any overlap between key variables. Marital status and feeling safe/unsafe after dark were excluded (the first because its effect was very small, the latter because it is more difficult to relate to punishing a burglar than is perceptions of the likelihood of burglary). The national burglary victimisation rate (the five-year measure) was added as a covariate on the assumption that this could influence individual attitudes.

Six models are shown in Table 4.5. The first applies to all cases in all regions (the overall model). Within this, to capture socio-cultural background, there is an indicator of global region, as well as a grouping of Anglophone countries. There are then separate models for each of five other regions – with Western Europe and the New World taken together as 'industrialised countries'. Eight common variables were entered in four stages. Gender, age, education and income were entered first. (Education and income were, as one would expect, correlated with each other, but not sufficiently so (especially in Africa and Latin America) to consider omitting income.) The second stage entered personal burglary victimisation, and the national rate of

Table 4.5 Log linear models explaining preference for imprisonment in relation to selected variables, all cases and five global regions (odds ratios)

	All cases	Industrialised countries	East & Central Europe	Asia	Africa	Latin America
Main effect	0.72*	0.48*	0.47*	1.21	1.81*	0.76
Gender (female is the reference category)						
Male	1.27*	1.40*	1.29*	1.08	0.87	1.81*
Education (high is the reference category)						
Low	1.24*	1.38*	1.18*	1.12*	0.91	1.61*
Income (high is the reference category)						
Low	1.01	1.13*	1.00	0.73	1.10	1.13
Age (40 + is the reference category)						
16–39	1.12*	1.32*	0.93*	1.35*	1.17*	0.86*
Victim of burglary (non-victim is the reference category)						
Yes	1.04	0.95	1.12	0.95	1.09	0.95
Burglary rate						
Covariate	1.02*	1.01	1.00	1.03*	1.01	1.01
Assessment of risk (low is the reference category)						
High	1.09*	0.94	1.28*	0.96	1.26*	0.99
Satisfied with the police (satisfied is the reference category)						
No	1.06*	1.26*	1.10	0.82	1.08	1.08

Region (the reference category for these regions is the 'main effect' above)

Western Europe	0.54*
New World	0.78*
East & Central Europe	0.56*
Asia	2.02*
Africa	2.21*
Latin America	0.94

(Reference category is Industrialised countries)

Non-Anglophone countries	0.56*	Western Europe without the UK and Malta
Anglophone countries	1.80*	Anglophone countries (New World, UK and Malta)

Note
*Indicates significance at p <0.5 level on a two-tail test.

burglary. The third stage entered perceived risk of burglary and satisfaction with the quality of local policing. The model for indus-trialised countries included a variable denoting 'Anglophone' countries (grouping the three UK countries, Malta and all four New World countries) since previous analyses has suggested that these are more punitive than other industrialised countries, possibly because of commonalities in legal tradition.

The parameters presented are the independent contribution of each variable. For each model there is a 'main effect' that is the odds ratio of choosing a prison sentence as against another sentence. For other variables (e.g. gender), the odds ratios are given relative to a reference category. For instance, in the overall model, men are 1.27 times more likely to opt for imprisonment than women, who are the reference category. The reference category for the regional variables in the overall model is the 'main effect'.

The 'main effect' results show large differences between the five regions. The industrialised and ECE countries are the least punitive. Latin America is near the overall average. Asia is above this average and Africa even more so. The 'region effect' in the overall model confirms the same results, although it additionally shows that the New World is more punitive than Western Europe as a whole – though certainly this reflects the particularly high punitiveness levels in the USA and Canada. Taking these Western Europe countries and the New World together in the second (industrialised countries) model, though, and grouping the four New World countries with the UK and Malta, shows a clear 'Anglophone effect'. The odds ratio for Anglophone countries equals 1.80, whereas that for the other industrialised coun-tries is much lower, at 0.56.

The importance of region in the overall model suggests that there is some overarching factor at play such that support for imprisonment is stronger in countries lower down on the social and economic scale. Figure 4.4 illustrates this by grouping the countries in terms of their values on the 1998 UN Human Development Index (HDI). The Anglophone countries are kept as a separate group. There is a clear increase in punitiveness as HDI values fall, with the divergence from the overall pattern coming only from the Anglophone countries.

Table 4.5 also shows that the effects of the other variables are not completely consistent over the regions.

- *Gender*. In four out of five of the global regions, men are more punitive than women, but this ranges from 1.08 times more in Asia (not statistically significant) to 1.61 times more in Latin America. The

Figure 4.4 Percentage supporting imprisonment, by Human Development Indicator scores.

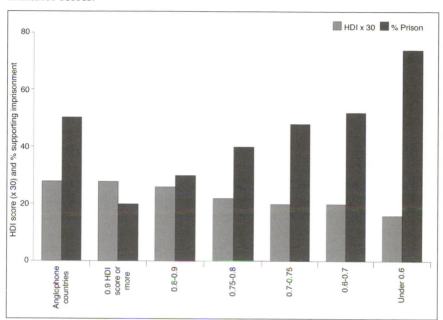

gender effect is in the other direction in Africa, but this is not statistically robust, taking other variables into account.

- *Education.* Overall, the less educated are 1.24 times more often in favour of imprisonment than others. This holds in four regions, being strongest in Latin America (1.61). Again, the effect is in the opposite direction in Africa but is not statistically robust.

- *Income.* There is no significant income effect in the overall model, and a significant one only in the industrialised countries where it seems that low income increases punitiveness, independent of poorer educational standing

- *Age.* People aged 16 to 40 are more punitive in the industrialised countries, Asia and Africa. But the reverse applies in East and Central Europe and Latin America. (Additional analysis with more refined age breakdowns showed much the same results.)

- *Burglary victimisation.* This does not show any significant effect in any region.

- *National burglary rate.* This only showed a significant effect in the overall model and in Asia.[5]

- *Perceived risk of burglary.* Respondents who regarded themselves as likely to be burgled in the coming year were more punitive in East and Central Europe and Africa only.

- *Satisfaction with the police.* Dissatisfaction with police performance only exerted an independent significant effect on punitiveness in the industrialised countries.

The overall thrust of these results, then, is that none of the key variables considered have the same effect on preference for imprisonment in all five global regions. It is hard to know why. It may reflect cultural differences, or perhaps some diversity in the significance of imprisonment for different groups of people in different jurisdictions.

Discussion

The ICVS is mainly known for its cross-national comparisons of victimisation (see, for example, van Dijk, 1999; van Dijk and Kangaspunta, 2000), with some of the other topics it covers having received less attention. With regard to attitudes to punishment, though, ICVS results provide unique information on people's views across a very wide range of countries. Indeed, there has been nothing approaching this scale of coverage outside the ICVS. The questions on attitudes to punishment have been subject to some previous analyses, but this chapter goes further.

The scope of the punishment questions is much more limited than the scope of countries covered. Restrictions on the size of the questionnaire (to keep costs down, and ensure adequate response) means that only burglary has been asked about – albeit a common offence, and one regarded with much the same seriousness in different countries. There remains plenty of scope for more comparative work. For instance, it would be valuable to assess whether there are differences in attitudes towards the punishment of juveniles as well as adults. Research in the UK shows that people are especially unhappy about how they believe the courts handle juveniles (Mattinson and Mirrlees-Black, 2000), although work in Canada shows that they nonetheless see imprisonment as less appropriate for them (Tuft and Roberts, 2002). It would also be useful to know more about what people in different countries think about the aims of punishment in terms of retribution, rehabilitation or deterrence. It would be illuminating, too, to assess whether the public belief that the courts are too lenient (a persistent finding of research in industrialised countries) holds up in a wider range of judicial contexts.

Four features of the results merit emphasis. The first is that this current analysis does not confirm any relationship between the level of public support for imprisonment and its use by the judiciary. Such a relationship has been found in ICVS analysis based on a smaller set of countries and using slightly different imprisonment data (or at least different reference periods). In the present analysis, though, even taking Western Europe and the New World together, there was only a very weak relationship between support for imprisonment and the frequency of its use. The lack of a broader relationship is notable since it seems more plausible than not that there should be some mirroring of public attitudes and judicial practice. It may be that a more precise measure of incarceration for burglars would generate different findings. Or it may be that current measures of imprisonment rates in some countries may not be sufficiently reliable.

A second feature of the results regards the correlates of punitiveness. With bivariate analysis, the dominant patterns were for higher levels of punitiveness among men, the less well educated, younger people, burglary victims, the more fearful and those dissatisfied with police performance. Yet results from many countries did not conform (albeit that some variation is to be expected simply due to sampling error). Multivariate analysis at the global region level confirmed some of the patterns, but dented the contribution of personal victimisation and dissatisfaction with police performance. Moreover, none of the key variables had the same effect on preference for imprisonment for respondents in all regions.

Setting measurement error aside, this suggests some cultural divergence that remains essentially unmeasured. The regional grouping in the ICVS comes nearest to capturing the socio-legal background against which respondents in different countries gave their views – and it is not of course very satisfactory in this regard. Social development, however, appears one facet of context that is of overarching importance in so far as there was more support for imprisonment in countries lower down on the UN Human Development Index. The greater punitiveness observed in Africa, Asia and Latin America is of course consistent with this. So too is the 'softening' of attitudes observed over time in those ECE countries which have participated in the ICVS more than once. It may well be that the greater degree of support for imprisonment in less developed countries reflects the fact that there are generally fewer non-custodial alternatives available, and greater difficulties in implementing them (Joutsen and Zvekic, 1994). Indeed, it is worth bearing in mind that even in advanced countries other options are far from well known. Hough and Roberts (1998), for instance, showed that when asked to identify as many community-based sanctions as they could, only a third of people in England and Wales mentioned probation, and even fewer mentioned a suspended sentence. In a recent Canadian study, too, Tuft and Roberts (2002) demonstrated that almost half of those who had initially chosen prison were prepared to support other options when these were explained to them (see also research by John Doble discussed elsewhere in this volume). Credible alternatives to prison, then, seem under-appreciated and it could well be that if people were more familiar with them, support for imprisonment would decline. Modernisation and social development will play some part in this.

Thirdly, the analysis does not support the hypothesis that experience of victimisation (even of burglary itself) increases support for imprisonment. This is an important finding (especially given some inconsistency in other studies) since hardline criminal justice policy is often justified by the claim that victims are the main proponents of a 'tougher' approach to sentencing. Those who seek improved services for victims, in contrast, tend to want to undermine the idea that victims are consistently punitive – both because it provides a more benign climate for arguing for better victim provision, and because it undermines the argument that victims should not play more of a part in sentencing procedures because they will be overly punitive.

Finally, the emphasis here on attitudes towards imprisonment should not obscure the level of support that community service attracts. The current data reveal that in 23 out of the 58 countries worldwide, more people supported community service than imprisonment, and in Western Europe, the New World and the ECE countries, 22 countries out of 37 did so. As political rhetoric about crime and punishment is fuelled by the idea of unshakeable and widespread public support for imprisonment, the support for community service in this global context is worth emphasising. This has been done before on the basis of ICVS results, and it bears being done again.

Appendix

Table A4.1 Details of samples used (type of sample, date of results, and sample size)

	Type of survey (other than national)	Date of results used	Sample size		Type of survey (other than national)	Date of results used	Sample size
Western Europe				*Asia*			
Austria		1996	1,507	Azerbaijan	city	2000	930
Belgium		2000	2,501	Cambodia	city	2001	1,245
Catalonia	regional	2000	2,909	China	city	1992	2,000
Denmark		2000	3,007	India	city	1996	1,200
England & Wales		2000	1,947	Indonesia	city	1996	1,400
Finland		2000	1,782	Japan		2000	2,211
France		2000	1,000	Mongolia	city	2000	944
Italy		1992	2,024	Philippines	city	1996	1,500
Malta		1997	1,000	*Africa*			
Netherlands		2000	2,000	Botswana	city	1997	644
Northern Ireland		2000	1,511	Egypt	city	1992	1,000
Portugal		2000	2,000	South Africa	city	1996	1,006
Scotland		2000	2,055	Tanzania	city	1992	1,002
Sweden		2000	2,001	Tunisia	city	1992	1,086
New World				Uganda	city	1992	1,023
Australia		2000	2,005	Zimbabwe	city	1996	1,006
Canada		2000	2,078	*Latin America*			
New Zealand		1992	2,048	Argentina	city	1996	1,000
USA		2000	1,000	Bolivia	city	1996	999

Table A4.1 *Continued*

	Type of survey (other than national)	Date of results used	Sample size
East and Central Europe			
Albania	city	2000	1,498
Belarus	city	2000	1,520
Bulgaria	city	2000	1,505
Croatia	city	2000	1,532
Czech Republic	city	2000	1,511
Estonia	city	2000	502
Georgia	city	2000	1,000
Hungary	city	2000	1,513
Kyrgyzstan	city	1996	1,750
Latvia	city	2000	1,002
Lithuania	city	2000	1,526
Macedonia	city	1996	700
Poland		2000	5,276
Romania	city	2000	1,506
Russia	city	2000	1,500
Slovakia	city	1997	1,105
Slovenia		2001	3,887
Ukraine	city	2000	1,509
Yugoslavia	city	1996	1,094

	Type of survey (other than national)	Date of results used	Sample size
Brazil	city	1996	1,000
Colombia	city	1997	1,000
Costa Rica	city	1996	1,000
Paraguay	city	1996	587

Table A4.2 Recommended punishments, by region and country

		% recommending different sentences					Average length of imprisonment (months)	
	Fine	Prison	Community service	Suspended sentence	Other sentence	Don't know	Those wanting prison	All respondents
Western Europe								
Austria	14	10	62	8	2	4	10	1
Belgium	11	21	57	5	3	3	17	3
Catalonia	15	7	65	1	2	9	23	1
Denmark	9	20	50	13	4	4	7	1
England & Wales	7	51	28	5	4	5	24	12
Finland	15	19	47	16	2	2	8	1
France	8	12	69	5	2	4	14	2
Italy	10	22	47	4	5	13	30	6
Malta	8	52	29	4	7	0	18	9
Netherlands	11	37	30	10	5	6	19	6
Northern Ireland	8	54	29	4	2	3	21	11
Portugal	9	26	54	1	6	4	23	6
Scotland	11	52	24	5	4	4	21	10
Sweden	11	31	47	4	3	4	11	3
New World								
Australia	8	37	35	10	4	5	15	5
Canada	9	45	32	3	7	3	22	10
New Zealand	10	26	51	3	7	4	16	4
USA	9	56	20	1	8	6	30	16

Changing Attitudes to Punishment

Table A4.2 *Continued*

| | % recommending different sentences | | | | | | Average length of imprisonment (months) | |
	Fine	Prison	Community service	Suspended sentence	Other sentence	Don't know	Those wanting prison	All respondents
East and Central Europe								
Albania	31	46	15	0	2	6	28	13
Belarus	11	43	32	1	5	8	45	19
Bulgaria	8	40	38	6	2	6	35	13
Croatia	6	22	55	7	3	7	38	7
Czech Republic	6	26	57	7	2	1	26	6
Estonia	6	30	51	8	3	3	7	7
Georgia	25	16	42	14	2	2	41	6
Hungary	6	29	44	9	7	4	30	8
Kyrgyzstan	15	27	35	21	2	0	46	12
Latvia	7	48	30	9	4	2	35	17
Lithuania	13	24	46	2	7	9	37	8
Macedonia	11	41	25	12	3	9	22	9
Poland	10	21	55	6	4	5	31	6
Romania	6	49	33	2	5	5	75	34
Russia	9	38	43	3	8	0	29	9
Slovakia	5	36	43	7	5	4	42	16
Slovenia	13	31	42	8	3	3	24	7
Ukraine	9	34	43	4	3	6	54	17
Yugoslavia	5	42	39	6	3	5	35	14

Asia								
Azerbaijan	36	24	19	12	4	3	42	10
Cambodia	17	64	4	6	7	3	97	61
China	3	84	7	2	4	0	62	51
India	10	67	13	2	1	8	37	24
Indonesia	2	68	10	3	10	6	25	20
Japan	17	51	19	1	0	13	19	10
Mongolia	11	40	35	3	6	5	32	12
Philippines	11	79	3	1	2	3	31	24
Africa								
Botswana	9	62	16	0	8	4	123	75
Egypt	6	66	8	1	20	0	44	28
South Africa	9	66	16	3	2	3	47	31
Tanzania	6	75	13	1	4	0	117	87
Tunisia	17	56	11	1	14	0	34	19
Uganda	8	80	7	1	4	0	51	41
Zimbabwe	8	79	6	2	2	2	63	49
Latin America								
Argentina	8	54	32	6	0	1	30	16
Bolivia	8	40	18	16	9	9	46	17
Brazil	0	44	54		0	2	26	11
Colombia	11	45	34	2	4	5	27	12
Costa Rica	7	52	27	2	7	5	49	24
Paraguay	7	58	22	3	6	4	48	27

Notes

1. In the main, each industrialised country has met its own survey costs, with much of the administrative overheads borne by the Dutch Ministry of Justice. The technical management of most of the surveys in industrialised countries has been carried out by InterView-NSS, a Dutch survey company. They subcontracted fieldwork to survey companies in the participating countries, maintaining responsibility for the questionnaire, sample selection and interview procedures. The data from the surveys have been integrated and processed by researchers at Leiden University.
2. Surveys in developing countries and in East and Central Europe were most funded by the Dutch government, the UK Home Office and the United Nations on an ad hoc basis.
3. The precise wording of the question was: 'People have different ideas about the sentences which should be given to offenders. Take for instance the case of a 21-year-old man who is found guilty of burglary/housebreaking for the second time. This time he has taken a colour TV. Which of the following sentences do you consider the most appropriate for such a case [read out]: fine, prison, community service, suspended sentence, and other sentence?'
4. Poland is included here in the group of East and Central Europe countries, though in some publications it has been included in the industrialised Western European countries. In the report of the second sweep of the ICVS, Czechoslovakia was also reported on as a western industrialised country (van Dijk and Mayhew, 1992).
5. In a separate overall model, omitting the regional variable, the national burglary rate showed a large, significant effect. This indicates both that burglary levels vary greatly across region and that they correlate with the attitude towards punishment. The burglary effect, though, is subsumed by the broader regional variable.

References

Alvazzi del Frate, A. (1998) *Victims of Crime in the Developing World*, Publication No. 57 (Rome: UNICRI).

Alvazzi del Frate, A. and van Kesteren, J. (forthcoming) *Criminal Victimisation in Urban Europe* (Turin: UNICRI).

Besserer, S. (2001) 'Attitudes towards sentencing in nine industrialized countries', in Paul Nieuwbeerta (ed.), *Crime Victimization in Comparative Perspective*. The Hague: Boom Juridische uitgevers, pp. 391–409.

Block, R. (1987) *A Comparison of Victimization, Crime Assessment and Fear of Crime in England and Wales, the Netherlands, Scotland and the United States*, paper presented to the Council of Europe Conference on the Reduction of Urban Security, Barcelona, Spain, 1987.

Hood, R. (1996) *The Death Penalty: A Worldwide Perspective* (Oxford: Oxford University Press).

Hough, M. and Roberts, J. V. (1998) *Attitudes to Punishment: Findings from the British Crime Survey*, Home Office Research Study No. 179 (London: Home Office).

Joutsen, M. and Zvekic, U. (1994) 'Noncustodial sanctions: comparative overview', in U. Zvekic (ed.), *Alternatives to Imprisonment in Comparative Perspective* (Chicago: Nelson Hall).

Kuhn, A. (1993) 'Attitudes to punishment', in A. Alvazzi del Frate, U. Zvekic and J. J. M. van Dijk (eds), *Understanding Crime: Experiences of Crime and Crime Control* (Rome: United Nations Interregional Crime and Justice Research Institute (UNICRI)), pp. 271–88.

Lenke, L. (1974) 'Criminal justice policy and public opinion towards crimes of violence', in *Violence and Society*, Collected Studies in Criminological Research, Vol. 11 (Strasbourg: Council of Europe), pp. 61–124.

Lynch, J. (1993) 'Secondary analysis of international crime survey data', in A. Alvazzi del Frate, U. Zvekic and J. J. M. van Dijk (eds), *Understanding Crime: Experiences of Crime and Crime Control* (Rome: United Nations Interregional Crime and Justice Research Institute (UNICRI)), pp. 175–89.

Mattinson, J. and Mirrlees-Black, C. (2000) *Attitudes to Crime and Criminal Justice: Findings from the 1998 British Crime Survey*, Home Office Research Study No. 200 (London: Home Office).

Maxfield, M. (1987) *Incivilities and Fear of Crime in England and Wales and the United States*, paper presented at the American Society of Criminology, Montreal, November 1987.

Mayhew, P. and van Dijk, J. J. M. (1997) *Criminal Victimisation in Eleven Industrialised Countries: Key Findings from the 1996 International Crime Victims Survey* (The Hague: Research and Documentation Centre, Ministry of Justice).

Newman, G. (1976) *Comparative Deviance: Perceptions of Law in Six Countries* (New York: Elsevier).

Roberts, J. V. (1992) 'Public opinion, crime, and criminal justice', in N. Morris and M. Tonry (eds), *Crime and Justice: An Annual Review of Research, Volume 16* (Chicago: University of Chicago Press), pp. 99–180.

Roberts, J. V. and Stalans, L. (1997) *Public Opinion, Crime, and Criminal Justice* (Boulder, CO: Westview Press).

Sanders, J. and Hamilton, V. L. (1992) 'Legal cultures and punishment repertoires in Japan, Russia and the United States', *Law and Society Review*, 26:1, pp. 117–38.

Schwarzenegger, C. (1989) 'Zurcher Opferbefragung: fragestellung, vorgehen und erste resultate', *Kriminologisches Bulletin de Criminologie*, 15, pp. 5–239.

Scott, J. E. and Al-Thakeb, F. (1977) 'The public's perceptions of crime: a comparative analysis of Scandinavia, Western Europe, the Middle East, and the United States', in C. R. Huff (ed.), *Contemporary Corrections: Social Control and Conflict* (Beverly Hills, CA: Sage), pp. 78–88.

Shinkai, H. and Zvekic, U. (1999). 'Punishment', in G. Newman (ed.), *Global Report on Crime and Justice* (New York and Oxford: Oxford University Press), pp. 89–120.

Skogan, W. (1993) 'Reactions to crime in cross-cultural perspective', in A. Alvazzi del Frate, U. Zvekic and J. J. M. van Dijk (eds), *Understanding Crime: Experiences of Crime and Crime Control* (Rome: United Nations Interregional Crime and Justice Research Institute (UNICRI), pp. 257–70.

Sprott, J. B. and Doob, A. N. (1997) 'Fear, victimisation and attitudes to sentencing, the courts and the police', *Canadian Journal of Criminology*, 39: July, pp. 275–91.

Tufts, J. and Roberts, J. V. (2002) 'Sentencing juvenile offenders: comparing public preferences and judicial practice', *Criminal Justice Policy Review*, 12:1, pp. 46–64.

Van Dijk, J. J. M. (1999). 'The experience of crime and justice', in G. Newman (ed.), *Global Report on Crime and Justice* (New York and Oxford: Oxford University Press), pp. 25–42.

Van Dijk, J. J. M. and Kangaspunta, K. (2000) 'Piecing together the cross-national crime puzzle', *National Institute of Justice Journal*, January 2000 (Washington, DC: National Institute of Justice).

Van Dijk, J. J. M. and Mayhew, P. (1992) *Criminal Victimization in the Industrialized World: Key Findings of the 1989 and 1992 International Crime Surveys* (The Hague: Ministry of Justice, Department of Crime Prevention).

Van Kesteren, J., Mayhew, P. and Nieuwbeerta, P. (2000) *Criminal Victimization in Seventeen Countries: Key Findings from the 2000 International Crime Surveys* (The Hague: Ministry of Justice, Department of Crime Prevention).

Walker, N. and Hough, M. (eds) (1988) *Public Attitudes to Sentencing: Surveys from Five Countries* (Aldershot: Gower).

Walmsley, R. (2002) *World Prison Population List*, 3rd edn, Home Office Findings 166 (London: Research, Development and Statistics Directorate, Home Office).

Zvekic, U. (1998) *Criminal Victimisation in Countries in Transition*, Publication No. 61 (Rome UNICRI).

Chapter 5

The evolution of public attitudes to punishment in Western and Eastern Europe

Helmut Kury, Joachim Obergfell-Fuchs and Ursula Smartt

Introduction

In the wake of the widespread social and political changes experienced by Europe during the 1990s, there has been a marked increase in crime rates, accompanied by mounting public fear, particularly in Eastern European states. This has resulted in both an increased sense of freedom and, on the other hand, increased East–West migration due to continuing domestic problems in the former Eastern Bloc countries (Kury and Obergfell-Fuchs, 1996). The largely uncensored free press in the East has merely increased levels of public anxiety. For example, ever-increasing competition between media moguls contributed to the extensive coverage of a few spectacular crimes, such as the murder of James Bulger by two ten-year-old boys in England in 1993.

Exaggerated crime reporting became increasingly common in most Western European industrialised nations, as was evident in the coverage of paedophilia and the 'witch-hunts' of sex offenders in Germany. Seeking retribution for these most serious offences, the press tends to promote a 'necessary' degree of punitiveness. In this context, the public's heightened emphasis on punishment over the last decade is perhaps only to be expected. This issue will be addressed in this chapter through a review of empirical findings from studies conducted in a number of Eastern and Western European countries.

The evolution of public attitudes to punishment: West Germany

One of the main problems associated with comparing data sets from different studies of public attitudes to punishment is that these surveys are often incompatible. For example, a number of victimisation surveys were conducted in West Germany during the 1970s, and included questions on attitudes to punishment. These surveys differed in a number of respects: for example, in their operationalisation of variables and their sample sizes. Inconsistent methodologies have thus reduced the opportunities to make international comparisons. We would even go so far as to say that, to date, there has been no reliable measurement of German attitudes to punishment. Moreover, the limitations of using data sets from victimisation surveys for the purposes of comparison are all the more evident with regard to research findings from some of the former socialist Eastern European states. In these countries, surveys of public attitudes to punishment are less common and less sophisticated than those conducted in Western Europe.

Some of the more sophisticated and representative data sets originate from commercial opinion poll institutes in the former West Germany (the German Federal Republic or FRG), and date back to 1950. In East Germany (the German Democratic Republic or GDR) these have been available only since 1992. When asked their views on capital punishment, German citizens were also always asked about their general attitudes to punishment (Noelle-Neumann and Köcher, 2002: 676). The most recent findings (published in 2002) reveal that in West German support for the death penalty dropped substantially between 1950 and 2000 (see Figure 5.1). More than half of the surveyed population (55 per cent) favoured the death penalty in 1950, compared with approximately a quarter in 2000 (23 per cent).

Research has shown that there is a high level of public support for capital punishment in countries that actually have the death penalty (Zvekic and Alvazzi del Frate, 1995). One explanation for this is that in these countries, the death penalty is seen simply as 'the way it is done' – that is, as a customary and familiar way of dealing with offenders convicted of the most serious crimes. The public, fearing a rise in crime, has generally viewed with scepticism the prospect of fundamental legislative change in this respect (i.e. the abolition of the death penalty). Public surveys conducted in West Germany after the Second World War found that the majority favoured the retention of capital punishment, albeit for the most serious crimes.

Despite the views of the public in this regard, the West German Parliament (*Bundestag*) abolished capital punishment with the new

Figure 5.1 Attitudes towards death penalty in East and West Germany.

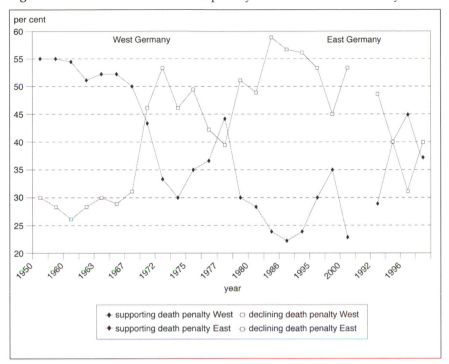

Basic Constitution of 1949. Subsequently, public support for the death penalty gradually diminished. A study conducted in 1971 found, for the first time, more opponents than proponents (46 per cent against and 43 per cent in favour). One year later, over half (53 per cent) of the citizens of the FRG were against capital punishment. Public attitudes appear to have changed in response to the exceptionally violent terrorist attacks by Baader-Meinhoff and Red Army Factions (RAF). From 1977 onwards, 44 per cent of the population were in favour of the death penalty, while 39 per cent opposed it. Thereafter, however, support for capital punishment sharply declined again, and by 1986 only 22 per cent favoured it. A further change in attitudes followed German unification in 1990: by 1996, support for the death penalty had risen to 35 per cent, by 2000 the support decreased to 23 per cent.

Explanations for the low levels of support for the death penalty towards the end of the 1980s – that is, before unification – can partly be found in the relative liberalism of government penal policy and the more general liberalisation and plurality of West German society.

During this period, alternative sanctions were introduced; furthermore, the traditional forms of punishment were called into question. Similarly, in the United States, Denmark and the Netherlands, extensive debates took place about the treatment and rehabilitation of offenders – particularly young offenders – in the 1970s and 1980s. For example, diversion methods, victim-offender mediation and restorative justice practices were the subject of intense discussion (see Kury and Lerchenmüller, 1981; Heinz and Storz, 1992).

The first administration of the International Crime and Victimisation Survey (ICVS) in 1989 (see van Dijk et al., 1990) revealed that German attitudes to punishment changed over this period. (Since West Germany only participated in this first wave of the survey any longitudinal comparisons were not possible.) The 1989 ICVS found that when asked to sentence a young recidivist burglar who had stolen a colour television (henceforth referred to as the 'TV thief'), only 13 per cent of German respondents favoured a prison sentence. This figure contrasts with an international average of 27 per cent across all 14 countries in that administration of the survey. Nine per cent of Germans (compared to the international average of 13 per cent) favoured a fine; and fully 60 per cent were in favour of a community sentence.

Swiss citizens expressed even less support for imposing a prison sentence (9 per cent) than the Germans, whereas the French (13 per cent), Norwegians (14 per cent) and Finns (15 per cent) supported imprisonment to approximately the same degree. In contrast, there was relatively strong support for a prison sentence in various other countries, including Spain (27 per cent), Canada (32 per cent), England and Wales (38 per cent) and the Netherlands (45 per cent). In the United States, over half the population (53 per cent) supported harsh, punitive prison sentences (see Table 5.1). When asked about the appropriate length of a prison sentence, the West German average was 11 months, longer than the Norwegian average (10 months) and the Swiss (six months). The average length of prison sentence selected in the United States was 38 months (see van Kesteren et al., 2000: 218).

However, such findings – and, in particular, the comparisons between the data sets – should be treated with caution. For example, as noted, the ICVS found that only 9 per cent of the Swiss sentenced the TV thief to prison; but only three years later, Schwarzenegger (1992) found that more than half (54 per cent) of the surveyed inhabitants of Canton Zurich favoured the death penalty (1992: 299ff). Stadler (1987) found that half the population of Canton Uri (51 per cent) also favoured capital punishment. This raises the important and complex issue of the context and manner in which questions about

Table 5.1   Public preferences for sanctions for recidivist burglar

Country	Fixed penalty fine (%)	Prison (%)	Community service (%)	Imprisonment length (%)
Germany	9	13	60	11
Australia	9	36	46	17
Belgium	13	26	38	24
Canada	11	32	39	14
England/Wales	11	38	38	20
Finland	19	15	37	15
France	10	13	53	11
The Netherlands	9	26	46	13
Northern Ireland	9	45	30	23
Norway	23	14	47	10
Scotland	14	39	34	19
Spain	23	27	24	36
Switzerland	12	9	57	6
USA	8	53	30	38
All countries	13	27	41	18

Source: ICVS, van Dijk et al. (1990).

'punitiveness' are posed. If questions are formulated in such a way that capital punishment is presented as a central issue, especially in those countries where the death penalty is abolished, then the results might be somewhat misleading. Hence answers to single-item questions should not be given too much weight in the overall analysis and interpretation of data.

At the end of 1989, after German unification and the opening of the Eastern borders, members of this research team conducted a representative victimisation survey in the former GDR and FRG of Germany. The ICVS items, such as questions about punishment of the TV thief, were included in this survey. A marked increase in punitive attitudes among the population emerged: 33 per cent favoured imprisonment for the TV thief, 17 per cent a fine, and 31 per cent community service. There was no major difference in terms of the length of prison sentences between East and West Germany (see Kury et al., 1996: 309ff). A quarter of the German population was 'very much in favour' of 'meaningful' punishment for the offender, which was seen as a way of combating crime.

In 1991/1992, we conducted an additional survey, involving comparable, representative samples from a West German town (Freiburg) and an East German town (Jena). In addition, smaller communities outside these two towns were also surveyed (see Kury et al., 2000). A list of 21 serious criminal offences was created. For each offence, respondents were asked to select an appropriate sanction, ranging from 1 – 'no response' to 8 – 'imprisonment'.

When questioned about the appropriateness of the death penalty, 34 per cent of the West German sample responded in favour. Support for the death penalty was influenced by various demographic factors, such as gender (36 per cent of men vs. 31 per cent of women in favour), age (27 per cent of 14 to 25 year olds compared to 52 per cent of those aged over 66 were in favour), and educational level (61 per cent of working-class respondents in favour vs. 15 per cent of university graduates).

Multivariate analyses revealed that support for harsher sanctions was influenced by a number of factors. These included perceptions of the police: for example, the belief that the rise in crime was caused by the leniency of the police. Other factors were a high income, a lack of experience of victimisation and political apathy (see Table 5.2).

During the late 1990s, there was an extensive public debate in Germany about punishment, fuelled by emotionally charged media coverage of a small number of dramatic sexual attacks on children.

Table 5.2 Linear multiple regression analysis: attitudes to sanctioning, Freiburg 1991

Variable	Beta-weight	T-value	p
Police leniency as reason for crime increase	0.23	9.62	<0.001
Interested in politics	−0.18	−8.39	<0.001
Hostility against foreigners	0.17	7.50	<0.001
Anomie	0.12	5.01	<0.001
Public order and security function of police	0.10	4.18	<0.001
Educational level	−0.09	−4.33	<0.001
Gender	−0.09	−3.78	<0.001
Feelings of security	−0.06	−2.62	<0.01
Income	0.03	1.51	0.13
Economic reasons for crime increase	−0.02	−1.08	0.28
Age	0.02	0.76	0.45
Victimisation	0.01	0.61	0.54
Public police duties	−0.01	−0.42	0.68
Neighbourhood satisfaction	0.00	0.22	0.83
Societal reasons for crime increase	0.00	0.19	0.85

$$R = 0.51; R^2 = 0.26; F_{(8,1656)} = 74.50^{***}$$

Over this period, the attitudes of the German public became increasingly punitive. By November 1996, 37 per cent were in support of capital punishment (42 per cent opposed). In relation to paedophiles, 60 per cent of the surveyed sample favoured the death penalty (22 per cent opposed). Half the population favoured the death penalty for murder following a kidnapping (31 per cent opposed) (Noelle-Neumann and Köcher, 1997: 767) by 2000 the general support for the death penalty decreased in Germany. Zitelmann (1998) cites a 1998 German opinion poll that found that 55 per cent of the sample favoured the death penalty for crimes such as sexual assault, rape and paedophilia. Public pressure for more punitive sanctions for serious crimes began to influence governmental penal policies during the 1990s. Most recently, the German *Bundestag* has introduced new statutory provisions relating to the punishment of sexual and violent offenders.

The evolution of public attitudes to punishment: East Germany

Some of the former socialist states, including East Germany (GDR), retained the death penalty in their criminal legislation until the late 1980s in order to support their political regimes. In 1987, the GDR declared that capital punishment was no longer essential for the defence of socialism (Hood, 1998: 749). Although the deterrent effectiveness of capital punishment was never established empirically, capital punishment retained its appeal for politicians. In these states, public attitudes to punishment and criminality were different to those held in the West. Public debate and discussions in the media about possible causes of crime and criminality dwindled when attention turned to the nature and extent of criminal offences. There were also considerable differences in recorded crime rates and the types and use of sanctions, linked to social differences between the East and West. Despite declining crime rates, the prison populations of a number of Eastern European countries increased, following the imposition of harsher penalties. As the press was largely controlled and censored, public debate about sentencing could not develop in the same way as in the Western democratic societies. These differences between East and West were exacerbated by the enormous divergence in economic development – particularly after the 'economic miracle' experienced by West Germany in the 1960s.

This economic boom was certainly not matched by the GDR or the other socialist states that did not have access to American aid (through the postwar Marshall Plan). This may have contributed to differing attitudes to offenders, and may explain the more punitive attitudes found in formerly socialist East European states. To test this hypothesis, the vast East–West German database from the *Bundeskriminalamt* (BKA) was used. At the historically crucial turning point of 1990, Kury et al. (1996) conducted the first victimisation and crime survey with BKA data sets. Before then, official data from the former socialist states were absent, as public surveys of victimisation were virtually unheard of. The findings of this study from the early 1990s must be viewed in the context of the optimism that prevailed in the former GDR, resulting from the recent collapse of the Berlin Wall and arrival of Western capitalism. At this time, the social problems that were to emerge later could not be anticipated. The East Germans' positive attitudes can be linked to the decrease in punitiveness that was manifest in pleas for 'softer' penal sanctions: 27 per cent per cent of former GDR citizens chose a prison sentence for the TV thief – well below the 33 per cent of West Germans. However, later studies did not reveal this kind of leniency among East Germans: when asked about the length of prison sentence for the young burglar, they generally favoured longer terms.

The Freiburg and Jena Study (see Kury et al., 2002), conducted about a year after the study just discussed, generated the following results: in the East German Jena, 58 per cent of respondents were in favour of capital punishment, compared to 34 per cent per cent of the West German Freiburgers. The authors' hypotheses regarding the relationship between repressive regimes, reduced pluralism and harsher attitudes to punishment were supported.

A multivariate analysis of the findings on attitudes to punishment showed that five variables in Jena (ten in Freiburg) had a statistically significant influence. More punitive attitudes were evident among those who also demanded an increase in police presence; among males; among those who felt unsafe; among respondents who did not link economic problems to a rise in crime; and among those with higher disposable incomes. Equally significant results were found in the Freiburg sample (see Table 5.3). Among the East German sample, the variable 'feelings of safety' was also significant, but this did not apply to the Freiburgers.

Those who expressed heightened feelings of fear of crime also demanded harsher sanctions. The study also revealed striking correlations between public attitudes to punishment and certain social traditions. One such example is provided by the relatively liberal attitude to abortion among Jena citizens as compared to the Freiburgers. This can be related to the fact that in the GDR the churches had no influence on state legislation, whereas there was an influential church lobby in the West. In contrast, the Jena sample showed a high

Table 5.3 Linear multiple regression analysis: attitudes to sanctioning, Jena 1991

Variable	Beta-weight	T-value	p
Public order and security function of police	0.13	5.50	<0.001
Gender	−0.12	−4.59	<0.001
Feelings of security	0.08	2.98	<0.01
Economic reasons for crime increase	−0.07	−2.76	<0.01
Income	0.06	2.65	<0.01
Age	−0.04	−1.70	0.09
Educational level	−0.04	−1.55	0.12
Societal reasons for crime increase	0.04	1.46	0.14
Public police duties	0.04	1.37	0.17
Interested in politics	−0.03	−1.28	0.20
Neighbourhood satisfaction	−0.03	−1.03	0.30
Police leniency as reason for crime increase	0.02	0.72	0.47
Hostility against foreigners	0.01	0.56	0.57
Anomie	0.01	0.53	0.60
Victimisation	−0.01	−0.22	0.83
$R = 0.20$; $R^2 = 0.04$; $F_{(5,1684)} = 13.43^{***}$			

degree of punitiveness in relation to cannabis use, resulting from the lack of open and liberal debate on the subject of illegal drug use in the East (see Figure 5.2). In the FRG, on the other hand, soft and hard drugs had always been differentiated.

In 1992, only two years after German unification, our research revealed that former East Germans placed a greater emphasis on capital punishment than their West German counterparts (29 per cent favoured the death penalty in the East, compared to 24 per cent in the West). Following unification, the East faced a considerable rise in crime and an accompanying increase in the fear of crime – along with various other hitherto unknown socio-economic problems. These included an increased threat of unemployment, a new competitive market economy, a vast rise in rented accommodation and reduced state responsibility for the individual. It comes as no surprise that punitive attitudes in the East increased more rapidly than in the West (Kury et al., 2000). By 1995, 40 per cent of former East Germans favoured capital punishment (compared to 30 per cent in the West).

A year later, in 1996, 45 per cent of East and 35 per cent of West Germans were in favour of capital punishment (see Figure 5.1) by 2000 the support for the death penalty had decreased to 37 per cent in East Germany and 23 per cent in West Germany. These findings are

Figure 5.2   Mean values of suggested sanctions for different types of offences – comparison between Freiburg and Jena.

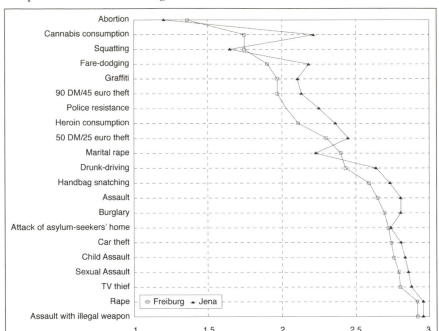

supported by the results of recent similar study by Reuband (2001), who surveyed residents of the former GDR towns of Chemnitz (Karl Marx Stadt), Dresden and Leipzig. Capital punishment was favoured by 40 per cent of respondents in Dresden, 44 per cent in Leipzig and 41 per cent in Chemnitz. Other studies carried out in the 1990s revealed similarly high degrees of punitiveness among East Germans (see also Kreuzer et al., 1993, who surveyed young people's attitudes to punishment).

A study by the Criminal Research Institute of Lower Saxony, which in 1992 examined elderly people's attitudes to crime and punishment, produced a range of responses to questions about sanctions for different offences. The sanctions selected ranged from cautions to complete discharge to imprisonment without parole (Bilsky et al., 1993). When asked about the offence 'grievous bodily harm' – involving the scenario of a 30-year-old offender whose victim had suffered a severe wound – more East than West Germans favoured the option of imprisonment without parole. Among the West Germans, 9 per cent of those under 60 years of age suggested imprisonment with no parole, as did 11 per cent of those aged over 60; among the East

Germans, the figures were 30 per cent and 29 per cent respectively – that is, three times higher. A comprehensive study of social change and criminality by Sessar (1997) also suggests that East German attitudes to punishment became more punitive during the 1990s. Sessar reported a marked increase in support for imprisonment between 1991 and 1993.

The results of the comparison between East and West Germany show the influence of political and economic conditions. Good conditions and an anticipation of positive future developments might lead to increasingly tolerant deviant behavior, while social and economic crisis leads to an increase in punitive attitudes. The vast social upheaval in East Germany was followed by increasing insecurity, an increase in unemployment and worsening economic conditions. This may explain the harsher punitive attitudes in comparison to West Germany. The results further showed that the East Germans choose fewer alternatives to imprisonment, probably because they are less familiar with these alternatives than the West Germans, where diversion or victim-offender mediation had become common during the preceding years. This suggests that public attitudes to punishment can be influenced by the actual sentencing patterns.

Attitudes to punishment in Eastern European countries

Poland

As previously stated, there is an absence of reliable data on attitudes to crime and punishment in East European countries. Poland, however, provides an exception to this, as it was included in the last wave of the ICVS (see van Kesteren et al., 2000: 218). The 1989 survey revealed a high degree of punitiveness among the Polish public: 42 per cent of respondents favoured imprisonment for the TV thief (van Dijk et al., 1990). Among the 14 countries surveyed, a higher degree of punitiveness was recorded only in Indonesia (67 per cent in support of imprisonment), the USA (53 per cent) and Northern Ireland (45.4 per cent). With regard to the length of imprisonment, 95 per cent of the Polish respondents were in favour of a year or more: the highest result of all the countries included in the survey.

It is worth noting that a correlation was found between more punitive attitudes to crime and the size of a country's prison population. At the time of the above study (ICVS 1989), the total prison population in Poland had risen to a staggering 265 per 100,000 inhabitants (van Dijk et al., 1990: 83). Subsequent surveys in Poland also revealed a high degree of punitiveness towards the TV thief. In

1992, 31 per cent of the Polish respondents favoured imprisonment (average across all countries was 27 per cent); but this compares to only 17 per cent in 1996 (average 30 per cent) and 21 per cent in 2000 (average 34 per cent). The length of imprisonment selected by Polish respondents was, however, well above the average. In 1992, Polish respondents suggested a minimum of 35 months in prison (compared to the survey average of 19 months); in 1996 they proposed 25 months prison (average 18 months), and in 2000, 31 months (average 19 months). It is possible that once Poland joins the European Union, public attitudes, influenced by Western custom and Western media, may start to converge with attitudes held by people in other Western nations.

Earlier Polish studies revealed high levels of punitiveness among the population. Kwasniewski and Kojder (1979) undertook several studies in this field during the 1960s and 1970s. The authors concluded that half of the Polish population generally supported severe punishments for offenders in the belief that these sanctions would guarantee a reduction in crime and the re-establishment of law and order. In 1966, 54 per cent of the Polish population favoured harsh forms of state punishment; this increased to 65 per cent in 1973, but dropped to 48 per cent by 1978. A further 31 per cent viewed corporal punishment (whipping) as an acceptable criminal sanction. This figure gradually declined (to 26 per cent in 1974 and 22 per cent in 1978), reflecting a general downward trend in punitive attitudes. In 1993, however, a sizeable minority of the population continued to support harsh corporal punishment: one-sixth believed in whipping, and one-eighth regarded cutting off an offender's hand as a suitable sanction for a thief (see Wojciechowska, 1994: 41).

Polish attitudes to capital punishment are well documented by opinion polls dating back to 1964. (Table 5.4 gives provides an overview of findings from 1964 to the late 1980s.) The death penalty was consistently supported, and only abolished with the new Polish Penal Code of 1998; however, it had not been implemented since 1990, and a moratorium had been formally introduced in 1995. That said, public support for the death penalty rose steadily – from 50 per cent in 1964 to 60 per cent in 1987 – and declined during the late 1980s, a time of rapid political change in Poland (support was recorded at 52 per cent in both 1988 and 1989). However, the number of 'undecideds' during this latter period was considerably higher than previously: 17 per cent were 'undecided' in 1964, compared to 20 per cent in 1988 and 22 per cent in 1989. In 1989 approximately a quarter (27 per cent) of the Polish population were opposed to capital punishment, compared to one-third in 1964 (33 per cent).

Table 5.4 Attitudes of Polish citizens towards the death penalty (in %)

Year	Support	Oppose	Undecided
1964	50	33	17
1966	58	29	13
1973	59	24	17
1974	60	31	9
1987	60.3	27.8	11.9
1988	51.8	28.3	19.9
1989	51.8	26.7	21.5
	Should the death penalty be abolished?		
	No	*Yes*	*Undecided*
1993	64	28	8
1995	62	32	6

Source: Krajewski (2001), p. 158.

The political and social strife of the late 1980s, coupled with general feelings of confusion and unrest among the Polish population, were reflected in attitudes to punishment. Feelings of social insecurity, an increasing fear of crime, and feelings of becoming disadvantaged because of the vast social changes might be seen as the background of punitiveness. In the early 1990s there was a steady increase in the percentage of the public favouring abolition of the death penalty: from 28 per cent in 1993 to 32 per cent in 1995. A polarisation of attitudes to capital punishment may have been due to the population's disappointment with political developments, which followed the initial euphoria of the democratic revolution of the early 1990s. Similar trends were evident within the former East Germany.

Rising crime rates in Poland may have contributed to the increasing punitiveness of the public. The crime rate rose by 85 per cent between 1988 and 1996, and was accompanied by a rise in fear of serious and violent crime. Between 1989 and 1996, for example, the number of officially recorded murders rose from 556 to 1,134; rape cases rose from 1,660 to 1,985; and armed robbery from 9,067 to 26,257 (see Markiewicz, 1997: 211). As with studies conducted elsewhere, a survey carried out in 1995 found a correlation between attitudes to capital punishment and socio-demographic variables. There was stronger support for the death penalty among men (67 per cent) than women (57 per cent); as there was among the less educated (abolition of the death penalty was supported by 28 per cent of those who had received only elementary education, and by 49 per cent of university graduates) (see Kury and Krajewski, 2002).

Russia

To meet the Council of Europe's requirement, the Russian government has promised to abolish capital punishment. However, as Hood (1998) points out, the Soviet Union has already abolished the death penalty on three occasions in the past: from 1917 to 1918, 1920 to 1921, and – for peacetime offences – from 1947 to 1950 (1998: 20). However, Gilinsky (2001) established that between 1921 and 1953 Russia executed approximately 19,484 persons (2001: 52). From 1961, the death penalty in the Soviet Union was applied not only to premeditated murder but also to certain economic crimes, aggravated rape and hijacking (see van den Berg, 1983: 154ff).

According to a UN survey, by 2001, 38 retentionist countries had become abolitionist. Of these, 18 were in the formerly Soviet Union-dominated Eastern Europe or former states of the Soviet Union itself (see Hood, 2001: 333). The Council of Europe's parliamentary assembly threatened to suspend the Ukraine if it succumbed to popular pressure to execute Anatoly Onuprienko, accused of murdering 52 people (*Economist*, 1999). The Russian Duma remains reluctant to abolish capital punishment altogether. Georgia abolished capital punishment on the initiative of its President Eduard Shevardnadze in 1997, two years before becoming a member of the Council of Europe in 1999. In Azerbaijan, which has a strong Islamic tradition, the death penalty was abolished in February 1993, as the result of a Bill introduced by the President in support of human rights (Hood, 2001: 338).

With the break-up of the Soviet Union and increased international political pressure for the complete abolition of the death penalty, the Russian Federation eventually adopted a new Constitution. Article 20(1) states that 'Everyone has the right to life', and Article 20(2) that 'Until such time as it is repealed, the death penalty may be imposed under Federal Law as an extreme measure of punishment for particularly serious crimes against life.' This constitutional decision clearly did not reflect public opinion: a poll established that only 28 per cent of Russians favoured retention of the death penalty (see Seliverstov, 1997). Russia's new Penal Code of 1996 severely curtailed the use of capital punishment. During that same year, the Russian Federation made a commitment to the Council of Europe to abolish capital punishment, in order to gain entry to the European Union. Since then, about 90 per cent of all death penalty appeals to the Russian President have been successful (1997: 60). In 1999, Russia's Constitutional Court made the dramatic decision that capital punishment was unconstitutional, and that only 'specialist execution courts' could thereafter impose a death sentence.

However, statistics on the use of the death penalty in Russia must be viewed with caution, since different criminological studies provide varying accounts. Kvashis (2001), for instance, calculated that approximately 1,890 executions were carried out in 1961, compared with just 100 in 1989. According to Schestakov (2001), the mere existence of the death penalty in Russia's Constitution has increased the overall severity of judicial sanctions: for example, extremely long prison sentences have been imposed (2001: 136). Executions apparently decreased in number after 1998 – to 'only' 131 (2001: 52). As Kvashis (2001) notes, capital punishment is not only merely an instrument of the criminal justice system and an element of the Russian Constitution, but also reflects certain socio-cultural phenomena. He argues that a country that employs the death penalty also encourages greater punitiveness in public attitudes. It thus has to be recognised that the abolition of capital punishment by states like Russia or East Germany (GDR) often goes against the tide of public opinion. The abolition of capital punishment at a time of rapid social and economic change, and accompanying ever-rising crime, can be interpreted by the public and politicians as a sign of the further weakening of the social order (see Hood, 2001: 339).

Seliverstov (1997) convincingly describes the relationship between the state's penal sanctions and Russian cultural norms in the following terms:

> Because of historically established social, political and ideological traditions and moral norms, forming the basis of Russian legal praxis, the use of imprisonment has been considered the most efficient response of society to a committed crime. To pass an alternative non-custodial sentence, for instance to impose a fine, is in everyday Russian thinking, as research shows, identified with releasing the offender from punishment. (1997: 59)

The new Russian Penal Code also introduced 'alternative sanctions' in the form of non-custodial sentences. It is assumed that there will be a growing acceptance of such diversion measures among Russians, mirroring attitudinal change in Western nations (see Roberts, this volume).

Czechoslovakia

The Czech Institute for Public Opinion Surveys has conducted opinion polls on attitudes to capital punishment since 1947 (see Kury and

Zapletal, 2002). The first study, conducted only in the states of Bohemia and Moravia, found 54 per cent of respondents to be in favour of retaining the death penalty. Just two months later the figure had dropped to 44 per cent – illustrating the potential unreliability of this kind of data collection. After a considerable time lapse, further studies were conducted in 1967 (Novotny and Kvasnicka, 1969). These found that 51 per cent of the surveyed population favoured the retention of capital punishment. Over the following 20 years of the totalitarian Czech regime, the abolition of the death penalty was never on the political and criminal justice agenda. The death penalty was abolished in the Czech Federal Republic following the introduction of democratic government in 1990. The Czech Institute for Public Opinion Surveys polled the population at regular intervals between 1992 and 1999, a period of rising crime, and found that 67 per cent of the population (rising to 76 per cent in 1999) favoured the reintroduction of the death penalty. By 2000, this figure had dropped to 61 per cent.

Romania

Following a similar pattern to the Czechoslovakian and East German processes of democratisation, Romania marked the fall of the tyrannical Ceaucesçu regime in December 1989 with the immediate abolition of the death penalty. As previously mentioned, public support for capital punishment existed alongside the state's use of this judicial instrument. This was established by Keil et al. (1999) who, in 1996, undertook a survey of attitudes to the death penalty in Bucharest. Over half (60 per cent) favoured the reintroduction of capital punishment. This was particularly prominent among the 'workers' included in the study (of whom 81 per cent supported reintroduction). Those who felt that crime was on the increase in their own neighbourhoods strongly believed that capital punishment would have crime preventive effects. Results similar to the Bucharest study were found in Finland and Estonia (see Aromaa and Ahven, 1999a: 24f).

Other Baltic States

More Estonians than Finns selected the imprisonment option for the TV thief (40 per cent as against 27 per cent) (see also Markina, 2001), and the Estonians were less in favour of the community service option (36 per cent as against 56 per cent). Once again, these findings should be considered against the backdrop of the relative ignorance of alternative forms of imprisonment. It is also worth noting that after the Second World War, the Finns were regarded as holding relatively punitive attitudes in comparison to their Scandinavian neighbours in Denmark, Norway and Sweden. These results, in turn, should be viewed in the context of the ongoing tension between Finland and the Soviet Union (see Lappi-Seppälä, 2000). Persistent Russian intimidation certainly influenced popular attitudes to punishment in Finland. Christie (1968) found that there was considerably less emphasis on harsher sanctions during peacetime (1968: 171).

Comparing the Estonian findings of 1993 with those of 1995, there are no substantial differences in public attitudes to punishment (see Aromaa and Ahven, 1999b: 114f). However, the 2000 results show a marked reduction in the punitiveness of the Estonian public. About 40 per cent of the 1995 sample wanted the TV thief imprisoned; this figure dropped to 23 per cent in 2000 (see Ahven et al., 2001: 34f). Over the same period, public support for community penalties grew: from 35 per cent in 1995 to 51 per cent in 2000. Compared to their Finnish counterparts, however, the Estonians still preferred longer prison sentences, and, in relation to the European results as a whole, the attitudes of the Estonians were about average (see van Kesteren et al., 2000: 218f). Kerezsi (2001) reported similar results for Hungary, where the population displayed increasingly punitive attitudes.

Discussion

The EU now has an official policy of promoting abolition of the death penalty around the world. This has put significant pressure on countries in Eastern Europe, most of which have abolished the death penalty with new constitutions and criminal legislation – and some of which have been among the strongest opponents of capital punishment over the past 12 years.

Although crime rates remained relatively stable in Central and Eastern European countries from the mid-1990s onwards, there has been a marked increase in the imprisonment rate in most of these states (see Joutsen and Walmsley, 1997: 233). At the same time, attitudes to punishment have become more punitive in a number of countries. The reasons for this are manifold, and partly lie in the political revolutions experienced by a number of Eastern European states. The political turbulence led to growing feelings of unease and fear of crime, coupled with increasing mistrust in governmental regimes, state systems and judicial control mechanisms. Public scepticism about the possible benefits of rehabilitative sanctions was greater than ever before. Hebenton and Spencer (2001) observed a growing 'crisis of confidence in the means and ends of the criminal justice system – albeit sometimes in complex ways' within the population they surveyed in England and Wales (2001: 81) (see also Tarling and Dowds, 1997; Hough and Roberts, 1998; Mattinson and Mirrlees-Black, 2000).

Similar findings have emerged from Western European nations such as Germany, where some spectacular cases of corruption within the political arena have led to growing public uncertainty (see Scheuch, 2002). Such mistrust in 'the system' can easily produce a culture in which simplistic problem-solving rhetoric takes root. Popular slogans such as 'zero tolerance', 'three strikes and you're out' and 'truth in sentencing' have great resonance among the general public. Britain's New Labour government of 1997 imported such ideas from the United States, and new legislative policies manifest in the Crime and Disorder Act 1998 – particularly relating to persistent young offenders – are promoted with the slogan 'No more excuses' (Home Office, 1997). There was overwhelming public support for harsh punishment, including long-term prison sentences, for the most serious and persistent offenders. Aspects of this Anglo-American approach to penal policy have been replicated by the German socialist (SPD) government that came to power in 1998.

Harsher penal sanctions have now become part of many Western European election manifestos, which present policies for 'getting tough' with the most serious offenders. The German state of Baden-Württemberg recently passed legislation that is intended to keep serious violent and sex offenders behind bars well *after* the completion of their prison sentences (*Sicherungsverwahrung bei Sexualstraftätern*). If the prison authorities believe that an offender will pose a 'substantial risk' to the public after his release from prison, he will be kept in custody for a longer period. This statutory provision has now been extended to all 16 federal German states. German politicians have been employing populist rhetoric such as 'locking up sex offenders for good' – which, together with the exaggerated media coverage of crime, subtly encourages punitive attitudes among the general public.

In the current punitive climate, it is difficult for policy-makers to promote alternative criminal sanctions, such as restorative justice or rehabilitative penal regimes, as these will not attract a great deal of support (and ultimately votes) from the public. Moreover, the rise in punitive attitudes in Western Europe has had parallels in Eastern Europe since the wave of democratisation in the late 1980s/early 1990s. In the East, a perceived rise in criminality has been accompanied by growing public unease about rising unemployment and the threat of poverty. Eastern European citizens have had to become accustomed not only to rapid political and social change, but also to new forms of deviance and criminal activity, such as international organised crime.

It is perhaps not surprising that the Eastern European and East German public continues to support the death penalty – often believing that capital punishment deters violent crime. However, this paper has demonstrated that detailed research, exploring attitudes to punishment in various countries, has produced some more perplexing results. It is important to inform the public about the problems of punishment and to show them better ways of handling the crime problem. Then the public might agree to at least some alternative measures which are both cheaper and effective.

References

Ahven, A., Tabur, L. and Aromaa, K. (2001) *Victims of Crime in Estonia 1993–2000*. Talinn and Helsinki: Ministry of Internal Affairs, Estonia and National Research Institute of Legal Policy, Finland.

Amnesty International (2000) 'The death penalty worldwide: developments in 1999', *AI Index: ACT 50/04/00*.

Aromaa, K. and Ahven, A. (1999a) 'Victims of crime in two Baltic countries. Finnish and Estonian data from the 1992/1993 International Crime Victimisation Survey' (ICVS), in K. Aromaa (ed.), *Eastern Crime. A Selection of Reports on Crime in the St. Petersburg Region and the Baltic Countries, 1993–1999*. Helsinki: National Researach Institute of Legal Policy, pp. 1–33.

Aromaa, K. and Ahven, A. (1999b). 'Victims of crime in times of change: Estonia 1993 and 1995', in K. Aromaa (ed.), *Eastern Crime. A Selection of Reports on Crime in the St. Petersburg Region and the Baltic Countries, 1993–1999*. Helsinki: National Research Institute of Legal Policy, pp. 73–123.

Bilsky, W., Mecklenburg, E., Pfeiffer, C. and Wetzels, P. (1993). *Persönliches Sicherheitsgefühl, Angst vor Kriminalität und Gewalt, Opfererfahrungen älterer Menschen*, 2nd edn. KFN-Forschungsberichte. Hannover: Kriminologisches Forschungsinstitut Niedersachsen.

Christie, N. (1968) 'Changes in penal values', *Scandinavian Studies in Criminology*, 2: 161–72.

Economist, The (1999) 'The cruel and ever more unusual punishment', 15 May, pp. 137–9.

Gilinskiy, Y. (2001) 'Crime control in the epoch of inclusive/exclusive', in J. Saar, A. Annist and A. Markina (eds), *Crime Control: Current Problems and Developments Prospect*. Tallinn: TPÜ Kirjastus, pp. 46–53.

Hebenton, B. and Spencer, J. (2001) 'Crime, offenders and policy developments in England and Wales: are there lessons for the Baltic states?', in J. Saar, A. Annist and A. Markina (eds), *Crime Control: Current Problems and Developments Prospect*. Tallinn: TPÜ Kirjastus, pp. 78–95

Heinz, W. and Storz, R. (1992) *Diversion im Jugendstrafverfahren der Bundesrepublik Deutschland*. Godesberg: Forum Verlag.

Home Office (1997) *No More Excuses – A New Approach to Tackling Youth Crime in England and Wales*. London: HMSO

Hood, R. (1998) 'Capital punishment', in M. Tonry, *The Handbook of Crime and Punishment*. New York: Oxford University Press, pp. 739–76.

Hood, R. (2001) 'Capital punishment. A global perspective', in *Punishment and Society*, 3(3).

Hough, M. and Roberts, J. (1998) *Attitudes to Punishment: Findings from the British Crime Survey*, Home Office Research Study No. 179. London: HMSO.

Joutsen, M. and Walmsley, R. (1997) 'Summary remarks and conclusions presented by the rapporteur general', in Helsinki United Nations Institute (HEUNI) (ed.), *Prison Populations in Europe and in North America. Problems and Solutions*. Helsinki: HEUNI, pp. 231–43.

Keil, T., Vito, G. F. and Andreescu, V. (1999) 'Perceptions of neighborhood safety and support for the reintroduction of capital punishment in Romania: results from a Bucuresti survey', *International Journal of Offender Therapy and Comparative Criminology*, 43(4): 514–34.

Kerezsi, K. (2001) 'Virtual criminals and real prison or is a prison building program requested in Hungary?', in J. Saar, A. Annist and A. Markina (eds), *Crime Control: Current Problems and Developments Prospect*. Tallinn: TPÜ Kirjastus, pp. 105–16.

Kojder, A. and Kwasniewski, J. (1981) 'Stosunek spoleczenstwa polskiego do zjawisk i zachowan dewiacyjnych' (Attitudes to punishment by Polish citizens towards deviance and deviance phenomena), in B. Holyst (ed.), *Opinia publiczna i srodki masowego przekazu a ujemne zjawiska spoleczne* (*Public Opinions. The Mass Media and Negative Social Phenomena*). Warsaw: Wydawn Prawnicze, pp. 85–106.

Krajewski, K. (1990) 'Opinia publiczna a problem kary smierci' (Public opinion towards the death penalty), *Panstwo i Prawo* (*State and the Law*), 9: 60–9.

Krajewski, K. (2001) 'Crime and Penal Policy in Poland in the Nineties', in J. Saar, A. Annist and A. Markina (eds), *Crime Control: Current Problems and Developments Prospects*. Tallinn: TPÜ Kirjastus, pp. 143–63.

Kreuzer, A., Görgen, Th., Krüger, R., Münch, V. and Schneider, H. (1993) *Jugenddelinquenz in Ost und West*. Bonn: Forum Verlag Godesberg.

Kury, H. and Krajewski, K. (2002) *Zur Strafmentalität der Bevölkerung: Das Beispiel Polen*. Forthcoming publication.

Kury, H. and Lerchenmüller, H. (eds) (1981) *Diversion – Alternativen zu klassischen Sanktionsformen*. Bochum: Brockmeyer.

Kury, H. and Obergfell-Fuchs, J. (1996) 'Crime development and fear of crime in postcommunist societies', in B. Szamota-Saeki and D. Wójcik (eds), *Impact of Political, Economic and Social Change on Crime and its Image in Society*. Warsaw: Zaklad Kryminologii, pp. 117–46.

Kury, H. and Zapletal, J. (2002 forthcoming) *Zur Einstellung der Bevölkerung zu Kriminalität und Strafen – Ein Vergleich vor allem zwischen Deutschland und der Tschechischen Republik*.

Kury, H., Obergfell-Fuchs, J. and Würger, M. (2000) *Gemeinde und Kriminalität – eine Untersuchung in Ost- und Westdeutschland*. Freiburg: Edition iuscrim.

Kury, H., Obergfell-Fuchs, J. and Würger, M. (2002 forthcoming) *Strafeinstellungen. Ein Vergleich zwischen Ost- und Westdeutschland*. Freiburg: Edition iuscrim.

Kury, H., Dörmann, U., Richter, H. and Würger, M. (1996) *Opfererfahrungen und Meinungen zur Inneren Sicherheit in Deutschland*, 2nd edn. Wiesbaden: Bundeskriminalamt.

Kvashis, V. (2001) 'Die Todesstrafe in Russland' (German unpublished manuscript on 'The death penalty in Russia'). Moscow.

Kwasniewski, J. and Kojder, A. (1979) 'Postawy mieszkancow Warszawy wobec zjawisk i zachowan dewiacyjnych' (Attitudes towards deviant behaviour and deviance phenomena of Warsaw citizens), *Studia Socjologiczne*, 1: 157–79.

Lappi-Seppälä, T. (2000) 'The fall of the Finnish prison population', *Journal of Scandinavian Studies in Criminology and Crime Prevention*, 1: 27–40.

Markiewicz, W. (1997) 'Means of regulating the prison population', in HEUNI (ed.), *Prison Populations in Europe and in North America. Problems and Solutions*. Helsinki: HEUNI, pp. 211–15.

Markina, A. (2001) 'Law and order issues in the election campaign in Estonia in 1999', in J. Saar, A. Annist and A. Markina (eds), *Crime Control: Current Problems and Development Prospect*. Tallinn: TPÜ Kirjastus, pp. 96–104.

Mattinson, J. and Mirrlees-Black, C. (2000) *Attitudes to Crime and Criminal Justice: Findings from the 1998 British Crime Survey*, Home Office Research Study No. 200. London: HMSO.

Noelle-Neumann, E. and Köcher, R. (1997) *Allensbacher Jahrbuch der Demoskopie 1993–1997*. Munich and Allensbach: K.G. Saur/Verlag für Demoskopie.

Noelle-Neumann, E. and Köcher, R. (2002) *Allensbacher Jahrbuch der Demoskopie 1998–2002*. Munich and Allensbach: K.G. Saur/Verlag für Demoskopie.

Novotny, C. and Kvasnicka, V. (1969) 'K problematice trestu smrti' (The problem with the death penalty), interni material. Prague. Unpublished manuscript.

Reuband, K.-H. (2001) 'Möglichkeiten und Probleme des Einsatzes postalischer Befragungen', *Kölner Zeitschrift für Soziologie und Sozialpsychologie*, 53(2): 307–33.

Schestakov, D.A. (2001) 'Die Todesstrafe in Rußland. Entwicklungen in den neunziger Jahren', *Monatsschrift für Kriminologie und Strafrechtsreform*, 84: 133–7.

Scheuch, E. K. (2002) 'Korruption als Teil einer freiheitlichen Gesellschaftsordnung. Oder: Die Kriminogenese eines kommunalen "Klüngels" ', *Kriminalistik*, 56: 79–91.

Schwarzenegger, C. (1992) *Die Einstellungen der Bevölkerung zur Kriminalität und Verbrechenskontrolle*. Freiburg: Edition Max-Planck-Institute.

Seliverstov, V. (1997) 'The impact of the new Criminal Code of the Russian Federation on the prison population', in HEUNI (ed.), *Prison Population in*

Europe and in North America. Problems and Solutions. Helsinki: HEUNI, pp. 59–65.

Sessar, K. (1997) 'Strafeinstellungen zum Umbruch', in K. Boers, G. Gutsche and K. Sessar (eds), *Sozialer Umbruch und Kriminalität in Deutschland.* Opladen: Westdeutscher Verlag, pp. 255–92.

Stadler, H. (1987) *Kriminalität im Kanton Uri. Eine Opferbefragung.* Entlebuch: Huber Druck AG.

Szumski, J. (1993) 'Fear of crime, social rigorism and mass media in Poland', *International Review of Victimology,* 2: 209–15.

Tarling, R. and Dowds, L. (1997) 'Crime and punishment', in R. Jowell (ed.), *British Social Attitudes: The 14th Report.* Aldershot: Ashgate.

United Nations (2001) *Capital punishment and implementation of the safeguards guaranteeing protection of the rights of those facing the death penalty. Report of the Secretary General.* Economic and Social Council E/NC. 15/2001/10.

van den Berg, G. P. (1983) 'The Soviet Union and the death penalty', *Soviet Studies,* 35: 154–74.

van Dijk, J. J. M., Mayhew, P. and Killias, M. (1990) *Experiences of Crime Across the World. Key Findings from the 1989 International Crime Survey.* Deventer and Boston: Kluwer Law and Taxation Publishers.

van Kesteren, J., Mayhew, P. and Nieuwbeerta, P. (2000) *Criminal Victimisation in Seventeen Industrialised Countries. Key Findings from the 2000 International Crime and Victimisation Survey (ICVS).* The Hague: Ministry of Justice.

Wojciechowska, J. (1994) 'Wzrost przestepczosci jako zrodlo obaw i niepokojow mieszkancow Warszawy' (Rise of criminality as a source of fear and intimidation of Warsaw citizens), *Przeglad Prawa Karnego (Review of the Penal Code),* 10: 32–42.

Zitelmann, R. (1998) 'Mehrheit plädiert für Todesstrafe. Umfrage: 55 Prozent wollen härteste Sanktion bei Kindesmord', *Die Welt,* 14 August.

Zvekic, U. and Alvazzi del Frate, A. (1993) 'Victimisation in the developing world: An overview. Preliminary key findings from the 1992 International Victim Survey', in A. Alvazzi del Frate, U. Zvekic and J. J. M. van Dijk (eds), *Understanding Crime. Experiences of Crime and Crime Control.* Rome: United Nations Interregional Crime and Justice Research Institute, pp. 51–86.

Zvekic, U. and Alvazzi del Frate, A. (eds) (1995) *Criminal Victimisation in the Developing World.* Rome: United Nations Interregional Crime and Justice Research Institute.

Chapter 6

Public and judicial attitudes to punishment in Switzerland[1]

André Kuhn

Introduction

One often hears and reads in the media that the criminal justice system is too lenient and that offenders are not treated as harshly as they deserve. On the other hand, judges respond that the public does not know enough about the law and the details of the individual criminal cases and is accordingly unable to express a reasoned opinion. In order to reconcile these two extreme positions, we will first try to determine if the so-called leniency of the judges, according to the public, corresponds to the reality of the public opinion. If this is the case, we shall examine why, and how, the gap between public and judges could be filled.

The goal of the study reported here was to determine the extent to which the severity of the sanctions imposed by judges is consistent with the desires of the public. But before being able to understand the relation between public and judicial attitudes to punishment, a way of measuring these two attitudes has to be defined. Several researchers have tried to measure either judicial attitudes to punishment (e.g. Walmsley, 2002; de Keijser, 2000; Kuhn, 2000) or public opinion towards the sentencing (e.g. French Ministry of Justice, 1998). But the systematic study of the relation between both of them seems to be a relatively recent topic.[2] Table 6.1 summarises some examples of recent, representative research.

A Swiss study

As Table 6.1 shows, several methods have been used to measure the difference between public and judicial attitudes to punishment. Some

Table 6.1 Previous research comparing public opinion and judicial practice

- *Graebner (1974)* analysed American nationwide data to determine whether the severity of sentencing varied from one region of the United States to another and, in this case, if the variation was related to public opinion. He observed that regional variation did exist and that public opinion was directly related to sentencing practices.
- *Roberts and Doob (1989)* report findings from a study which compared the incarceration rates favoured by the public with actual incarceration rates for a number of common offences. These researchers found a high degree of overall concordance between the two populations.
- *Van Dijk et al. (1990)* measured judicial attitude to punishment by the imprisonment rate[1] in 14 countries and, on the other hand, public attitudes to punishment by the proportion of the respondents of the first international crime victims survey who favoured a prison sentence for a 21-year-old recidivist burglar who stole a television.[2] They observed a strong correlation ($r = 0.61$) between both attitudes. In other words, the countries in which judges imposed harsh sentences were also those where the public opinion was the most punitive.[3]
- *Ouimet (1990)* presented five fictional cases to 235 court practitioners and 299 members of the general public in Montreal. Each respondent was asked to impose a sentence on the five offenders. This study revealed that the general public was more severe than court practitioners by a ratio of about 1.5 to 1. In addition, the demographic characteristics of the respondents (e.g. sex, age, family income) were unrelated to punitive attitudes.
- *Tremblay, Cordeau and Ouimet (1994)* employed the same design and included new variables in their analyses. They observed that both sets of respondents differed in the degree of responsibility that they attributed to the five offenders and that attitudes towards punishment co-varied with the degree of knowledge of the criminal justice system.
- *Indermaur (1994)* interviewed 410 Perth residents, 17 judges, and 53 offenders about sentencing in Australia. He observed that the three samples had very different views on the goals of sentencing. While the public favoured incapacitation, the judges seemed to prefer deterrence and the offenders favoured rehabilitation.
- *Rossi, Berk and Campbell (1997)* asked a sample of 1,500 Americans about the sentences they would like to see imposed for different offences, in order to explore the correspondence between public opinion and the Federal sentencing guidelines.[4] Although only a modest degree of concordance emerged at the individual level, the median sentences favoured by the public corresponded quite closely to the guidelines for almost all types of offences – with the exception of drug trafficking, where the public tended to be less punitive than the guidelines.
- *Hough and Roberts (1998)* presented a summary of a case of burglary to a representative sample of the British population and showed that the public would sentence the offender almost the same way – or even milder – than the

judges. Furthermore, about 80 per cent of these respondents thought that the sentences delivered by the judges were too lenient and that the latter did not do a good job. A similar finding has been found in Poland[5] where the public generally asked for longer sentences but when confronted with actual cases, imposed more lenient sentences.

- *Beyens (2000)* compared views of magistrates on punishment with these of the general public in Belgium. To do so, she used the International Crime Victimisation Survey question asking which sentence the respondents would prefer in the case of a young recidivist burglar who had stolen a television.[6] The main result was that the public seemed more willing to impose alternatives to imprisonment (especially community service order) than the interviewed judges: 63 per cent of the latter delivered a prison sentence, whereas only one of five respondents from the public asked for it.

---

[1]For a definition of the prisoner rate and a comparative table on the prisoner rate across the world, see Kuhn (2000) and Walmsley (2002).

[2]The question used in the international victimisation surveys is the following: 'People have different ideas about the sentences which should be given to offenders. Take for instance the case of a 21-year-old man who is found guilty of a burglary for the second time. This time he has taken a colour TV. Which of the following sentences do you consider the most appropriate for such a case: fine, prison, community service, suspended sentence or any other sentence?' If the respondent chose a prison sentence, he or she is asked on its length; see for example van Dijk et al. (1990): 168, questions 30a and 30b.

[3]However, such a result does not demonstrate that the relationship is constant. Therefore, the question of whether public opinion influences judges or if the severity of the sanctions influences public opinion remains unanswered.

[4]On guidelines, see Gottfredson et al. (1978) and Wilkins (1987).

[5]See Szymanowska and Szymanowski (1996), as well as Kury and Krajewski (2000), cited in Kury (2000).

[6]See van Dijk et al. (1990: 168), question 30a and 30b, as well as note 2 above.

---

researchers simply asked respondents if they thought the sanctions imposed by judges were too harsh, adequate, or too lenient. All studies that used this question have concluded that the public considered judges to be too lenient.[3] Another method involves presenting respondents with real cases (that have already been sentenced by a court) and asking about the sanctions they would have liked to impose on the offenders. A third method involves presenting the same scenarios to a sample of the public *and* a sample of judges. This methodology is attractive because it controls all the relevant variables (such as the offender's previous convictions). Nevertheless, this technique also contains an important disadvantage: judges may respond differently when confronted with fictional cases contained in a questionnaire than when facing real offenders. The research reported in this chapter employed this last method.

Drawing upon actual cases, we created four scenarios containing all the information necessary to impose a sentence (e.g. a detailed description of the offence, characteristics of the offender and the

victim). A representative sample of 654 Swiss judges[4] and a representative sample of the Swiss population (606 people) were then asked to
impose a sentence on the four offenders. Since all respondents had the
same cases, any differences in the severity of their sentences must
reflect differences between the populations.[5]

The four cases are those of a recidivist driver who drove at 232 km/h
on a highway limited to 120 km/h (case A), a recidivist burglar who
committed a robbery (case B), a first-time rapist (case C) and a bank
clerk who stole one million Swiss francs from his bank (case D).

The judges' questionnaire was submitted to the sample of judges in
May 2000. In addition to the four criminal cases, some demographic
variables and a question about the goals of the penal sanctions were
included in order to measure the punitive *attitudes* of the respondents.
The participation rate was 44 per cent (290 valid questionnaires). The
public study was conducted through a computer-assisted telephone
interview (CATI) methodology in October 2000. In addition to all the
items contained in the judges' questionnaire, additional demographic
variables were included, as well as a question about people's views of
the criminal justice system. The participation rate was 72 per cent.

The samples

Among the 290 judges 219 were from the German part of Switzerland
(76 per cent), 64 from the French part (22 per cent), and seven from the
Italian region of the country (2 per cent). Since the Italian-speaking
sample was too small to be analysed separately we have added them
to the French-speaking respondents, and we then talk about the 'Latin
part of Switzerland'.[6] Approximately one-quarter of the judges were
female. The age of the respondents varied between 31 and 70 with an
average of 50 years.

With regard to the public survey, 287 interviews were conducted in
the German part of Switzerland and 319 in the French part of the
country.[7] Within both of these sub-samples, the quotas of gender and
age were respected. Therefore, a total of 295 men and 311 women were
interviewed. Among those 606 respondents, 293 (48 per cent) live in
cities with more than 100,000 inhabitants, 197 (33 per cent) in towns
with 3,000 to 100,000 inhabitants, and 116 (19 per cent) in smaller
locations. With regard to their nationality, 503 respondents (83 per
cent) were Swiss citizens,[8] whereas 103 (17 per cent) were foreign
residents. Forty-seven per cent of the interviewees indicate that they
lived in a modest household, whereas 49 per cent of the respondents
had the impression of living comfortably.[9] Finally, with regard to the

self-evaluated political position, 116 (19 per cent) people took a right-wing position, 85 (14 per cent) a centre position, and 172 (28 per cent) a left-wing position.[10]

Findings

The following hypotheses were tested:

1. Do public and judicial attitudes to punishment vary according to the gender of the respondents?

2. Do public and judicial attitudes to punishment vary according to the age of the respondents?

3. Do public and judicial attitudes to punishment vary from one part of the country to another?

4. Are public attitudes to punishment more punitive than the judicial opinions?

Table 6.2 shows the average prison terms delivered by the judges in the four cases. Several judges expressed a preference for a suspended prison term, preferred even a fine, or would have added to their prison term either a fine or a financial compensation (case C), the seizure of the car (case A) or of the stolen amount of money (case D), a confinement measure (case B), the withdrawal of the driving licence (case A), etc. For the following analyses we only took into account the (suspended or unsuspended) prison term the respondent intended to deliver to the different offenders.

Table 6.2 Average length (in months) of prison sentences delivered by a sample of Swiss judges in the four cases

| | Average length (in months) | By gender | | By region | |
		Men	Women	German part	Latin part
Case A (driver)	6	6	7	6	6
Case B (burglar)	11	12	10	12*	10*
Case C (rapist)	45	45	46	45	46
Case D (bank clerk)	27	27	26	26	29

*The difference is statistically significant: $p < 0.05$.

Table 6.3 Average length (in months) of prison sentences delivered by a sample of Swiss citizens in the four criminal cases

| | Average length (in months) | By gender | | By region | |
		Men	Women	German part	French part
Case A (driver)	12	10	13	11**	18**
Case B (burglar)	14	13	14	12**	19**
Case C (rapist)	59	60	59	56*	73*
Case D (bank clerk)	21	18	23	19*	28*

*The difference is statistically significant ($p < 0.05$).
**The difference is statistically significant ($p < 0.01$).

This table indicates that, in spite of important individual differences between judges in the sentences they deliver for the same case, a certain uniformity exists between the average length of the prison terms delivered by female and male judges, and also between the average sentence delivered in the German part of the country and elsewhere. We shall return to this issue later in the chapter. Table 6.3 shows the average prison terms desired by the public in the same four criminal cases.

As can be seen, the public was generally more punitive than the judges in three of the four cases, although they were more lenient towards the bank clerk who stole one million Swiss francs (case D). In addition, the French-speaking respondents are more punitive than the German speakers and women more than men, with the exception of the case of the rapist.

With regard to the goals of the sanctions according to the public, one observes that rehabilitating the offender is the preferred purpose (supported by 38 per cent of the respondents), followed by protecting society (26 per cent), punishment (21 per cent) and helping offenders to become aware of the committed offence (20 per cent). Further, considered as less important, one finds other goals such as individual deterrence (13 per cent), general deterrence (6 per cent), public order (4 per cent) and social balance (4 per cent). A small percentage (3 per cent) of the public believed that prison was useless and 1 per cent believed that it even promoted the commission of crimes.

Attitudes to punishment and gender

No differences between male and female judges emerged with respect to the sanctions. Therefore, our first hypothesis is not supported. Even the scenario involving a rapist failed to generate differences according to gender. This result is probably strongly influenced by the jurisprudence. Nor were there any significant differences between men and women, with regard to the purposes of sentences. Among the public, the results are quite different. With the exception of the case of the rapist, women were systematically (but not significantly) more punitive than men. At the attitudes level, i.e. the goals of the sanctions, there were no statistically significant differences between men and women.

Attitudes to punishment and age

Like gender, age did not significantly influence the sentences delivered by the judges. This is true for the four cases. Therefore, like the first one, our second hypothesis is not verified. Furthermore, age does not influence at all the choice of the hierarchy of the goals attributed to the sanctions.

With regard to the public, the results are slightly different from those concerning the judges. If age does not influence the punitive attitudes in cases B (burglar) and D (bank clerk), speeding is sentenced more severely by the older respondents,[11] whereas the rapist is punished more severely by the younger interviewees.[12] Preferences for the main goals of the sanctions were uninfluenced by the respondents' age.

Attitudes to punishment and regional origins

Once again, the responses of the judges reveal a high degree of homogeneity. With the exception of the burglar (case B) – on whom the German-speaking judges imposed a more punitive sanction than their French- and Italian-speaking colleagues – no significant differences emerged between the judges in relation to their regional origin. However, if one looks at the *attitudes* level, one observes that the German-speaking judges assigned a higher level of importance to individual deterrence, whereas the Latin judges preferred punishment. This difference is highly significant.

The results from the public sample are very clear: the French-speaking inhabitants of the country are largely and significantly more punitive than the German-speaking residents. This difference will come as no surprise to Swiss criminologists, as it is a constant finding in national studies.[13]

With regard to the goals of the sanctions, a larger proportion of French-speaking respondents (9 per cent against only 2 per cent of the German-speaking ones) think that the deprivation of liberty is not useful and may even be counterproductive (since it could lead to criminal behaviour). In the French part of Switzerland, respondents believed that sanctions are intended to help offenders to become self-conscious of their offending (34 per cent), as well as to punish the offender (26 per cent), whereas the Swiss-Germans were more likely to favour rehabilitation (43 per cent) and incapacitation (29 per cent).

Attitudes to punishment and other variables

Overall the size of the living agglomeration, the civil status and the professional activity did not significantly influence attitudes to punishment. On the other hand, foreign residents were more punitive than the Swiss citizens and interviewees living in a modest household are more punitive than those who live comfortably. Finally, the respondents with the lowest level of education are more punitive than the better educated ones.

Difference between public and judicial attitudes to punishment

With regard to the attitudes towards the goals of the sanctions, judges and the public seem to agree on the high importance of rehabilitation and punishment, and the low importance of the satisfaction of the victim as a goal of sentencing. However, the similarities between both judges and public end here. Judges assigned more importance to specific deterrence, whereas the public significantly preferred incapacitation.

With regard to the sentences imposed, with the exception of case D, Tables 6.2 and 6.3 show that the public seems to be more punitive than the judges;[14] this finding is consistent with previous research. The public leniency towards the bank clerk who stole more than one million Swiss francs from his employer shows that the public is not ready yet to consider the white-collar crime as a very serious form of offending.

While the public were in aggregate more punitive than the judges in three of our four cases, this finding needs some important qualification. Our measure of punitiveness – the *average* length of the prison terms imposed by judges and by the public – leaves open the possibility that the public's average may be affected by a small proportion of respondents with very extreme views. To check this, we examined the proportions of the public that would deliver less- and more-punitive sanctions than the average sanction delivered by the judges.

Table 6.4 shows that a majority of the public would be satisfied with the average sentences imposed by the judges. As they imposed less

Table 6.4 Proportion of the public who would impose sentences which are less and more punitive than the average prison sentence imposed by the judges

	Proportion of the public who would be less punitive than the judges (%)	Proportion of the public who would be more punitive than the judges (%)
Case A (driver)	67	33
Case B (burglar)	59	41
Case C (rapist)	51	49
Case D (bank clerk)	79	21

punitive sanctions than judges, most people would even be satisfied if judges imposed shorter prison terms. This unexpected result is probably the most interesting finding of the present study, because it shows that the high imprisonment rates are due to a small number of respondents who favoured the imposition of very long prison terms.

We decided to describe this minority of particularly punitive people and to compare them to the majority of less punitive respondents. As our sample of the public is relatively small, it was difficult to find significant differences between the two groups. However, a correspondence analysis[15] enabled us to find some discriminating variables. The particularly punitive respondents are characterised by the fact that they are inhabitants of large cities,[16] living in economically disadvantaged households,[17] without clear political affiliations,[18] unable to answer the question on the appropriate – or inappropriate – harshness of the current criminal justice system[19] and with a poor level of education.[20] Therefore, three of our five discriminating variables[21] tend to show that the most punitive people are those suffering from a lack of knowledge of the criminal justice system.

Conclusion

This study has shown that in terms of preferred average prison terms for specific cases, the Swiss public are more punitive than their judges. However, this finding reflects a skewing of the average by a small proportion of highly punitive respondents; the majority of respondents actually proposed sentences that were more *lenient* than those of the judges. As with previous research,[22] this study shows that public attitudes to punishment vary according the degree of knowledge of the criminal justice system; the more ignorant of the judiciary, the more punitive people are. An important element of the findings from this study is the start that it has made in describing that minority of the public who are highly punitive in their views, on the one hand, and poorly informed about justice, on the other. As the high average sanction among the public is due to this small group of very punitive people, engaging the public as a whole is not necessary to improve the situation; a change in public attitudes to punishment could be obtained by changing this small group of highly punitive people.

The target group of such an intervention seems to live in large cities, to be economically and educationally disadvantaged and to be relatively uninterested in politics. As this description seems to correspond to some of those people who read populist newspapers and watch television, one strategy for tackling their misperceptions of the criminal justice system would be to address them through their preferred media. Therefore, to avoid a growing misunderstanding of their work, criminologists and judges will, in the future, have to simplify their message and write articles for very popular newspapers and/or to participate in TV shows.

Notes

1. This research has been conducted with the financial assistance of the Swiss National Science Foundation. For further details, the final report can be found at the following Internet address: http://www.unil.ch/penal/qui/Kuhn/FNRS.htm.
2. On this matter see, for example, Killias (1991: 384), Kury (2000: 213), Glick and Pruet (1985) and Beckett (1997a and 1997b). Beckett shows that even if the public attitude to punishment is consistent with the judicial, that does not always mean that the first influences the second, but may also be an effect of judicial attitudes on public opinion. The title of her 1997a paper ('Political preoccupation with crime leads, not follows, public opinion') says a lot on that matter. But Mande and English (1989), as well as Roberts (1992: 162), believe that public opinion may have an indirect influence on judges.
3. As Roberts (1992) notes 'The question has never failed to generate the result that the majority of the public . . . expressed their desire for harsher penalties. In fact, this question concerning sentencing severity generates a higher consensus than any other issue in criminal justice'. See also Kury and Ferdinand (1999: 375).
4. The judicial sample was constructed in order to take into account criteria such as the linguistic representation.

5. For application examples of the simulated judgments method, see Ouimet (1990), Opp and Peuckert (1971) and Peters (1973).
6. Switzerland (about seven million inhabitants) is composed of about 71 per cent of Swiss-Germans, about 25 per cent of French-speaking people, and about 4 per cent of Italian-speaking persons. On most subjects, the latter resemble the people from the French part of the country.
7. This choice to make a disproportional sample where the French part of the country is over-represented leads us to have to make some weighting by analysing the data. The results presented below are all weighted results.
8. Twenty-five of them have a second nationality in addition to the Swiss one.
9. The 4 per cent missing are those who refused to answer this question.
10. Two hundred and eighteen respondents (36 per cent) said they do not have a political opinion and 15 (3 per cent) refused to answer the question.
11. $r = 0.15$, $p < 0.01$.
12. $r = -0.14$, $p < 0.01$.
13. See Killias (1989) for a discussion of this phenomenon.
14. This tendency is highly significant ($p < 0.01$) in cases A and C, but not significant in case B. Case D is the exception to the rule, with a public that is less punitive than the judge ($p < 0.05$).
15. We used the HOMALS procedure (e.g. homogeneity analysis).
16. This variable is discriminating in the four cases, as well as for the total length of the imposed prison sentences (e.g. the addition of the four prison sentences imposed by a same person).
17. This variable is discriminating in cases A, B, D as well as for the total length of the imposed prison sentences.
18. This variable is discriminating in cases B and D.
19. This variable is discriminating in case C and for the total length of the imposed prison sentences.
20. This variable is discriminating in case D.
21. The poor level of education (which probably includes a poor level of judicial knowledge), the impossibility of answering the question about the adequacy of the sentences imposed by the judges (indicating a poor knowledge of the criminal justice system), and the absence of political opinion (indicating that the respondents are not interested in the political realities and may therefore not have the knowledge needed to make a decision in the field of criminal justice).
22. See, for example, Walker and Hough (1988), Tremblay et al. (1994), Roberts (1997: 255), Hough and Roberts (1998 and 1999), and Wemmers (1999); contra, see Bohm and Vogel (1994).

References

Beckett, K. (1997a) 'Political preoccupation with crime leads, not follows, public opinion', *Overcrowded Times*, 8(5): 1, 8–11.

Beckett, K. (1997b) *Making Crime Pay: Law and Order in Contemporary American Politics*. New York: Oxford University Press.

Beyens, K. (2000) *Straffen als sociale praktijk. Een penologisch onderzoek naar straftoemeting (Sentencing as a Social Practice. A Penological Research on Sentencing)*. Brussels: VUBPress.

Bohm, R. M. and Vogel, R. E. (1994) 'A comparison of factors associated with uninformed death penalty opinions', *Journal of Criminal Justice*, 22(2): 125–43.

de Keijser, J. W. (2000) *Punishment and Purpose: From Moral Theory to Punishment in Action*. Amsterdam: Thela Thesis.

Dodge, Y., Mehran, F. and Rousson, M. (1990) *Statistique*. Neuchâtel: Presses Académiques.

French Ministry of Justice (1998) *A l'ombre du savoir: Connaissances et représentations des Français sur la prison*. Paris: Ministère de la Justice, Travaux et Documents no. 52.

Glick, H. R. and Pruet, G. W. (1985) 'Crime, public opinion and trial courts: an analysis of sentencing policy', *Justice Quarterly*, 2(3): 319–43.

Gottfredson, D. M., Wilkins, L. T. and Hoffman, P. B. (1978) *Guidelines for Parole and Sentencing*. Lexington (MA): Lexington Books.

Graebner, D. B. (1974) 'Judicial activity and public attitude: a quantitative study of selective service sentencing in the Vietnam War period', *Buffalo Law Review*, 23(2): 465–98.

Hough, M. and Roberts, J. V. (1998) *Attitudes to Punishment. Findings from the British Crime Survey*, Home Office Research Study No. 179. London: Home Office.

Hough, M. and Roberts, J. V. (1999) 'Sentencing trends in Britain: public knowledge and public opinion', *Punishment and Society*, 1(1): 11–26.

Indermaur, D. (1994) 'Offenders' perceptions of sentencing', *Australian Psychologist*, 29(2): 140–4.

Killias, M. (1989) *Les Suisses face au crime*. Grüsch: Rüegger.

Killias, M. (1991) *Précis de criminologie*. Berne: Staempfli.

Kuhn, A. (1993) 'Attitudes towards punishment', in A. Alvazzi del Frate, U. Zvekic, J. J. M. van Dijk (eds), *Understanding Crime: Experiencies of Crime and Crime Control*. Rome: UNICRI, pp. 271–88.

Kuhn, A. (2000) *Détenus: Combien? Pourquoi? Que faire?* Berne: Haupt.

Kury, H. (2000) 'Gemeingefährlichkeit und Medien – Kriminologische Forschungsergebnisse zur Frage der Strafeinstellungen', in S. Bauhofer, P.-H. Bolle, V. Dittmann (eds), *'Gemeingefährliche' Straftäter – Délinquants 'dangereux'*. Coire: Rüegger, pp. 193–236.

Kury, H. and Ferdinand, T. (1999) 'Public opinion and punitivity', *International Journal of Law and Psychiatry*, 22(3–4): 373–92.

Kury, H. and Krajewski, K. (2000) 'Zur Strafmentalität der Bevölkerung: Ein Vergleich zwischen Deutschland und Polen' (Freiburg im Br.), manuscrit non publié à paraître probablement dans H. Kury, J. Obergfell-Fuchs, M. Würger (2001) *Punitivität, Strafeinstellungen und Sanktionspraxis*. Freiburg im Br.: Iuscrim.

Mande, M. J. and English, K. (1989) *The Effect of Public Opinion on Correctional Policy: A Comparison of Opinions and Practices*. Denver, CO: Colorado Division of Criminal Justice.

Opp, K.-D. and Peukert, R. (1971) *Ideologie und Fakten in der Rechtsprechung: Eine soziologische Untersuchung über das Urteil im Strafprozess*. Munich: Goldmann.

Ouimet, M. (1990) *Tracking down Penal Judgment: A Study of Sentencing Decision-Making among the Public and Court Practitioners*. Newark, NJ: Rutgers University Publications.

Peters, D. (1973) *Richter im Dienst der Macht*. Stuttgart: Enke.

Roberts, J. V. (1992) 'Public opinion, crime, and criminal justice', in M. Tonry (ed.), *Crime and Justice: A Review of Research*, vol. 16 (Chicago: University of Chicago Press), pp. 99–180.

Roberts, J. V. (1997) 'American attitudes about punishment: myth and reality', in M. Tonry and K. Hatlestad (eds), *Sentencing Reform in Overcrowded Times: A Comparative Perspective*. Oxford: Oxford University Press, pp. 250–5.

Roberts, J. V. and Doob, A. (1989) 'Sentencing and public opinion. Taking false shadows for true substance', *Osgood Hall Law Journal*, 27: 491–515.

Rossi, P. H., Beck, R. A. and Campbell, A. (1997) 'Just punishments: guideline sentences and normative consensus', *Journal of Quantitative Criminology*, 13(3): 267–90.

Szymanowska, A. and Szymanowski, T. (1996) *Öffentliche Meinung in Polen über manche pathologischen oder kontroversen Verhaltensweisen sowie Straftaten und deren strafrechtlichen Kontrolle* (traduit du polonais) (Varsovie).

Tremblay, P., Cordeau, G. and Ouimet, M. (1994) 'Underpunishing offenders: towards a theory of legal tolerance', *Canadian Journal of Criminology*, 36(4): 407–34.

van Dijk, J. J. M., Mayhew, P. and Killias, M. (1990) *Experiences of Crime across the World*. Deventer (NL) and Boston: Kluwer.

Walker, N. and Hough, M. (eds) (1988) *Public Attitudes to Sentencing: Surveys from Five Countries*. Aldershot: Gower, Cambridge Studies in Criminology LIX.

Walmsley, R. (2002) *World Prison Population List*, 3rd edn, Findings No. 166. London: Home Office Research, Development and Statistics Directorate (traduction française de la première édition parue dans *Bulletin de Criminologie* (1999) 25(2): 55–75).

Wemmers, J. A. M. (1999) 'Victime notification and public support for the criminal justice system', *International Review of Victimology*, 6(3): 167–78.

Wilkins, L. T. (1987) 'Disparity in dispositions: the early ideas and applications of guidelines', in M. Wasik and K. Pease (eds), *Sentencing Reform: Guidance or Guidelines?* Manchester: University Press, pp. 7–21.

Chapter 7

Public support for correctional rehabilitation in America: change or consistency?[1]

Francis T. Cullen, Jennifer A. Pealer,
Bonnie S. Fisher, Brandon K. Applegate, and
Shannon A. Santana

Introduction

Virtually everyone agrees that the public in the United States harbours punitive views toward offenders. Liberals are troubled by such opinions. Believing that the American criminal justice system punishes too much (Clear, 1994; Currie, 1998), they argue that harsh attitudes reflect the distorted assumption that offenders receive lenient sentences. Citizens are portrayed as being manipulated by the media and by politicians into believing that most crime is violent and most offenders are dangerous – visions that encourage the embrace of 'get tough' policies. Conservatives, on the other hand, welcome the punitive views expressed by the public. Believing that the American criminal justice system punishes too little (Bennett, DiIulio and Walters, 1996), they see the public as making the rational assessment that punishments need to be increased. The rash of 'get tough' policies in the United States – which has been steadily spreading over the past two decades – is portrayed as a sensible agenda that will achieve greater justice for victims and greater protection of public safety.

The consensus belief in the 'punitive public' draws support from a range of survey data. Although there has been some slippage in advocacy recently (due to concern over the discovery of wrongfully convicted offenders on death row), Americans' support for capital punishment has fluctuated between 66 per cent and 80 per cent over the past 25 years. During this same time period, about four in five

Americans also have agreed in poll after poll that the 'courts in this area' do not 'deal harshly enough with criminals' (Cullen, Fisher and Applegate, 2000). Similarly, when survey respondents are presented with vignettes describing different offences and are asked to prescribe a sanction for the offenders in question, they favour incarceration and often recommend lengthy prison terms (Jacoby and Cullen, 1998). As Warr (2000: 22) notes, 'Americans overwhelmingly regard imprisonment as the appropriate form of punishment for most crimes'. To be sure, other research shows that these punitive sentiments are not rigidly held and can be moved downward when respondents are given more information (e.g. the costs of prisons) and other sentencing options (e.g. community sanctions) (Cullen et al., 2000; Roberts and Stalans, 1997; Thomson and Ragona, 1987; Turner et al., 1997). Nonetheless, there is little doubt that Americans are generally supportive of imposing stiff penalties on the criminally wayward (Innes, 1993).

However, this belief in the 'punitive public' is often accompanied by the collateral and mistaken notion that Americans are hostile to another potential goal of the criminal sanction: offender rehabilitation (Cullen, Cullen and Wozniak, 1988). On the surface, this assumption makes sense. 'Punishment' and 'rehabilitation' are often juxtaposed as competing correctional ideologies in which support for one view is tantamount to the rejection of the other. In policy and academic debates, where sides are taken and analytical distinctions are emphasised, this characterisation is generally accurate; there are, in short, supporters of punishment and supporters of rehabilitation. With regard to the public, however, it is not clear that attitudes are so dichotomous. As will be seen below, citizens often support multiple correctional goals simultaneously, seeing both punishment and rehabilitation as important. Especially in policy debates, this social construction of the public as exclusively punitive has served to mask the diversity of views on corrections that people actually express.

It is also relevant that the entire 'get tough' movement in the United States – a policy agenda that has been in vogue for three decades – can be viewed as representing a rejection of the rehabilitative ideal (Cullen and Gendreau, 2000; Cullen and Gilbert, 1982). This assumption, however, appears to be only partially correct. Even as crime policies have become more punitive, it is not clear that a majority of citizens have ever abandoned their belief that the correctional system should engage in offender treatment.

Thus, until the early 1970s, rehabilitation reigned as the dominant correctional worldview. Criminologists and policy-maker elites were virtually unanimous in stating that 'offender treatment' *should* be the goal of the correctional system. By the mid-1970s, however, the hegemony of rehabilitation as a guide for correctional policy and practice was fractured. Liberals opposed rehabilitation because of a belief that it justified extensive discretion by judges and correctional officials – people who could not be trusted to use this discretion in a just, non-coercive way. In short, rehabilitation was seen to victimise offenders. Conservatives opposed rehabilitation because of a belief that rehabilitation allowed offenders to be 'coddled' and prematurely freed to roam the community in the pursuit of crime. In short, rehabilitation was seen to victimise citizens (Cullen and Gilbert, 1982).

In the end, liberals' concerns that offenders were being oppressed were swept aside, and the conservative critique of rehabilitation, with its embrace of harsh sanctions, prevailed. Rising prison populations and a spate of 'get tough' laws – passed in virtually every corner of the United States – followed. In the absence of public protest, it seems reasonable to conclude that public attitudes tracked this policy change away from support for rehabilitation and toward support for punishment. Indeed, it became fashionable to ask, 'Is rehabilitation dead?' (Allen, 1981; Cullen et al., 1988; Cullen, Golden and Cullen, 1983; Rotman, 1990). However, this conclusion – that the 'get tough movement' signalled public disillusionment with rehabilitation – did not turn out to be accurate. As we will show shortly, the results from a 2001 national survey in the United States suggest that support for correctional rehabilitation remains extensive.

Due to the lack of longitudinal data, it is difficult to determine in any finely calibrated way whether – and if so, how much – public support for rehabilitation has shifted. Various polls have asked one type of question over time: 'What should be the goal of prisons?' The responses typically include 'rehabilitation', 'punishment' and 'protection of society' (or 'crime prevention/deterrence'). In 1968, fully 73 per cent of the respondents in a Harris poll selected 'rehabilitation' in a forced-choice answering scheme. By 1982, the percentage choosing the rehabilitation option had declined to 44 per cent (Cullen et al., 2000: 49). Two surveys using this question, which were conducted a decade apart in Cincinnati, Ohio, found that support for rehabilitation declined from 55 per cent in 1986 to 33 per cent in 1995 (Cullen et al., 1990; Sundt et al., 1998). A 1996 statewide study in Ohio reported that 41 per cent of the sample endorsed the rehabilitation option (Applegate, Cullen and Fisher, 1997). Using a slightly different response set, a 1996 national poll found that 48 per cent of the respondents favoured rehabilitation (Cullen et al., 2000). We should note that there is some evidence that American support for rehabilitation at the *sentencing* phase – as opposed to what is done with offenders once they are under correctional supervision – is low; 'just deserts' or 'retribution' seem much more influential at this stage (Gerber and Engelhardt-Greer, 1996). Still, more systematic research is needed to disentangle public opinions about sentencing from those about corrections.

We can draw two conclusions from these findings. First, it seems likely that support for rehabilitation as the dominant goal of corrections declined between the latter part of the 1960s and the 1980s (see also Innes, 1993; Pettinico, 1994). What we do not know, however, is whether the overwhelming endorsement of offender treatment near the end of the 1960s represented a long-term, stable pattern of public opinion or a departure from lower levels of support for rehabilitation that existed before and after this unusual period in American history. It is instructive that, at this time (1966), more Americans also opposed than favoured capital punishment – a view that has not prevailed before or since this juncture (Cullen et al., 2000).

Second, even with the ostensible decline in support for rehabilitation, offender treatment remained a reasonably popular goal of prisons. In nearly every study, the rehabilitation option secured more public support than either the punishment or protection of society options (Cullen et al., 2000). Furthermore, a forced-choice question can reveal some things, such as which goal is most important to respondents, but it can mask other things, such as whether the public supports multiple correctional goals. Notably, when asked to rate only whether rehabilitation as a single principle is 'an important goal of prisons' – as opposed to how it compared to other punishment-oriented goals – most survey respondents answer in the affirmative. For example, in a 1996 statewide Ohio survey, over 80 per cent of the public rated rehabilitation either as 'very important' (45 per cent) or as 'important' (38 per cent) (Applegate et al., 1997).

Data from other sources also reinforce the conclusion that the American public sees rehabilitation as an integral purpose of the correctional enterprise. Thus, studies have presented respondents with statements about rehabilitation – asking, for example, whether rehabilitation programmes are a 'good thing' or 'should be expanded' – and then have instructed them to rate the extent to which they 'agreed' or 'disagreed' with the ideas expressed. High percentages of the public typically respond with sentiments favourable to offender treatment (see, for example, Applegate et al., 1997; Cullen et al., 1988; Doble Research Associates, 1995a; Johnson, 1994; see also Flanagan, 1996). Surveys also reveal that citizens believe that rehabilitation programmes are 'helpful' to offenders. Respondents, however, tend to express less confidence that violent offenders will be rehabilitated (Sundt et al., 1998; see also Pettinico, 1994). Yet even these reservations vary by the phrasing of the question being answered. In a 1996 national poll, for example, a clear majority of respondents answered that 'most' (15 per cent) or 'some' (46 per cent) of the 'criminals who commit violent crimes' could be 'rehabilitated, given early intervention with the right programme' (Flanagan, 1996: 80). Finally, although more limited in number, other studies have presented respondents with vignettes describing an offence and then have queried whether the offender should be rehabilitated in some way. Again, support for rehabilitation in this research is consistent (Applegate et al., 1997; McCorkle, 1993).

The existing research also is clear in showing that public support for the rehabilitation of juveniles is particularly strong (Applegate et al., 1997; Cullen et al., 2000; Cullen et al., 1983; Doble Research Associates, 1995b; Gerber and Engelhardt-Greer, 1996; Moon et al., 2000; Steinhart, 1988; Sundt et al., 1998). Similarly, recent surveys reveal that citizens support a range of early intervention programmes with children at risk of delinquency or already involved in offending (Cullen et al., 1998; Moon, Cullen and Wright, forthcoming). When asked whether they would prefer to try to reduce crime by building more prisons to incapacitate offenders or by using programmes with children to prevent them from 'growing up to become criminals', about three in four respondents – if not more – choose the early intervention option (Cullen et al., 1998; Fairbank, Maslin, Maullin & Associates, 1997; Resources for Youth, 1998).

In short, research conducted over the past two decades reveals consistent support for rehabilitation as a correctional goal. In this chapter, we attempt to build on the extant research by reporting the results of a national survey that we conducted on public views about correctional issues. Previous studies have been limited in at least one of two ways. First, national-level studies have typically involved asking respondents only one or two items – thus being brief 'polls' rather than systematic 'surveys'. Second, community-wide and state-wide studies have often (but not always) included detailed measures of correctional attitudes. However, the generalisability of the results has been circumscribed by the restricted geographical location of the sample. In this project, we have attempted to overcome the limitations of past research by undertaking a systematic survey of public opinion on correctional issues using a national-level sample. Our study also has the advantage of supplying the most recent (2001) data available on what the public in the United States thinks about rehabilitation. Again, the key finding we report is that public support for offender treatment appears to be extensive. Accordingly, we suggest that there has been, and is likely to be, a fairly high level of *consistency* in Americans' endorsement of rehabilitation as an integral part of the corrections enterprise.

The current study

To secure a national sample, we relied on Survey Sampling, Inc. to conduct a simple random sample of 1,000 phone and non-phone households for America's 50 states and the District of Columbia. Following Dillman's (1978) 'Total Design Method', the study was designed to include three waves of questionnaires and a follow-up reminder letter to the respondents after the first wave of surveys were mailed. We also sent a pre-contact letter to inform the sample members that a survey would be forthcoming. A token (a pen) was included in the first mailing. Finally, an effort was made to contact all non-respondents by telephone following the second mailing. Of those contacted, 123 were returned due to addresses that were no longer valid. In all, 349 surveys were returned, for a response rate of 40 per cent of eligible sample members. Of these surveys, 329 were usable.

The relatively modest response rate raises potential concerns about whether the composition of the respondents accurately represents the larger population, a consideration that could introduce bias into the results reported here. This worry is best addressed within the context of the issue we are investigating: whether the public still supports rehabilitation. That is, is there anything about those responding to the survey that would artificially inflate support for rehabilitation? In general, we would expect that support for treatment would be associated with sample members who were liberal politically and non-punitive in orientation. Although socio-demographic characteristics typically do not explain substantial amounts of variation in correctional views, support for rehabilitation tends to be higher among women, minorities, and the young (Applegate, 1997; Applegate et al., 1997). Notably, the respondents in the current survey do not have characteristics that would make them, as a group, overly inclined to embrace the rehabilitative ideal.[2]

As we will see below in Table 7.1, the sample showed clear support for the punishment of offenders. Questions included in another portion of the survey (not included in this chapter) revealed that 74 per cent favoured the death penalty and that 54 per cent felt that the 'courts in this area' did not 'deal harshly enough with criminals' (41 per cent stated the courts' harshness was 'about right', but only 5 per cent stated the courts acted 'too harshly'). In terms of socio-demographics, the sample had characteristics that, if anything, would make it lean against rehabilitation. Hence, the respondents were disproportionately male (66 per cent), white (83 per cent) and old (mean age of 55 years of age). Finally, we should add that although appropriate caution should be exercised due to the response rate, the findings reported here are consistent with the existing research on public opinion about corrections (Applegate, 1997; Cullen et al., 2000).

Our research strategy here is to use various ways of exploring support for rehabilitation. We begin by reporting whether the respondents embraced punishment as a correctional outcome. We then examine how the sample members rated the goals of prisons both in forced-choice questions and in questions that instructed the respondents to rate each goal separately. Building on previous research (Cullen et al., 1983; Cullen et al., 1988; Dunaway and Cullen, 1991), the respondents were also asked to rate statements about rehabilitation using a six-point scale ranging from 'strongly disagree' to 'strongly agree'. These results are presented below. Finally, we examine support for juvenile rehabilitation and for early intervention programmes.

The correctional ideology of the American public

Table 7.1 reports the extent to which respondents endorsed ideas about just deserts, the use of punishment for crime control, incapacitation and prisons as a means of reducing crime. Using a six-point Likert scale, the sample members rated each of the items listed in Table 7.1. The percentage who selected one of three 'agree' responses is presented in the table (i.e. those who answered 'agree slightly', 'agree', or 'agree strongly').

Consistent with previous research, punitive sentiments are apparent. Thus, 9 out of 10 respondents agreed that 'criminals deserve to be punished' and that offenders should be incarcerated so that 'innocent citizens' would be protected from 'criminals'. Almost 6 out of 10 said that 'punishing criminals is the only way' to prevent future offending, and 7 out of 10 rejected the idea that incarceration 'doesn't make much sense' because prisons are 'schools of crime'. Furthermore, in Table 7.2 (see the third column of data), it can be seen that high proportions of the sample rated 'punishment' and 'protect society' as important goals of prisons. Some ambivalence, however, is apparent with regard to

Table 7.1 Public support for punishment (percentages reported)

	% agree*
1. Criminals deserve to be punished because they have harmed society.	92
2. Punishing criminals is the only way to stop them from engaging in more crimes in the future.	59
3. We should put criminals in jail so that innocent citizens will be protected from criminals who victimise them – rob them – if given the chance.	91
4. Since most criminals commit crimes over and over again, the only way to protect society is to put these criminals in jail and throw away the key.	48
5. Putting people in prisons does not make much sense since it will only increase crime because prisons are schools of crime.	29
6. Sending criminals to jail will not stop them from committing crimes.	65

*The 'agree' category includes the responses 'agree slightly', 'agree', and 'agree strongly'.

whether the respondents believed that incarceration will 'stop them from committing crimes'; 2 out of 3 agreed that 'jail' may not diminish future offending (see Table 7.1). One interpretation is that although citizens see prisons as effectively incapacitating offenders, they are less sure about whether the prison experience itself deters once an inmate is returned to the community.

Support for rehabilitation as a goal of prisons

As noted, Table 7.2 presents data on the degree to which the public supports rehabilitation as a goal of prisons. The questions used in this study are drawn from the 1968 Harris survey (Harris, 1968). Like the Harris poll, we asked what the respondents thought 'is' the main emphasis of prisons and then what they thought 'should be' the main emphasis of prisons. We also include, in the third column of data, how citizens rated the 'importance' of each goal one by one. The percentages reported in Table 7.2 are those in the sample who answered 'important' or 'very important'. The other two response categories in the four-point Likert scale were 'a little important' and 'not important at all'.

Less than 20 per cent of the sample believed that rehabilitation 'is the main emphasis of most prisons'. It is noteworthy, however, that 55.3 per cent stated that rehabilitation 'should be' the principal purpose of

Table 7.2 Public support for the goals of prisons (percentages reported)

	Main emphasis is	Main emphasis should be	Importance of each goal*
1. Rehabilitation – trying to rehabilitate the individual so that he might return to society as a productive citizen.	19	55	87
2. Punishment – punishing the individual convicted of crime.	31	14	86
3. Protect society – protect society from future crimes he might commit.	34	25	93
4. Not sure.	16	6	—

*Reporting the percentage stating that the goal is 'important' or 'very important'.

incarceration. Taken together, fewer than 4 out of 10 respondents selected either 'punishment' or 'protect society' as their preferred option. By way of comparison, the level of support for rehabilitation in our 2001 survey fell below that reported in the 1968 Harris poll (73.0 per cent) but matched or was higher than the level found in most other surveys conducted in the past two decades (Cullen et al., 2000: 49).

Equally revealing is how the respondents defined the 'importance' of rehabilitation as a correctional goal. As reported in Table 7.2, 87.0 per cent of the sample stated that rehabilitation was either 'important' (33.4 per cent) or 'very important' (53.6 per cent). Again, the public also manifested support for 'punishment' (86.4 per cent) and for 'protect society' (93.4 per cent). It appears that Americans believe that correctional institutions should fulfill multiple goals, not only punishing and incapacitating offenders but also rehabilitating them.

Specifying support for rehabilitation

The survey instrument contained a number of statements about various aspects of rehabilitation, which are listed in Table 7.3. Again, these items were rated using a six-point Likert scale. The 'agree' responses for each of the ten items rated are presented.

The striking feature of the findings in Table 7.3 is that a high percentage of the respondents agreed with each item. For eight of the ten items, the percentage of agreement equals or exceeds 88 per cent; in no case does the percentage dip below 69 per cent. Across all ten items, the mean percentage of agreement is 87 per cent.[3]

Table 7.3 Public support for rehabilitation (percentages reported)

	% agree*
1. It is a good idea to provide treatment for offenders who are in prison.	92
2. It is a good idea to provide treatment for offenders who are supervised by the courts and live in the community.	88
3. We should try to rehabilitate men who have broken the law.	92
4. We should try to rehabilitate women who have broken the law.	93
5. Rehabilitation programmes should be available even for offenders who have been involved in a lot of crime in their lives.	69
6. The best way to rehabilitate offenders is to give them a good education.	71
7. The best way to rehabilitate offenders is to teach them a skill that they can use to get a job when they are released from prison.	89
8. The best way to rehabilitate offenders is to try to help them change their values and to help them with the emotional problems that caused them to break the law.	88
9. It is important to try to rehabilitate adults who have committed crimes and are now in the correctional system.	88
10. It is important to try to rehabilitate juveniles who have committed crimes and are now in the correctional system.	98

*The 'agree' category includes the responses 'agree slightly', 'agree', and 'agree strongly'.

Substantively, a consistent degree of support is shown for rehabilitating offenders both in prison and in the community, for rehabilitating male and female inmates, for rehabilitating adult and juvenile offenders, and for rehabilitating offenders through vocational training, internal psychological change, and education (though less so). Even for offenders 'who have been involved in a lot of crime in their lives', nearly 7 out of 10 respondents agreed that rehabilitation was an appropriate correctional response.

Support for juvenile rehabilitation

The public clearly endorses rehabilitation as a, if not the, main purpose of juvenile corrections. Thus, item 10 in Table 7.3 reveals that 98 per cent of the sample 'agreed' that 'it is important to try to rehabilitate juveniles who have committed crimes and are now in the correctional system'. In fact, the mean for this item – again, on a six-point scale – was 5.3.

Table 7.4 Public support for the goals of juvenile prisons (percentages reported)

	Main emphasis should be	Importance of each goal*	Very important goal
1. Rehabilitation – trying to rehabilitate the individual so that he might return to society as a productive citizen	80	97	73
2. Punishment – punishing the individual convicted of a crime.	8	76	44
3. Protect society – protect society from future crimes he might commit.	8	85	25
4. Not sure	4	—	—

*The goal is 'important' or 'very important'.

Table 7.4 summarises the respondents' views on the goals of juvenile imprisonment. When asked what the 'main emphasis' should be, 4 out of 5 members of the sample in a forced-choice response set selected 'rehabilitation' over 'punishment' and 'protect society'. When asked to rate the importance of each goal one by one, there was support for punishment and protect society. Even so, 97 per cent of the sample stated that rehabilitation was an 'important' goal. Furthermore, 73 per cent indicated that rehabilitation was a 'very important' goal; in contrast, the percentage rating punishment and protect society as 'very important' was, respectively, 29 and 48 percentage points lower.

Support for early intervention programmes

Table 7.5 summarises views toward a range of early intervention programmes, including family-based programmes, pre-school and school-based programmes, and after-school programmes. It is noteworthy that support for these interventions is almost universal. Every programme was supported by at least 89 per cent of the sample. Moreover, the percentage of the respondents selecting 'favour strongly' (number six on the Likert scale) ranged from a low of 32 per cent to a high of over 50 per cent.

Finally, we replicated a question asked previously about whether the public supports building more prisons or early intervention as a preferred crime control strategy (Cullen et al., 1998; Fairbank et al., 1997; Resources for Youth, 1998). The 'prison option' was stated this

Table 7.5 Public support for early intervention programmes (percentages reported)

	Favour*	Favour strongly
1. Giving special treatment services to troubled kids who are growing up in families where the parents neglect or abuse kids.	94	37
2. For parents who have kids who get into trouble at school or in the community, programmes that show these parents how to discipline, guide and support their children more effectively.	94	37
3. When youths are first convicted of a crime, programmes that require the youths and their parents to participate in rehabilitation programmes so that the problem causing the behaviour can be dealt with.	96	51
4. Expanding pre-school programmes, such as Head Start, that are aimed at preparing children from disadvantaged and troubled families for school.	89	32
5. Programmes that are set up in schools that have teachers identify youths who have behavioural problems, and that then try to provide psychological services to youths so that they do not develop into delinquents, and later into adult criminals.	90	34
6. Programmes that are specifically aimed at keeping delinquent youths in school, so that they do not drop out of school and spend their time on the streets.	93	41
7. After-school programmes to provide youths whose parents work with educational and recreational activities.	95	37

*The 'favour' category includes the responses 'favour slightly', 'favour', and 'favour strongly'.

way: 'Spending tax dollars to build more prisons so that more criminals can be locked up for longer periods of time'. The 'early intervention option' was stated this way: 'Spending tax dollars on programmes that try to prevent crime by identifying delinquent youths early in life and rehabilitating them so that they do not grow up to be criminals'. In a forced-choice answering scheme, the results were revealing: 86 per cent of the respondents chose the 'early intervention' option, while only 14 per cent chose the 'prison option'.

Conclusion: the tenacity of the rehabilitative ideal

The results reported here are fully consistent with the research that has appeared over the past two decades (Cullen et al., 2000). Four conclusions are possible. First, the American public clearly harbours punitive sentiments. Citizens embrace the concept of 'just deserts', support punishment as a goal of corrections, and view prisons as a tool to protect society through incapacitation – even if they have doubts about whether imprisonment 'stops criminals from committing crime'. Second, support for correctional rehabilitation remains firm. The commonly held idea that 'Americans have largely soured on the idea of rehabilitation' (Lacayo, 1997) is inaccurate. Thus, over 55 per cent of the sample agreed that rehabilitation 'should be the main emphasis' of prisons. In the Likert-type items, about 9 out of 10 respondents stated that 'it is a good idea to provide treatment for offenders' in prison, in the community, and in the correctional system. Third, support for juvenile rehabilitation was pronounced. Indeed, 8 out of 10 respondents selected rehabilitation as the 'main goal' of juvenile prisons. Fourth, support for early intervention programmes was even higher, with the public advocating a variety of programmes and favouring prevention over imprisonment as a strategy for reducing crime.

Again, these results are not unexpected, given that similar findings have been reported in a variety of surveys that have examined one or another of these issues (Cullen et al., 2000). But the high degree of support for rehabilitation is remarkable in light of the degree to which policy elites and criminologists have excoriated rehabilitation for many, many years. Although there is likely some slippage in support for offender treatment since the 1960s – a period in which liberalism was normative, whereas today we speak in belittling tones of the 'L Word' – the data are clear in showing that rehabilitation remains an integral component of American correctional ideology. But why? That is, after all the attacks on rehabilitation, why is the rehabilitative ideal still supported by the public? Why have attitudes remained largely consistent during this period?

We can offer three possible reasons for the tenacity of the rehabilitative ideal. First, compared to most other Western industrial nations, the United States is a religious nation – so much so that Wald (1992: 8) terms the US's degree of religiosity a 'conspicuous exception'. For example, 96 per cent of Americans express a belief in God, two-thirds report they are members of a church or synagogue, and 3 out of 5 say that religion is a 'very important' part of their lives (Applegate et al., 2000: 720). Some religious beliefs – those that are fundamentalist –

increase punitive sentiments, but others are associated with a belief in forgiveness and, in turn, the advocacy of offender rehabilitation (Applegate et al., 2000). Integral to this religious worldview is the notion of redemption – that is, that it is virtually never too late for a 'soul to be saved' or for an 'individual to change'. Recall that when developed some 200 years ago, prisons were appealing because their inventors argued that these institutions had the power to transform the lawless into the law-abiding. This is why they were originally called 'penitentiaries' (Rothman, 1971). Later, when sacred labels were largely banished from the public sphere, institutions were not simply called 'prisons' or 'justice centers' but rather 'correctional institutions'. As the choice of these terms illuminates, the narrative that offenders can be 'saved' or 'corrected' is deeply embedded within American culture.

Second, although Americans embrace the ideal of individual rights and mistrust government power, they also are eminently utilitarian. Appeals to doing 'what works' are thus effective. At least part of the potency of the 'get tough' movement in the United States has been its promise to 'do something' about crime and criminals. Many liberal proposals during this period were unconvincing because they emphasised giving offenders more justice (i.e., rights), reducing the length of prison sentences, and placing more offenders under community supervision – albeit with no clear sense of what such supervision would entail. None of these proposals provided a persuasive rationale that they would, either alone or in concert, blunt crime rates. Conservative commentators, however, offered a clear prescription for reducing crime: lock up as many offenders as possible for as long as possible (see, for example, Bennett et al., 1996). This policy agenda had face validity: if offenders were behind bars, they could not victimise people in the community.

The appeal of rehabilitation is that it, too, offers to afford societal protection – and to do so with an element of humanity. Implicit in offender treatment is a utilitarian exchange. Thus, offenders are given treatments that improve their psychological, human and social capital in exchange for their criminal propensities being reduced if not transformed into prosocial tendencies. In short, unlike other liberal policy proposals, rehabilitation is potentially utilitarian because it seeks not only to improve offenders but also to advance public safety. In colloquial terms, one can always ask: 'Do you want offenders to be rehabilitated or to come out of prison two or three years later worse than when they went in?' For utilitarians – that is, for Americans – the answer is 'obvious'.

Third, Americans are often portrayed as embracing a strong belief in individualism, a view that should make them believe that crime is a choice and that such wayward conduct would be less likely if choosing it was made less attractive through the threat of harsh punishments (see Bellah et al., 1985; Cao and Cullen, 2001; Hamilton and Sanders, 1992). Although accurate to a degree, it is also the case that the public in the United States attributes crime to a variety of causes – including, for example, poor family upbringing, emotional disturbance, abuse and neglect, poor education, peer influence, and economic hardship (Cullen et al., 1985; Roberts and Stalans, 1997). To the extent that beliefs about crime causation and policy prescriptions are linked logically, then Americans are likely to see rehabilitation as necessary to reverse the consequences of being exposed to criminogenic conditions beyond offenders' control. This does not mean that citizens will excuse crime, see it as not involving free choice, or abandon 'get tough' thinking – only that they will believe that a full solution to reducing criminal involvement must also involve 'doing something about' the untoward influences that have moved a person into crime. Rehabilitation, of course, is the one correctional approach equipped to address these underlying crimi-nogenic influences. Accordingly, it 'makes sense' to those Americans – the clear majority – who view crime as having multiple causes.

The constant support for rehabilitation is of considerable policy significance. The two main arguments against correctional treatment are that 'it does not work' and that, in any case, 'the public will not support it' (Cullen and Moon, 2002). In reality, the empirical evidence is now increasingly strong that rehabilitation programmes are effective in reducing offender recidivism, especially if they conform to what researchers have shown are the components or 'principles' of effective treatment interventions (Cullen, 2002; Cullen and Gendreau, 2000; Gendreau, 1996). In contrast, although there is evidence that prisons have an incapacitation effect (Spelman, 2000; cf. Clear, 1994; Currie, 1998), there is virtually no empirical support for the conclusion that 'get tough' correctional programmes (e.g. boot camps, scared straight programmes, intensive probation supervision, electronic monitoring) have any impact on reoffending (Cullen et al., 2002). In short, if offender change is the goal, rehabilitation – not punishment – is 'what works' in corrections (see also Andrews and Bonta, 1998; Cullen, 2002; Cullen and Gendreau, 2000; McGuire, 2001; MacKenzie, 2000). We should note as well that the evidence showing the effectiveness of a variety of early intervention programmes is now extensive (Currie, 1998; Farrington, 1994; Tremblay and Craig, 1995).

The growing consensus that rehabilitation-oriented intervention is 'what works' to change offenders thus leads to the second policy barrier: 'Well, members of the public won't support it anyway. All they want to do is to punish criminals'. Once constructed, social realities are difficult to deconstruct. In the United States, the widely held view that the public is exclusively punitive potentially constrains the pursuit of progressive policy alternatives in many jurisdictions. Politicians and other policy-makers woefully and persistently misperceive public views on crime control. As Roberts and Stalans (1997: 294) note, this distortion is 'asymmetrical: politicians and policy-makers assume that members of the public are more hawkish regarding crime policies than is in fact the case'. What is worse, these officials seek not only to respond to the 'public will' but also to capitalise upon it to secure political capital (Beckett, 1997). The result is a disquieting spiral in which punitive sentiments – real enough but not the full nature of what the public thinks about crime – prompt political officials to implement harsh policies and then to stir up and intensify citizens' support for their 'get tough' agenda.

The value of public opinion data such as those reported here is that they provide an empirical counterpoint to the unchallenged belief that the public is vengeful and 'out for blood'. They suggest that the public wants the correctional system to serve a larger social purpose (Allen, 1981) and not be reduced to warehousing offenders or to a cold-hearted instrument for inflicting what Clear (1994) poignantly calls 'penal harm'. A first step in combating the 'myth of the punitive public' (Cullen et al., 1988) is in publicising public opinion data showing that citizens advocate a more balanced approach to crime – one that exacts an appropriate measure of just deserts and protects the public from the truly dangerous but that also makes a concerted effort to rehabilitate and restore to the community those who need not be ensnared in a life in crime (see also Sundt, 1999). Although a daunting task, the assumption that the public only wants to punish must not be allowed to persist as a taken-for-granted 'truth'. Again, it is important to realise that the data are on the side of those who wish to take up this challenge. We can legitimately report that 'rehabilitation works better than punishment and that the public supports it'.

Finally, the tenacity of the rehabilitative ideal – the constant endorsement by citizens across decades and periods of dramatic social change – reveals that belief in offender treatment is not transitory but part of the worldview of Americans. This is an important lesson. When criminologists and liberals rejected rehabilitation in the late 1960s and 1970s, they had no alternative correctional narrative that the public would 'buy' (Cullen and Gendreau, 2001). They failed to understand that rehabilitation is a *cultural resource* that those with a progressive political leaning can use to justify policies that are both efficacious and humane. Borrowing a phrase once used in conversation by Elliott Currie, the logic of rehabilitation creates 'ideological space' in which to implement progressive crime policies. 'Rehabilitation' is something that the public finds familiar and persuasive, and thus programmes justified by this rationale 'make sense' and have a measure of legitimacy. To ignore this reality is to forfeit the one correctional ideology that retains the power to stand toe-to-toe with 'get tough' thinking and, at least on occasion, to emerge from the fight victorious.

Notes

1. This research was sponsored by a grant from the University Research Council of the University of Cincinnati.
2. Thus more respondents self-identified as Republicans (38 per cent) than as Democrats (35 per cent); 30 per cent declared their political party to be Independent. When asked to rate their 'own political views', 41 per cent selected the mid-point of 'moderate'; 42 per cent fell to the 'conservative' side of the mid-point, whereas only 17 per cent fell to the 'liberal' side of the mid-point.
3. The mean score for each item was equal to or in excess of 3.9 on the six-point agree–disagree scale; for eight of the ten items, the means were 4.6 or higher.

References

Allen, F. A. (1981) *The Decline of the Rehabilitative Ideal: Penal Policy and Social Purpose*. New Haven, CT: Yale University Press.

Andrews, D. A. and Bonta, J. (1998) *The Psychology of Criminal Conduct*, 2nd edn. Cincinnati: Anderson.

Applegate, B. K. (1997) 'Public support for rehabilitation: a factorial survey approach'. Unpublished dissertation, University of Cincinnati.

Applegate, B. K., Cullen, F. T. and Fisher, B. S. (1997) 'Public support for correctional treatment: the continuing appeal of the rehabilitative ideal', *Prison Journal*, 77(3): 237–58.

Applegate, B. K., Cullen, F. T., Fisher, B. S. and Vander Ven, T. (2000) 'Forgiveness and fundamentalism: reconsidering the relationship between correctional attitudes and religion', *Criminology*, 38(3): 719–53.

Beckett, K. (1997) *Making Crime Pay: Law and Order in Contemporary American Politics*. New York: Oxford University Press.

Bellah, R. N., Madsen, R., Sullivan, W. M., Swidler, A. and Tipton, S. M. (1985) *Habits of the Heart: Individualism and Commitment in American Life*. Berkeley, CA: University of California Press.

Bennett, W. J., DiIulio Jr, J. J. and Walters, J. P. (1996) *Body Count: Moral Poverty and How to Win America's War Against Crime and Drugs*. New York: Simon & Schuster.

Cao, L. and Cullen, F. T. (2001) 'Thinking about crime and control: a comparative study of Chinese and American ideology', *International Criminal Justice Review*, 11: 58–81.

Clear, T. R. (1994) *Harm in American Penology: Offenders, Victims, and Their Communities*. Albany, NY: State University of New York Press.

Cullen, F. T. (2002) 'Rehabilitation and treatment programs', in J. Q. Wilson and J. Petersilia (eds), *Crime: Public Policies for Crime Control*, 2nd edn. Oakland, CA: ICS Press, pp. 253–89.

Cullen, F. T. and Gendreau, P. (2000) 'Assessing correctional rehabilitation: policy, practice, and prospects', in J. Horney (ed.), *Criminal Justice 2000: Volume 3 – Policies, Processes, and Decisions of the Criminal Justice System*. Washington, DC: US Department of Justice, National Institute of Justice, pp. 109–75.

Cullen, F. T. and Gendreau, P. (2001) 'From nothing works to what works: changing professional ideology in the 21st century', *Prison Journal*, 81(3): 313–38.

Cullen, F. T. and Gilbert, K. E. (1982) *Reaffirming Rehabilitation*. Cincinnati: Anderson.

Cullen, F. T. and Moon, M. M. (2002) 'Reaffirming rehabilitation: public support for correctional treatment', in H. E. Allen (ed.), *Risk Reduction: Intervention for Special Needs Offenders*. Lanham, MD: American Correctional Association, pp. 7–25.

Cullen, F. T., Cullen, J. B. and Wozniak, J. F. (1988) 'Is rehabilitation dead? The myth of the punitive public', *Journal of Criminal Justice*, 16(:): 303–17.

Cullen, F. T., Fisher, B. S. and Applegate, B. K. (2000) 'Public opinion about punishment and corrections', in M. Tonry (ed.), *Crime and Justice: A Review of Research*, Vol. 27. Chicago: University of Chicago Press, pp. 1–79.

Cullen, F. T., Golden, K. M. and Cullen, J. B. (1983) 'Is child saving dead? Attitudes toward juvenile rehabilitation in Illinois', *Journal of Criminal Justice*, 11(1): 1–13.

Cullen, F. T., Clark, G. A., Cullen, J. B. and Mathers, R. A. (1985) 'Attribution, salience, and attitudes toward criminal sanctioning', *Criminal Justice and Behavior*, 12(3): 305–11.

Cullen, F. T., Pratt, T. C., Miceli, S. L. and Moon, M. M. (2002) 'Dangerous liaison? Rational choice theory as the basis for correctional intervention', in A. R. Piquero and S. G. Tibbetts (eds), *Rational Choice and Criminal Behavior: Recent Research and Future Challenges*. New York: Taylor & Francis, pp. 279–96.

Cullen, F. T., Skovron, S. E., Scott, J. E. and Burton Jr, V. S. (1990) 'Public support for correctional treatment: the tenacity of rehabilitative ideology', *Criminal Justice and Behavior*, 17(1): 6–18.

Cullen, F. T., Wright, J. P., Brown, S., Moon, M. M., Blankenship, M. B. and Applegate, B. K. (1998) 'Public support for early intervention programs:

implications for a progressive policy agenda', *Crime and Delinquency*, 44(2): 187–204.

Currie, E. (1998) *Crime and Punishment in America*. New York: Metropolitan Books.

Dillman, D. A. (1978) *Mail and Telephone Surveys: The Total Design Method*. New York: John Wiley & Sons.

Doble Research Associates (1995a) *Crime and Corrections: The Views of the People of Oklahoma*. Englewood Cliffs, NJ: Doble Research Associates.

Doble Research Associates (1995b) *Crime and Corrections: The Views of the People of Oregon*. Englewood Cliffs, NJ: Doble Research Associates.

Dunaway, R. G. and Cullen, F. T. (1991) 'Explaining crime ideology: an exploration of the parental socialization perspective', *Crime and Delinquency*, 37(4): 536–54.

Fairbank, Maslin, Maullin & Associates (1997) *Resources for Youth California Survey*. Santa Monica, CA: Fairbank, Maslin, Maullin & Associates.

Farrington, D. P. (1994) 'Early developmental prevention of juvenile delinquency', *Criminal Behaviour and Mental Health*, 4(3): 209–27.

Flanagan, T. J. (1996) 'Reform or punish: Americans' views of the correctional system', in T. J. Flanagan and D. R. Longmire (eds), *Americans View Crime and Justice: A National Opinion Survey*. Thousand Oaks, CA: Sage, pp. 75–92.

Gendreau, P. (1996) 'The principles of effective intervention with offenders', in A. T. Harland (ed.), *Choosing Correctional Interventions that Work: Defining the Demand and Evaluating the Supply*. Newbury Park, CA: Sage, pp. 117–30.

Gerber, J. and Engelhardt-Greer, S. (1996) 'Just and painful: attitudes toward sentencing criminals', in T. J. Flanagan and D. R. Longmire (eds), *Americans View Crime and Justice: A National Opinion Survey*. Thousand Oaks, CA: Sage, pp. 62–74.

Hamilton, V. L. and Sanders, J. (1992) *Everyday Justice: Responsibility and the Individual in Japan and the United States*. New Haven, CT: Yale University Press.

Harris, L. (1968) 'Changing public attitudes toward crime and corrections', *Federal Probation*, 32(4): 9–16.

Innes, C. A. (1993) 'Recent public opinion in the United States toward punishment and corrections', *Prison Journal*, 73(2): 220–36.

Jacoby, J. E. and Cullen, F. T. (1998) 'The structure of punishment norms: applying the Rossi-Berk model', *Journal of Criminal Law and Criminology*, 89(1): 245–312.

Johnson, B. (1994) 'To rehabilitate or punish? Results of a public opinion poll', *American Jails*, 8: 41–5.

Lacayo, R. (1997) 'Teen Crime', *Time*, 21 July: 26–9.

McCorkle, R. C. (1993) 'Research note: punish and rehabilitate? Public attitudes toward six common crimes', *Crime and Delinquency*, 39(2): 240–52.

McGuire, J. (2001) 'What works in correctional intervention? Evidence and practical implications', in G. A. Bernfeld, D. P. Farrington and A. W. Leschied (eds), *Offender Rehabilitation in Practice: Implementing and Evaluating Effective Programs*. Chichester, UK: John Wiley & Sons, pp. 25–43.

MacKenzie, D. L. (2000) 'Evidence-based corrections: identifying what works', *Crime and Delinquency*, 46(4): 457–71.

Moon, M. M., Cullen, F. T. and Wright, J. P. (forthcoming) It takes a village: public willingness to help wayward youths, *Youth Violence and Juvenile Justice*, 1(1).

Moon, M. M., Sundt, J. L., Cullen, F. T. and Wright, J. P. (2000) 'Is child saving dead? Public support for juvenile rehabilitation', *Crime and Delinquency*, 46(1): 38–60.

Pettinico, G. (1994) 'Crime and punishment: America changes its mind', *Public Perspective*, 5(6): 29–32.

Resources for Youth (1998) *Mapping California's Opinion*. San Rafael, CA: Resources for Youth.

Roberts, J. V. and Stalans, L. J. (1997) *Public Opinion, Crime, and Criminal Justice*. Boulder, CO: Westview Press.

Rothman, D. J. (1971) *The Discovery of the Asylum: Social Order and Disorder in the New Republic*. Boston: Little, Brown.

Rotman, E. (1990) *Beyond Punishment: A New View of the Rehabilitation of Criminal Offenders*. New York: Greenwood Press.

Spelman, W. (2000) 'What recent studies do (and don't) tell us about imprisonment and crime', in M. Tonry (ed.), *Crime and Justice: A Review of Research*, Vol. 27. Chicago: University of Chicago Press, pp. 419–94.

Steinhart, D. (1988) *California Opinion Poll: Public Attitudes on Youth Crime*. San Francisco: National Council on Crime and Delinquency.

Sundt, J. L. (1999) 'Is there room for change? A review of public attitudes toward crime control and alternatives to incarceration', *Southern Illinois University Law Journal*, 23(4): 519–37.

Sundt, J. L., Cullen, F. T., Applegate, B. K. and Turner, M. G. (1998) 'The tenacity of the rehabilitative ideal revisited: have attitudes toward offender treatment changed?', *Criminal Justice and Behavior*, 25(4): 426–42.

Thomson, D. R. and Ragona, A. J. (1987) 'Popular moderation versus governmental authoritarianism: an interactionist view of public sentiments toward criminal sanctions'. *Crime and Delinquency*, 33(2): 337–57.

Tremblay, R. E. and Craig, W. M. (1995) 'Developmental crime prevention,' in M. Tonry and D. P. Farrington (eds), *Building a Safer Society: Strategic Approaches to Crime Prevention-Crime and Justice: A Review of Research*, Vol. 19. Chicago: University of Chicago Press, pp. 151–236.

Turner, M. G., Cullen, F. T., Sundt. J. L. and Applegate, B. K. (1997) 'Public tolerance for community-based sanctions', *Prison Journal*, 77(1): 6–26.

Wald, K. D. (1992) *Religion and Politics in the United States*. Washington, DC: Congressional Quarterly.

Warr, M. (2000) 'Public perceptions of and reactions to crime', in J. F. Sheley (ed.), *Criminology: A Contemporary Handbook*. Belmont, CA: Wadsworth, pp. 13–31.

Chapter 8

Attitudes to punishment in the US – punitive and liberal opinions

John Doble

Over the past fifteen years or so, two profound shifts in US public opinion about crime and criminal justice have occurred. The first led to a host of 'get tough' or 'punitive' measures such as mandatory minimum sentencing, 'three-strikes' laws, repressive drug laws and community notification for sex offenders. Recently, however, public support for more progressive ideas seems to be on the rise, as evidenced by referenda in various states that decriminalise marijuana or require treatment instead of incarceration for low-level drug offenders who are also addicts. As well, a number of states are reconsidering their mandatory minimum sentencing laws. The report of a national public opinion survey (Hart Research Associates, 2002) noted that: 'Public opinion has shifted substantially on the question of whether to take a pre-emptive approach to crime reduction by addressing the underlying causes, or whether to focus on deterrence through stricter sentencing' (p. 13).

In 1994, Americans were almost equally divided in their responses to this question: 48 per cent favoured addressing the causes of crime, while 42 per cent preferred a punitive approach to offenders. Since then, there has been significant movement toward the progressive view. According to a Hart Research Associates survey, the public now favours dealing with the roots of crime over strict sentencing by a margin of 65 per cent to 32 per cent. As well, the chapter by Francis Cullen and his colleagues in this volume attests to the significant degree of public support for rehabilitation of offenders among members of the public.

Such shifts in public attitudes have led policy-makers to gravitate toward ideas such as restorative justice, greater use of alternative sentences and expanded rehabilitative efforts, including treatment instead of incarceration for certain types of drug offenders. There has also been a movement towards the amendment, or even repeal of three-strikes laws and other forms of mandatory minimum sentencing. But while there have undoubtedly been changes in public opinion, the underlying architecture of the public's thinking about crime, its causes and remedies has been more constant and logically consistent than a cursory review of the polling data might suggest.

In the mind of the American people, attitudes that *seem* contradictory may be based on an alternate conceptualisation of the problem, a public 'framing' of the issue that is different from the frame of reference employed by policy experts and political leadership. Understanding how the public frames an issue, as well as the logic underlying that framing, will help us attain a better understanding of public opinion and contribute to our ability to map out public thinking, instead of merely taking a snapshot of public opinion at successive points in time. Over the past ten years, Doble Research Associates have conducted a series of quantitative and qualitative investigations into the nature of American attitudes to punishment. The results have shown considerable consistency across studies and states. This chapter reviews some of this research and places the findings in the context of research on these issues from other countries.

Framing the issues: the public's perspective

In the field of criminal justice, the public has a conceptualisation of the issue that is fundamentally different from that which is used by experts. The public's view is neither better nor worse, just qualitatively different. For example, criminal justice experts have long debated the nature of the highest priority in dealing with lawbreakers: should we punish, incapacitate, rehabilitate offenders, or try to deter other potential offenders from violating the law in the future? Depending on their answer to this question, experts advance a list of policy instruments to achieve their top priority. Public opinion surveys routinely follow this logic by asking people which of several competing sentencing goals is most important. For example, the recent Peter Hart survey asked the American public to identify their top priority for dealing with crime from among the following possibilities: prevention, rehabilitation, punishment or enforcement. However, there is evidence that this expert conceptualisation is fundamentally inconsistent with the framework employed by the public. This is clear from surveys that

Table 8.1 Public support for goals of the corrections system

Possible goals	Very important (%)	Fairly important (%)	Not that important
Punish offender	89	9	1
Require offenders to pay back their victims or society	87	10	3
Discourage would-be criminals from breaking the law	86	12	2
Rehabilitate offenders so they will become productive members of society	68	22	8

address responding to crime on a general level as well as polls which ask about the specific purposes of sentencing.

Public favours multiple sentencing goals

In a 1995 survey in North Carolina conducted by Doble Research Associates, large majorities said that each of four goals of the correctional system is very important: punishing offenders (89 per cent), requiring offenders to pay back their victims (87 per cent), and discouraging would-be offenders from breaking the law (86 per cent). As can be seen in Table 8.1, a smaller, but nonetheless very substantial majority of 68 per cent also endorsed rehabilitation; only 8 per cent dismissed this goal as 'not that important' (Doble Research Associates, 1995a).

While the North Carolinians could have rank-ordered these four goals, it is clear from Table 8.1 and also from what people said in focus groups that all four aims were regarded as important. Indeed, respondents saw the four goals as complementary in nature and not competitive. For example, people said that rehabilitation is not only humane but also *instrumentally* valuable, because offenders who are rehabilitated are less likely to reoffend. A woman in a Charlotte focus group explained that she favoured treatment *in order to reduce crime* because, 'nine times out of ten, [the offender's] problem was related to their crime.' Similarly, a Greenville woman said, 'I'd say, let's give an offender [drug or mental health] treatment to get him straightened out so he knows what he's doing' (Doble Research, 1995a).

People also said that restitution would help reduce crime rates because prison hardens offenders, whereas alternatives might promote rehabilitation. According to the public, an offender who makes restitution to his victim might understand how hurtful his offence had been. This might touch his conscience, thereby making him less likely to reoffend. In a 1999 study in Vermont, a woman from Brattleboro said: 'I'd make [a shoplifter] go back to the store and apologise. That would be very hard for a person. It would be very embarrassing. And maybe [he should] have to do so many hours worth of work [at the store], cleaning, shining the glass in the cases, something' (Doble and Greene, 2000).

If offenders performed community service, people said, others would see them working hard and giving back to their victims and to the community. As a result, potential offenders might be deterred from committing a crime. In fact, many participants perceived community service to be more demanding than a brief term of custody during which, people believe, offenders sit around all day, watching TV or playing cards. Finally, making restitution and performing community service might help offenders learn new skills or promote the development of a stronger work ethic. 'Most offenders never learned the work ethic,' said a woman from Newport, Oregon, adding that doing something productive 'would get them a work ethic and see some sense of achievement at the end of the day.' In North Carolina and other states then, it was participants' sense, and inferentially the general public's sense, that all four of these sentencing goals should be accomplished simultaneously. Only when all goals are being pursued can the criminal justice system accomplish its primary mission – which is to reduce crime and provide as much protection as possible for law-abiding citizens.

Trying to understand or map the architecture of people's thinking by looking only at what is most important may yield a result that is incomplete and misleading. If people simultaneously deem more than one goal to be vital, asking them which goal is 'most important' can be likened to asking someone who is hungry, thirsty, cold and tired, what is most important: food, water, warmth or rest. The answer will be essentially meaningless if the person's real goal is not to have one, but all four of their needs met. And met not as ends in themselves but in order to do something else – live in an ordinary, day-to-day sense, or in this context, live with as little crime as possible.

These findings are consistent with surveys conducted in other countries. The Home Office Sentencing Review in England and Wales surveyed the public about the purposes of sentencing and found substantial support for multiple sentencing goals, including deterrence, punishment, denunciation and restitution, to name but a few (Home Office, 2001). When Canadians were asked to identify the purposes of

Table 8.2   Purposes relevant to sentencing serious offenders (Canada)

	% of sample
To provide a punishment that reflects the seriousness of the offence	86
To discourage the offender from committing further crimes	85
To prevent the offender from committing further offences by imprisoning him	82
To discourage others from committing crimes	81
To show society's disapproval of the crime	80
To provide restitution to the victim	70
To rehabilitate the offender	70

Source: Roberts and Doob (1989).

sentencing, the results demonstrate the same point: people see multiple purposes as relevant. Table 8.2 presents the responses of Canadians when asked to identify the purposes relevant to sentencing serious offenders.[1] As can be seen, support for all principal sentencing purposes is high. It is particularly noteworthy that fully 70 per cent of the sample supported the purpose of rehabilitation, even for serious offenders, a finding consistent with the research reported by Francis Cullen and his colleagues in this volume.

The co-existence of 'punitive' and 'liberal' attitudes

Numerous studies by Public Agenda, a non-partisan research organisa-tion, and Doble Research since the late 1980s have found clear, consensus-levels of public support for making far greater use of alternative sentences, or intermediate, non-carceral sanctions, for an array of offenders, especially non-violent offenders, but also with some certain violent offenders (see chapter by Roberts, this volume). These studies also found that such support coexists in the public mind, within the public's framing of the issue, along with an array of more 'punitive' views, which were, especially in the 1980s and early 1990s, ascendant and consequently more visible and politically dominant. Here too, the public simultaneous-ly favours what some experts might see as contradictory attitudes.

Using what it called a Citizen Review Panel, a forerunner of Fishkin's 'deliberative poll' (see Fishkin, 1995; Hough and Park, this volume), in 1988, the Public Agenda brought together a geographically and demographically representative quota sample of 420 people from across Alabama to meet for three hours in six locations across the state to consider what to do with convicted offenders (see Doble and Klein, 1989). Participants were given a list of 23 cases involving offenders who had committed crimes ranging from joyriding to rape. In each case, participants were told only three things: the gender and age of the offender (21 of the offenders were men, and 21 of them were between 21 and 25, while the other two were 15 years old), and the number of previous convictions each had committed. Upon arrival, before any kind of educational intervention, participants filled out a lengthy questionnaire listing the 23 cases; for each case, they were asked to impose sentence using only two sentencing options: prison or probation. Initially, majorities wanted to incarcerate 18 of the 23 offenders.

After an educational intervention, which consisted of a 20-minute Public Agenda video describing an array of alternative sanctions the state was considering (intensively supervised probation or what was called 'strict probation' (ISP), restitution, community service, house arrest and boot camp) and then participating in a 90-minute discussion led by an impartial moderator, participants were asked to resentence the 23 offenders, this time with seven sentencing options: prison and probation, along with the five intermediate sanctions. When they had more options, majorities wanted to incarcerate only 4 of the 23 offenders. One was sentenced to 'regular probation' and the other 18 to another alternative sanction. The significant shifts following the information are presented in Figure 8.1. These trends confirm findings from other countries, where support for alternatives to imprisonment increases when people are simply given information about these sanctions (see Roberts, in this volume).

The Public Agenda study, published in 1989, was only the first of many showing broad, deep public support for this approach. In a subsequent (1995) telephone survey Doble Research asked a cross-section of 800 people in North Carolina whether they favoured or opposed having their state make greater use of eight 'less expensive' alternative sentences or intermediate sanctions for *non-violent* offenders. Huge majorities – ranging from 82 per cent to 98 per cent – said that the state should make greater use of each one (Doble Research Associates, 1995a) – see Table 8.3.

It is significant that both the North Carolina survey and the Public Agenda study found strong public support for making much greater use of alternative sentences *coexisting* in the public mind with more punitive attitudes. In Alabama, roughly three-quarters of the public endorsed the position that the majority of offenders should serve some time in prison. Approximately the same percentage expressed support

Figure 8.1 Comparison of sentencing: pre- and post-intervention questionnaire.

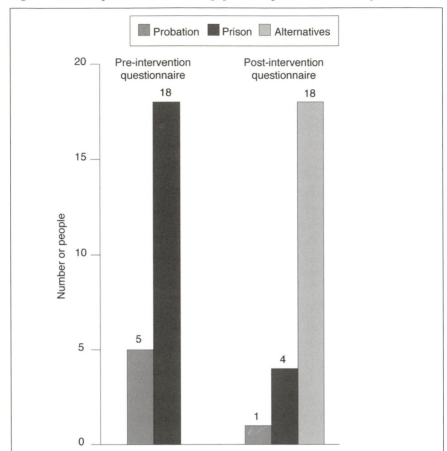

for executing offenders convicted of murder, 'if prisons were over-crowded'. At the same time, as a solution to prison overcrowding in the pre-tests, 84 per cent endorsed a search for alternative, less expensive sanctions that were harsher than prison – see Table 8.4.

The results were remarkably similar in North Carolina. Clear support emerged for the punitive sentencing option of making prison sentences longer: almost two-thirds of the sample supported this strategy. At the same time, almost the entire sample (93 per cent) endorsed the use of boot camps, community service and restitution as a means of reducing prison overcrowding (Doble Research Associates, 1995a).

In Delaware and Pennsylvania in the early 1990s, Public Agenda found the same pattern: large majorities favoured mandatory mini-

Table 8.3   The use of alternative sentences instead of prison

Should North Carolina make greater use of:	*Favour* (%)	*Oppose* (%)
Restitution where offenders must pay back the victims of their crime	98	2
Community service where offenders must do unpaid work such as cut brush or pick up litter	97	3
Boot camp where for 90 days offenders must get up early and work hard all day under strict supervision and strong discipline	97	3
Strict probation where offenders must see a probation officer once a week. It includes unscheduled visits and mandatory drug testing	89	11
Treatment centres where offenders work at their regular job but are locked up at night and must attend mandatory drug treatment, job training, or high school classes	88	10
Day reporting centres where offenders must report in person each morning, and their activities are monitored throughout the day	88	12
House arrest where offenders must, by electronic monitoring, stay at home except to go to work or school	88	18
Halfway houses where offenders are locked up at night but can go to work or school during the day	82	16

Source: Doble Research Associates (1995a).

mum sentencing laws both before *and* after the educational intervention. But at the same time, large majorities also called for a *much* greater use of non-carceral, alternative sentences for a wide array of offenders.

The same pattern emerges with respect to rehabilitation. In Alabama in 1988, before any educational intervention, 77 per cent said the state should place 'more emphasis' on 'efforts to rehabilitate convicted offenders' (as opposed to 'less emphasis', 4 per cent, or 'about the same emphasis', 10 per cent). In the post-test, after the educational intervention, the 420 Alabamians were given a list of arguments for and against a much greater use of alternative sentences and asked whether they agreed or disagreed with each one. By a margin of 85 to 6 per cent, they agreed that offenders sentenced to an alternative were more likely to be rehabilitated. And so here Alabamians' support for alternatives grew out of their view of the important goals of corrections, which in turn stemmed from their sense of which measures would reduce crime in the state (Doble and Klein, 1989).

Table 8.4 The coexistence of 'punitive' and 'progressive' attitudes in Alabama, 1988

Statement	Agree (%)
'Punitive' attitudes:	
In the past year, the crime rate in my area has been increasing (pre-test)	83
Vast majority of offenders should serve at least some time in prison (pre-test)	77
If state prisons were overcrowded, we should use capital punishment more often for the most serious crimes such as murder (pre-test)	72
Co-existing with 'progressive' attitudes	
If state prisons were overcrowded, we should find new ways to punish offenders that are less expensive than prison but harsher than probation (pre-test)	84
To reduce prison overcrowding, 'place many who would normally go to prison in less expensive programs such as strict probation, house arrest, boot camp, etc.' (post-test)	85

In Alabama, Delaware and Pennsylvania, political leaders who supported a greater use of alternatives were concerned about prison overcrowding and the cost of incarceration, and they were seeking less expensive punishment options. They felt that the public, which they believed to be perennially concerned about government spending and excessive taxation, would favour using alternatives for the same reason. But in each of those states, the public favoured a much greater use of non-carceral, alternative sentences, not so much to reduce overcrowding or to save money, but because the alternatives made sense to them, made sense on their own merits in that offenders would simultaneously be punished, make restitution and have a much, much better chance of being rehabilitated. Here again, there was a gap between politicians and the public, with each bringing a different framework and a different set of priorities to bear on the issue.

The depth of the public's commitment to rehabilitation from the late 1980s

One way of ascertaining the depth of the public's commitment to any proposed reform is by exploring the trade-offs that people are willing to accept in order to achieve the reform. Using this approach, Doble Research asked a number of questions about rehabilitating convicted offenders in state-wide surveys in Oregon, Oklahoma and North Carolina.

In a 1995 survey in Oregon, 88 per cent favoured, and 62 per cent strongly favoured, *mandatory* treatment for offenders with drug and alcohol problems, even if it involved greater expense to the state. In Oklahoma, more than two-thirds of the respondents favoured the creation of more mental health treatment and educational opportunities for prison inmates, while 76 per cent favoured *mandatory* treatment for all drug addicts, even if both steps resulted in more state spending. In North Carolina, 79 per cent favoured psychiatric treatment for every mentally ill inmate, once again, even if it cost more money.

Most importantly, people who favoured mandatory treatment were not particularly optimistic about its efficacy. In Oklahoma, people were asked: 'For every 10 addicts who complete a drug treatment program, how many are successfully rehabilitated?' Only 19 per cent said 5 or more, while 62 per cent said 'a definite minority, 3 of 10 or fewer'. Oklahomans had a somewhat more optimistic, but nonetheless guarded, view about the efficacy of alcohol treatment, with 50 per cent saying '3 or fewer' are 'successfully rehabilitated upon completing treatment'.

The depth of the public's commitment to rehabilitation is further evidenced by the results of a more recent qualitative study of public opinion about the least popular group of lawbreakers, sex offenders. Four focus groups, each with a demographically representative cross-section of about a dozen people, were conducted in the fall of 1998 in Burlington, Vermont. In those sessions, participants were told that incarcerated sex offenders in Vermont usually receive about two hours of treatment a week for two to three years, which is far more treatment than most states provide. Group members unanimously favoured much more treatment. ' "Two hours a *day* is more like it," one man said to general agreement.' Clearly, then, people want to do more than simply punish this group of offenders (Doble and Greene, 2000).

When asked why they endorsed so much additional treatment, people said that since almost all sex offenders would be released one day, they would, absent effective treatment, pose a danger to the community and in particular its most vulnerable members. When those in the focus group were asked how effective treatment would be if it were offered every day, nearly all said it would be ineffective most of the time. They favoured treatment because they saw more treatment as humane and, more important, as a means to reduce crime. A woman said, 'If one person out of five is rehabilitated, it [i.e. the cost and expense of additional treatment] is worth it.' This finding demonstrates that the public does not wish to abandon rehabilitation, even for sex offenders.

Explaining the apparent conflict between punishment and rehabilitation

Poll results showing that the public simultaneously favours punitive and progressive approaches might lead some analysts and political leaders to conclude that instead of coherence, public opinion reflects inconsistency. While there can be no doubt that the public's under-standing of this issue, or for that matter any other complex issue, is at best fragmentary and incomplete, there are other explanations as to why such 'punitive' and 'progressive' views coexist in the public mind.

As noted, the first explanation stems from the framework that the public brings to the issue and the fact that most people see no conflict between a greater emphasis on rehabilitation and taking a punitive approach. A second reason why people look so favourably on using alternatives at the same time that they hold 'punitive' views involves their beliefs about prison life and its effects. Asked to rate the job performance of the department of corrections in terms of four areas: punishing offenders, requiring offenders to make restitution, rehabili-tating offenders and deterring would-be criminals, more than 4 out of 5 Pennsylvanians gave corrections a rating of only 'fair' or 'poor' in each area. In Delaware, a majority said that instead of working productively or taking classes, most prison inmates sit around all day, watching TV or playing cards and basketball. In a 1995 focus group, a woman from Charlotte, North Carolina said, 'They [prison inmates] have it better than some of us – weights, cable TV, phones, field trips. It's not prison, it's summer camp.' A Greenville, North Carolina man said, 'Some of them will go back to prison because it's an easier life' than what they face on the outside.

Because of what people believe goes on behind bars, many conclude that a prison sentence is unlikely to either deter or rehabilitate. In Oregon, nearly three-quarters of the sample said the threat of going to prison in Oregon has 'little' or 'no' deterrent effect. 'Jail time alone will not help an offender. It will just harden him,' said a man from Eugene, Oregon. 'Why put them in prison when statistics show that when we put people in a bad atmosphere, they come out with more aggression?' said a woman from Greenville, North Carolina. In Oklahoma, 66 per cent said that when prison inmates are released, they are usually *more* dangerous than they were going in. 'Prison is like a crook's college,' said a man in a focus group in Tulsa.[2]

Public perceptions regarding the causes of crime

Beliefs about the causes of crime also underlie public thinking on this issue. In Delaware in 1993, Public Agenda gave people a list of 16 possible causes of crime and asked how important each one was. A sample of 432 demographically and geographically representative participants was virtually unanimous in naming illegal drug use as the most important cause (see Table 8.5). But majorities of respondents also named a host of other problems including the breakdown of the family, especially among the poor, a lack of education/poor schools, alcohol abuse, gangs, handgun availability and poverty as major causes. Much smaller numbers named each of the following: bad or greedy people (46 per cent), insufficient emphasis on basic law and order (39 per cent) and judges who are too lenient (39 per cent). According to the Public Agenda report, 'Delawareans believe the causes of crime are rooted in the state's – and in the nation's – social problems.'

Table 8.5   The causes of crime, Delaware, 1991

Possible causes/one of most important/major cause of crime	%
Illegal drug use	94
Breakdown of family, especially among poor	71
Lack of education/poor schools	67
Alcohol abuse	67
Gangs and gang warfare	66
Availability of handguns	64
Poverty and economic hardship	63
Low self-esteem	63
Lack of employment opportunities	54
Belief that crime pays	54
Bad or greedy people	46
Lenient judges	39
Not enough emphasis on basic law and order	39
Not enough police	28
Racial discrimination/prejudice	27
Mental illness	23

Source: Doble, Immerwahr and Richardson (1991).

Responses are the same across the nation. In 1993, and again in 2000, the Gallup organisation asked Americans to rate the importance of a number of possible causes of crime. In both periods the use of drugs was identified as 'critical' or 'very important' by 9 out of 10 respondents, with approximately two-thirds choosing 'critical' (Sourcebook of Criminal Justice Statistics, 2000). Lack of jobs for the young, racism in society and the availability of guns were also cited by significant proportions of respondents in both time periods (Sourcebook of Criminal Justice Statistics, 2000). Similar findings emerge in other countries as well (see Roberts and Stalans, 1997, for a review).

And so, in a study in which mandatory minimum sentencing remained popular before and after an extensive educational intervention, a cross-section of 400 Delawareans, according to Public Agenda, also felt that, to lower the crime rate, 'we must address the underlying social problems related to chronic poverty and broken family structures', which in turn of course lead to chronic drug abuse and alcoholism.

The boundaries of political permission

Public opinion about a policy issue establishes what social scientist Daniel Yankelovich (see Yankelovich, 1991) calls 'the boundaries of political permission', the limits or borders within which public policy will be supported, or tolerated, by the public. In a democratic society, leadership is ultimately accountable to the public will. Regardless of the issue, leaders who formulate public policy outside these boundaries of permission may see the public suddenly repudiate that policy and replace it with a radically different approach. Ideas such as term limits, tax cuts and a patient's Bill of Rights have each, over the past few years, been driven by public opinion that was dissatisfied with the status quo. In each case, shifting public opinion changed the political landscape and established new boundaries of permission. Regarding criminal justice, it was public opinion that led to the enactment of a host of policies, including mandatory minima, 'three strikes' laws, Megan's Law, the Brady Bill and the assault weapons ban.

But during the years when the American public seemed to favour only a 'punitive' approach, there was also broad and deep public support for an array of more progressive policies. In particular, the public favoured placing more emphasis on rehabilitation in general, including greatly expanded drug and alcohol treatment, and support for using non-carceral, community-based or alternative sentences with an array of non-violent offenders and even some violent ones. In effect, public opinion was misread by pundits and political leaders.

The recent Peter Hart/Open Society Institute argues that public opinion has undergone a significant transformation and that instead of long prison sentences and a purely punitive approach, the public 'now endorses a balanced, multifaceted solution that focuses on prevention and rehabilitation in concert with other remedies'. But the public has always favoured a balanced approach. It was their inability to block out the noise and static that prevented some experts and political leaders from more accurately understanding what Americans truly wanted.

It would be regrettable if the mistakes of the 1980s were repeated in the twenty-first century. While the American people now undoubtedly favour greater emphasis on prevention and other progressive approaches, they also favour what the Hart/OSI survey calls 'a *balanced* approach' that includes being tough with the most violent and dangerous offenders while simultaneously increasing the effort to rehabilitate those offenders the public believes can be turned around without serious risk to the community. A policy agenda, no matter how 'punitive' or 'progressive', that disregards either set of public attitudes will eventually run aground.

Notes

1. Another question asked respondents about the sentencing of minor offenders and although the pattern of support for specific purposes differed, the same trend emerged: people endorsed multiple sentencing goals (see Roberts and Doob, 1989).
2. Many people share the view of a Salem, Oregon, woman who identified the cause of crime as follows: 'Our problem seems to be throwing people in prison without providing [the rehabilitative] services [that are necessary] to help break the cycle.' A Charlotte, North Carolina, man said, 'We can spend money to incarcerate them again and again, or we can give them an opportunity to develop that [sense of] self-worth that says, I'm somebody who can do something.'

References

Doble, J. and Greene, J. (2000) *Attitudes towards Crime and Punishment in Vermont: Public Opinion about an Experiment with Restorative Justice*. Englewood Cliffs, NJ: Doble Research Associates.

Doble, J. and Klein, J. (1989) *Punishing Criminals. The Public's View. An Alabama Survey.* New York: Edna McConnell Clark Foundation.

Doble, J., Immerwahr, S. and Richardson, A. (1991) *Punishing Criminals. The People of Delaware Consider the Options.* New York: Edna McConnell Clark Foundation.

Doble Research Associates (1994) *Crime and Corrections: The Views of the People of Vermont.* Englewood Cliffs, NJ: Doble Research Associates.

Doble Research Associates (1994) *Public Opinion about Sex Offenders and Community Notification in the State of Vermont.* Englewood Cliffs, NJ: Doble Research Associates.

Doble Research Associates (1995a) *Crime and Corrections: The Views of the People of North Carolina.* Englewood Cliffs, NJ: Doble Research Associates.

Doble Research Associates (1995b) *Crime and Corrections: The Views of the People of Oklahoma.* Englewood Cliffs, NJ: Doble Research Associates.

Fishkin, J. S. (1995) *The Voice of the People.* New York: Vait-Baillou Press.

Home Office (2001) *Making Punishments Work. Report of a Review of the Sentencing Framework for England and Wales.* London: Home Office.

Peter D. Hart Research Associates (2002) *The New Politics of Criminal Justice.* Washington, DC: Peter D. Hart Research Associates.

Roberts, J. V. and Doob, A. N. (1989) 'Sentencing and public opinion: taking false shadows for true substances', *Osgoode Hall Law Journal*, 27: 491–515.

Roberts, J. V. and Stalans, L. S. (1997) *Public Opinion, Crime and Criminal Justice.* Boulder, CO: Westview Press.

Sourcebook of Criminal Justice Statistics (2000) Online edition available at www.albany.edu/sourcebook/.

Yankelovich, D. (1991) *Coming to Public Judgment. Making Democracy Work in a Complex World.* Syracuse, NY: Syracuse University Press.

Chapter 9

How malleable are attitudes to crime and punishment? Findings from a British deliberative poll

Mike Hough and Alison Park

Introduction

The contours of public attitudes in Western countries about crime and punishment have been increasingly well mapped over the last two decades. A consistent pattern has been established across many different countries, showing dissatisfaction with lenient sentencing and cynicism about the competence of sentencers. Yet in parallel with these findings are others that show support for community penalties, ambivalence about the use of custody for any but the most serious offences, and sentencing preferences that in reality are often consistent with judicial practice.

Resolving the tensions between these two sets of findings can be accomplished in two ways. First (as Loretta Stalans observes in her contribution to this volume), it is important to recognise that people can be genuinely ambivalent in their opinions. Many people recognise, for example, that imprisonment is a damaging and destructive experience while wanting court sentences to carry a penal weight that they regard as proportionate to the seriousness of the offence. Just as sentencers do, the public wants sentencing to achieve a multiplicity of aims, including retribution, deterrence, rehabilitation and reparation (cf. Doble, this volume). The apparent competition between sentencing aims is as much a function of survey design than attitudinal incoherence.

Second, there is widespread and systematic public ignorance about crime and justice, which is demonstrably a source of public criticism of the courts (e.g. Hough and Roberts, 1999, 2002; Mattinson and

Mirrlees-Black, 2001). People underestimate the severity of sentencing practice. Many believe that courts are retreating from the use of imprisonment, when the reverse is the reality; and most overestimate the gravity of crime problems, at least in so far as they are reflected in trends and in the proportion of crime that is violent (see Roberts and Stalans, 1997, for a review). It comes as no surprise, then, that the public is frustrated with the performance of sentencers.[1]

The position should not be overstated, however. In many jurisdictions there are likely to be practices that would remain unpalatable to the general public no matter how well explained. British examples would include the gap between nominal sentences and time actually served (with most prisoners serving half their nominal sentence in custody), the treatment of witnesses and victims by the judicial system and current practice in relation to offenders who have breached conditions of community penalties.

These findings present politicians and sentencers with a difficult balance to strike in responding to public opinion. However tempting in electoral terms, it is scarcely legitimate to respond to public anger by increasing the severity of sentencing – where this anger is grounded in misperception and misunderstanding. On the other hand, some response to public dissatisfaction can hardly be avoided, if it is accepted that systems of criminal justice will work only if they command a reasonable degree of popular support.

The most obvious and rational option is to try to correct those public misperceptions that lie at the heart of public disenchantment with criminal justice, and to try and explain to the public how sentencing actually operates in practice. However, this raises questions about the practicability of changing public attitudes on a large scale. Is it even possible to change public opinion in this area? There are two sets of relevant empirical questions:

- Can enduring changes in attitudes be achieved among those segments of the population that have the lowest opinions of the criminal justice system?

- If so, what are the best ways of doing so?

As discussed above, there is a growing literature demonstrating that people will modify their attitudes to justice when provided with more information about the issue in hand. For example, people's sentencing preferences are less 'prison-centric' when they are informed properly about non-custodial options (Roberts, this volume; Doble, this volume;

Hough and Roberts, 1998). When people have an opportunity to assess actual sentencing decisions, armed with all the necessary details of the case, they often find these decisions perfectly acceptable (Doob and Roberts, 1988).

Beyond these field experiments, however, there is a dearth of literature that addresses questions about ways of achieving *widespread* and *enduring* change. This chapter presents the results of one of few studies that do so. It took the form of a televised 'deliberative poll' which was conducted in 1994. The main results were widely publicised at the time in the television programme, and key findings were presented in Fishkin (1995). We carried out secondary analysis of the data set in 2001, to examine further the nature of the attitudinal changes which took place,[2] and we have presented results here and in Park and Hough (2002). As we shall discuss in more detail below, the 1994 deliberative poll allows measurement of both *immediate* and *long-term* attitudinal change. This chapter presents information only on the latter. For our purposes it is of only passing interest to know that attitudes can be modified for a matter of hours or days; whether enduring change can be achieved is of rather more policy significance.

The deliberative poll technique

The deliberative poll reported here was the first in England, carried out in 1994. It was mounted by James Fishkin in collaboration with the National Centre for Social Research[3] and Channel 4 Television, one of the main British broadcasting channels. Fishkin, an American political scientist, developed deliberative polls as a means of capturing a more thoughtful version of public opinion than conventional sample surveys (Fishkin, 1995; Fishkin et al., 2000). Deliberative polls were envisaged as a means of identifying the attitudes and policy preferences that the general population would hold if they had the time and energy to inform themselves properly about the issues and to develop an intellectual position. In essence, they involve assembling a large nationally or locally representative group of participants who are briefed by experts about the topic under consideration. Participants then hold detailed group discussions on the issue and the evidence they have heard. Before the event, and at its conclusion, their attitudes are measured in some detail, to yield indices of both 'tutored' and 'untutored' views.

As a tool to *change* public attitudes to sentencing, the deliberative poll obviously has a very restricted application. The numbers of people that can be reached through the very labour-intensive and costly process are limited. When the results are televised, as in this case, there may be some secondary benefits, in that viewers are drawn into the deliberative process, albeit at one stage removed. Even as a way of establishing what properly informed and properly considered opinion would look like, the method is open to criticism. It has been argued, for example, that the changes in attitudes that arise in deliberative polls are more a consequence of the experience of special treatment – a form of 'Hawthorne Effect' – than the deliberative experience itself.[4] It is also possible, if not likely, that the results depend simply on the quality of the advocacy of the politicians and experts who brief the deliberative poll participants.[5]

Finally, critics have suggested that whatever the *desirability* of having a well-informed and thoughtful public, deliberative polls are irrelevant as politicians need to take account of the reality of public opinion as it emerges from 'snapshot' public opinion polls, in which the respondent has neither sufficient information nor opportunity to reflect on the issue.

Whatever conclusion one may reach about deliberative polls as a means of correcting the 'democratic deficit' in conventional politics, such polls can provide a laboratory setting for learning more about public opinion. They can shed light on the differences between people's uninformed or untutored views, and the more considered views which they hold after they have had an opportunity to absorb information and discuss the issues with others. Depending on how they are organised, these polls can also tell us about the durability of attitudinal changes.

Surprisingly, the findings of the British deliberative poll on crime and punishment have not been analysed and described in detail since the 'headline' findings were broadcast in a Channel 4 television programme – until the Esmée Fairbairn Foundation funded the analyses reported here and in Park and Hough (2002).

The 1994 deliberative poll on crime

The first stage of the deliberative poll involved the creation of a national probability sample of the electorate, in which 869 respondents were interviewed about their views on crime and punishment. After the interview, all respondents were invited to take part in a televised weekend event in Manchester, a large city in the North West of England. The 297 people who attended were statistically representative of the larger group who had responded to the initial survey.

Before arriving in Manchester, they were sent briefing materials that introduced the issues at stake. The format of the weekend involved presentations by criminal justice practitioners, academics, an ex-prisoner and politicians from all three main political parties. There were opportunities to cross-question the speakers, as well as extensive group discussions. (Participants were randomly divided into groups within which they discussed their views and possible policy options under the guidance of a trained group moderator.) After the weekend, participants once again completed the questionnaire. Finally, some ten months later, participants were again re-interviewed in order to assess the durability of any changes in their views; completed questionnaires were received from 241 of the 297 people who took part in the event.

Attitudes before the deliberative poll event

At the time of first contact (that is, before the weekend), the sample had quite eclectic views on crime control. For instance, over two-thirds (68 per cent) thought that 'teaching children the difference between right and wrong' would be a very effective way of helping prevent crime in Britain. Only slightly fewer (64 per cent) thought that more police on the beat would be very effective. There was also a clear awareness of the role that broader socio-economic factors (particularly poverty and unemployment) can play in crime. Thus when people were asked to rank six different possible ways of reducing crime, over 8 out of 10 people opted for 'reducing unemployment and poverty' as one of their three chosen options. Moreover, nearly half thought this would be the *most* effective way to reduce crime, more than double the proportion who opted for giving police greater powers (19 per cent) or making sentences stiffer and building more prisons (14 per cent).

As with the public elsewhere, the deliberative poll sample also had tough-minded views about sentencing. There was, for instance, an overwhelming view that a life sentence should mean imprisonment for the offender's natural life ('life should mean life') and that courts should give 'tougher sentences to criminals'; over 8 out of 10 people agreed with each of these statements. By contrast, there was little support for sending fewer people to prison and opinion was divided over the extent to which prison should be reserved only for those who are 'hardened criminals' or who pose 'a danger to society'. Although there was a belief that prisons can have a rehabilitative role, when forced to choose between government focusing its energies on punishment or reform of criminals, people's preference was for punishment

(55 per cent vs. 36 per cent).[6] A clear exception to this punitive set of views about sentencing related to the punishment of young first-time offenders; only a very small minority of the sample thought this group deserved custodial sentences.

Who thought what?

There were marked differences between the views of particular groups. In particular, older people tended to be more authoritarian and punitive than younger ones, as did tabloid readers when compared with broadsheeet readers. Education also appears to make a difference; those with A-level[7] or higher qualifications tended to be less tough-minded in their views. Finally, the respondent's location also emerged as strongly linked to attitudes, with those in cities tending to be more punitive and authoritarian than those in other areas.

These factors all tended to emerge even when a wide range of other social characteristics (including experience of crime) were taken into account. So, if we were we to caricature the sort of person who holds extremely tough-minded views about crime control (favouring, for instance, harsher sentences, more police on the beat and firmer discipline in schools) we would be thinking of an elderly tabloid reader living in a city. However, these factors are independent of one another – young tabloid readers will be relatively punitive as well, as will elderly broadsheet readers.

Did information and debate achieve durable change in people's views?

After the weekend event people's views shifted in a more liberal and less punitive direction on many – but by no means all – measures. This effect was still evident when respondents were surveyed ten months later – although the difference was sometimes a little more muted. In this analysis we have presented only the changes from the period before the deliberative poll until the survey carried out ten months later. Additional findings on the changes occurring immediately after the deliberative poll can be found in Park and Hough (2002).

Table 9.1 shows changes in attitudes towards various ways of controlling crime over the ten-month period from *before* the deliberative poll until the second interview. The rows in bold type show statistically significant changes (Wilcoxon signed ranks test, p < 0.01 in

Table 9.1 'Very effective' ways of reducing crime: before deliberative poll and ten months later

	Very effective	Effective	Neither effective nor ineffective	Not effective	Total
Teaching children the difference between right and wrong					
Before	67	27	4	2	100%
After	62	32	4	2	100%
More police on the beat					
Before	**65**	**26**	**6**	**3**	**100%**
After	**48**	**38**	**10**	**4**	**100%**
Firmer discipline in schools					
Before	52	34	8	6	100%
After	45	39	11	5	100%
Parents spending more time with their children					
Before	52	33	13	2	100%
After	50	42	7	1	100%
Stiffer sentences generally					
Before	**50**	**28**	**16**	**7**	**100%**
After	**36**	**31**	**17**	**15**	**100%**
Reduce unemployment					
Before	44	39	11	7	100%
After	38	51	9	3	100%
People making their property more secure					
Before	**41**	**49**	**8**	**3**	**100%**
After	**32**	**43**	**17**	**8**	**100%**
Sending more offenders to prison					
Before	**36**	**23**	**21**	**20**	**100%**
After	**21**	**21**	**31**	**26**	**100%**
More schemes like neighbourhood watch					
Before	**35**	**45**	**14**	**5**	**100%**
After	**24**	**49**	**20**	**7**	**100%**
Less violence and crime on television					
Before	34	33	17	16	100%
After	23	42	19	16	100%

1. Base: 237 (minimum).
2. Bold rows show statistically significant differences.
3. Don't knows excluded.
4. Cases with missing data in either sweep excluded.

Table 9.2 Attitudes towards prisons and prison sentences: before deliberative poll and ten months later

	Strongly agree	Agree	Neither agree nor disagree	Disagree	Total
The courts should send fewer people to prison					
Before	6	23	22	50	100%
After	6	30	20	44	100%
Prison life should be made tougher and more unpleasant					
Before	33	37	13	17	100%
After	38	39	8	16	100%
Only hardened/dangerous criminals should be sent to prison					
Before	18	24	11	47	100%
After	20	30	9	42	100%
All murderers should be given a life sentence					
Before	61	22	8	10	100%
After	51	20	8	21	100%
Courts should give tougher sentences to criminals					
Before	39	44	11	6	100%
After	35	41	15	10	100%
Life sentences should mean life					
Before	63	26	8	4	100%
After	65	22	4	9	100%
Prison should try harder to reform people rather than just punishing them					
Before	32	49	9	10	100%
After	32	47	14	8	100%

1. Base: 234 (minimum).
2. Bold rows show statistically significant differences.
3. Don't knows excluded.
4. Cases with missing data in either sweep excluded.

each cases). There seems to have been a shift away from support for tough sentencing, preventive patrol and situational prevention, as exemplified by improved security and neighbourhood watch.

Table 9.2 presents findings on attitudes towards prisons and prison sentence. As in Table 9.1, all statistically significant changes are in bold; all changes are in the same direction: there was significantly less support for sending people to prison and for heavier sentences (Wilcoxon signed ranks test, $p < 0.05$) and for mandatory life sentences for murders ($p < 0.01$). There was more support for reserving custody only for high-risk offenders, though the difference did not quite reach statistical significance ($p = 0.09$).

Support for community penalties remained largely unchanged. Four items were put to respondents, in which they were asked to agree or disagree with the following statements:

1. More offenders should be kept out of prison, but made to report regularly to probation officers.

2. More offenders should be kept out of prison, but made to spend a certain number of days helping people in the community.

3. Kept out of prison, but made to do military service for a period of time.

4. Kept out of prison, but made to get training and counselling.

All items had majority support both before and after the deliberative poll; support was more tentative for the probation and military service options, and stronger for community service and training/counselling. Support increased a little over the ten months for probation, community service and counselling as alternatives to imprisonment, but none of these changes were statistically significant.

Table 9.3 examines changes over the ten-month period in attitudes towards the sentencing of young offenders. Respondents were asked how much they favoured four ways of dealing with a first-time burglar less than 16 years of age. With the exception of the community service option, which enjoyed substantial – and unchanging – support, Table 9.3 shows quite large, statistically significant changes over the ten-month period, all in the same direction: people were less likely to favour a formal or punitive response (Wilcoxon signed ranks test, $p < 0.01$ in all three cases).

The final set of questions on attitudes to punishment asked how the government should act if it were forced to choose between different policies (see Table 9.4). They were given three pairs of alternative options:

1. Concentrating more on *punishing* criminals or on trying to *reform* them

2. Concentrating on attacking crime at its *roots* or giving more money to the *police, prisons and courts.*

3. Relying on *ordinary people* to protect their own property or giving more money to the police to prevent burglaries and thefts.

Over the ten-month period there were statistically significant changes in responses to the first two pairs of options. People shifted away from

Table 9.3 Attitudes towards the sentencing of young offenders: before deliberative poll and ten months later

'Suppose a child under 16 commits a burglary for the first time. How much are you in favour or against each of the following ways of dealing with them?'	Strongly in favour	In favour	Neither in favour nor against	Against	Strongly against	Total
Make them do community service						
Before	34	48	6	9	3	100%
After	34	46	9	8	3	100%
Give them a strict warning but leave them to their parents to sort out						
Before	16	31	18	31	6	100%
After	20	39	13	21	7	100%
Send them to a secure institution for young criminals						
Before	12	20	20	34	14	100%
After	10	13	12	46	19	100%
Send them to an ordinary prison						
Before	5	3	13	44	35	100%
After	2	3	6	37	52	100%

1. Base: 226 (minimum).
2. Bold rows show statistically significant differences.
3. Don't knows excluded.
4. Cases with missing data in either sweep excluded.

Table 9.4 Attitudes towards government crime prevention policy : before deliberative poll and ten months later

'If the government had to choose, should it concentrate more on . . .'	Definitely option (a)	Probably option (a)	Doesn't matter either way	Probably option (b)	Definitely option (b)	Total
(a) Punishing criminals or (b) trying to reform criminals?						
Before	37	17	7	12	27	100%
After	34	11	7	15	32	100%
(a) attacking root causes or (b) giving money to police, prisons and courts?						
Before	62	13	4	5	16	100%
After	73	8	2	4	13	100%
(a) relying on ordinary people or (b) giving money to police for prevention?						
Before	15	11	8	16	51	100%
After	12	8	11	21	49	100%

1. Base: 224 (minimum).
2. Bold rows show statistically significant differences.
3. Don't knows excluded.
4. Cases with missing data in either sweep excluded.

punishment towards reform (p<0.05) and away from criminal justice expenditure towards investment in 'root cause' prevention (p=0.051). There was no change in views about the third option.

To summarise the results relating to attitudinal change, it is clear, first of all, that there were significant and enduring shifts over the ten months between recruitment to the deliberative poll weekend and completion of the follow-up. Secondly the statistically significant changes were systematic, in that all were in the same direction – involving reduced support for imprisonment and punitive sentences and greater support for rehabilitation and prevention aimed at 'root causes'. Thirdly – although we have not presented the results here – the changes can be attributed to the deliberative poll event with some confidence, in that changes in the same direction, usually of a great magnitude, were found in the survey completed by respondents at the end of the deliberative poll event.

Change at the individual level

So far we have concentrated on change at the aggregate level – examining, for example, changes in the overall percentage of respondents who favoured stiffer sentences. However, it would be a mistake to imagine that all the change that occurred was in one direction. This section examines what proportion of the sample changed their attitudes in which directions.

In order to make the material more manageable, we have constructed four scales that summarise key dimensions on which attitudes to punishment and crime control appeared to vary in our data. The scales were constructed using factor analysis, a statistical technique which identifies whether there are one or more apparent sources of commonality to the answers given by respondents to a set of questions (see Park and Hough, 2002, for further details on the components of each scale and their reliability). The four scales covered the following dimensions:

- reducing crime through better discipline and firmer punishment;
- toughening up court sentences and prison regimes;
- imprisoning young offenders to control crime;
- extending the use of reparative or rehabilitative community punishments.

Table 9.5 Changes over time in scale scores: before deliberative poll and ten months later

Scale	More liberal (%)	Unchanged (%)	Less liberal (%)	Net liberal shift
Support for imprisoning juvenile first-time burglars	51	33	17	+34
Reducing crime through better discipline and firmer punishment	44	41	16	+28
Using more reparative/rehabilitative community punishments	44	21	35	+9
Toughening up court sentences and prison regimes	28	52	20	+8

Base: 225 (minimum).

Table 9.5 places people in one of three categories for each scale: 'more liberal', 'less liberal' and 'no change'. For all four scales there were sizeable proportions of people shifting on both directions. Although there were majorities or near majorities of people whose views became more liberal, this does not mean that the majority of the sample experienced some sort of Damascene conversion. Most of those whose views changed simply moderated their attitudes, for example that tougher sentencing would be 'effective' rather than 'very effective' in reducing crime.

Who changed their views?

A key question for policy purposes is whether there are any systematic patterns to be found in the characteristics of people whose views softened in response to the deliberative process. If policy regards it as desirable to reduce public attachment to highly punitive penal policies, it is important to establish which groups are open to change. The first point to make is an obvious one, which nevertheless creates dilemmas for our analysis. To be defined as potentially open to change, a person has to hold a particular set of attitudes, and room – headroom, one might say – to shift these attitudes in the desired direction. If, for the sake of argument, the policy interest is in identifying those whose views might shift in a liberal direction, there is little value in targeting those who already show limited support for imprisonment. Put simply, there is no point in preaching to the converted.

Ideally, we would wish to identify the factors that differentiate those who softened their originally tough-minded views from those who remained steadfast in their more punitive views. However, because of the relatively small number of people who took part in the deliberative poll weekend, we cannot do this. Instead we focus upon comparing those who liberalised their views with the rest of the sample. It should be stressed that the rest of the sample includes both those with little room for further attitudinal change (that is, whose views were already fairly liberal) and those who had room but did not do so. Whatever the disadvantages of this approach, it does at least mirror the likely position of any 'real-world' strategy to change public opinion, which will have to identify those with the potential for change *only* on the basis of demographic information.

In analysing scales individually, we found few statistically significant predictors of preparedness to liberalise views. Table 9.6 shows the percentages of different social and demographic groups who, as measured by the four scales, shifted away from punitive or tough-minded positions over the ten-month period after the event.

The most striking – and intuitively plausible – finding is that people with A-levels are more likely to have changed their attitudes towards more liberal positions in relation to all four scales. We would interpret this finding as indicating that people who are good at absorbing and processing information are more likely to respond to it. (One might argue the converse, that better educated people will have had more opportunities to test and refine their views, and will thus be less willing to change them – but the data do not support this.) This apart, there is little consistency between the scales in the profile of people who seem open to change. On some, for example, men were more likely to have shifted their views (crime control and sentencing), but women were more likely to shift in relation to custody alternatives and the appropriateness of prison for juvenile offenders. It is notable, however, that the groups who changed the most were not always those whose original positions were the most punitive or authoritarian. For instance, young people and those with A-level plus qualifications tended to have more liberal views on many of the scales than their older, or less well qualified, counterparts. But, despite this, on some of the scales it was precisely the young and the well qualified who were the most likely to shift their positions in a liberal direction.

We conducted logistic regression analysis to identify which factors emerged as statistically significant predictors of attitude change. A number of themes emerged. The first relates to the importance of education and knowledge. Education, as Table 9.6 implied, does prove

Table 9.6 Percentage of people who liberalised their attitudes, by demographic group

Scale	Alternatives to custody (%)	Prison for juvenile burglars (%)	Tougher sentences (%)	Authoritarian crime control (%)
Age				
18–44	50	49	28	47
45+	38	53	28	41
Sex				
Men	38	46	32	51
Women	49	55	24	38
Qualification level				
A-levels	49	58	38	47
Lower qualifications	41	47	24	43
Socio-economic group				
Non-manual	44	57	26	43
Manual	44	42	27	46
Newspaper readership				
Reads tabloid	48	47	27	44
Reads other/no paper	41	53	28	44
Area of residence				
Rural	45	48	28	47
Elsewhere	43	53	28	41
Knowledge about sentencing				
Low or Medium	45	56	26	42
High	43	51	33	49

Base: 225 (minimum).

to be linked to attitude change, but only significantly so in relation to sentencing. On this issue we find that those with A-levels were more likely to have shifted their views in a liberal direction than those without, even though they already have a considerably more liberal stance than average. However, a very different picture emerges in relation to giving young offenders custodial sentences; this time the best predictor of change was having *limited* knowledge about the criminal justice system. This characteristic was initially linked to being particularly punitive on this issue; after discussion and debate it seems that this group's views changed somewhat.

Respondents' gender was also linked to changing views, but again in rather contradictory ways. Women were more likely than any other group to adopt more liberal views about the various possible alternatives to custody (such as community punishments) but men were the most likely to have developed more liberal attitudes towards crime control.

Finally, newspaper readership emerges as strongly linked to a person's openness to attitudinal change in one scale, relating to alternatives to custody. Those who read tabloid papers were more prepared to shift their views. The implication is that tabloid papers may foster and sustain positive attitudes towards imprisonment which are amenable to change in the deliberative process.

To summarise this set of findings, we found two characteristics among those who seem to have liberalised their views as a result of the weekend event. First, an important section of those who changed were those who started off with markedly authoritarian or punitive views (although this was not always the case – sometimes it was those with more liberal views who changed the most). Secondly, those who changed often appeared to require some intellectual capacity to absorb and process information, as indicated by their level of educational attainment. However, we must be wary of over-interpreting our data as the numbers of people who participated in the deliberative poll does limit our analysis.

Conclusions

This analysis allows us to come to some fairly firm conclusions about the malleability of public opinion in this field; it also allows us to draw rather more tentative conclusions about the reasons for change, and in turn this allows us to speculate about the value of deliberative polls.

Malleable attitudes?

It is clear that there were enduring and systematic shifts in public attitudes. There was a net movement towards 'liberal' or less punitive positions. By no means all respondents who changed their views did so in the same direction, however, and movement was much greater on some items than on others. Nevertheless, it is clear that there was measurable and durable change. In itself, this is a finding of some importance. It suggests that public attitudes to punishment are not simply an immutable constraint within which politicians and criminal justice practitioners are forced to operate.

It is also clear that the attitudinal shift can be attributed to the deliberative poll weekend itself. Sceptics might cast around for an independent source of influence – for example a marked shift in the climate of British debate about law and order in the ten months following the deliberative poll. However, at the time (1994–95) British politicians were *increasingly* engaged in a battle to 'out-tough' their opponents on crime issues in the run-up to an election in which crime played a significant part. And in any case the ten-month changes were actually rather less marked than those that occurred over the course of the deliberative poll weekend, as measured by the questionnaire completed at the end of the event. It is more appropriate to think in terms of a large-scale, but short-term, shift that left a smaller but nevertheless measurable long-term change.

It is much harder, of course, to say precisely what caused the change. Rewatching the television programme seven years after its original screening, we found that some of the politicians and practitioners were clearly charismatic communicators and others were not. Our impression is that the quality of the advocacy in their presentations was at least as important as the factual information they presented to the audience. It is possible that some specific pieces of apparently unassailable evidence were presented very persuasively, and became a shared reference point for each discussion group.[8] However, we obviously cannot test this idea empirically – almost a decade after the event.

On the other hand, a great deal of time during the deliberative poll event was spent in small-group discussion, and the personal engagement of participants in this process might have been as powerful an agent for change as the polished and attractive performances of experts and politicians. It seems likely that the process of testing one's opinions in an arena such as the deliberative poll event might well lead people to moderate their views, and develop an appreciation of the complexity of the issues. If – as seems intuitively likely – extreme views are more a feature of 'penal hawks' than of 'penal doves', then any moderating process would also be a liberalising one.

The problem in translating these findings into practical action is that those with the 'need to change' and those with the 'capacity to change' may be only partially overlapping groups. Certainly this is suggested by our analysis of attitudes held by respondents at the outset of the event. We would thus be pessimistic about the payoff of a *highly* targeted strategy to inform and educate those members of the public at the very tough-minded end of the attitudinal spectrum. It may be more realistic to think in terms of achieving smaller changes across a broader cross-section of the population.

There is also the risk, of course, in a highly targeted strategy, of unintended consequences. We have mentioned that there was change in both directions as a result of the weekend event, with a minority of people *hardening* their attitudes. Certainly, when we asked participants to indicate whether or not they thought their views had changed as a result of the weekend, one common response was that the weekend had increased their *awareness* of crime and the impact it has on some communities (rather than simply affecting their views about punishment). Perhaps some of this group developed more punitive views as a result. However, the small number of cases means that it is even more difficult to characterise this group than it is to describe those who liberalised their views. Nonetheless, there is a real possibility that using social marketing techniques to promote less punitive penal policies could backfire.

The role and future of deliberative polls

What can we say about the deliberative poll as a means of offsetting the 'democratic deficit' whereby political decision-making is distorted by people's uninformed and unthinking views? This analysis provides further confirmation of the idea that people's unconsidered or 'top of the head' opinions differ from those which they hold after they have been more fully informed and have had a chance to consider the issues. There remains the possibility that the changes that we have documented are the result of effective advocacy rather than deliberation. Regardless of this, however, the results imply that too much credence tends to be given to the results of polls that manage to chart only people's unreflecting views.

However, deliberative polls must have only limited value as a tool for *routinely* testing 'informed opinion'. If done on the scale that this one was, the cost is prohibitive. If they are conducted with fewer participants, then one rapidly encounters problems of generalisability. Our own analysis shows that even with samples of almost three hundred people, conclusions are often rather tentative.

There is also the problem that when poorly conducted, deliberative polls may demonstrate little more than the power of advocacy. If the intention is to reflect public opinion as it would be if it were *better informed* and *thoughtful*, then one has to be certain that the process was conducted in a dispassionate and objective way. There need to be ways of containing the impact of the charismatic communicator, and of ensuring that the panels of experts are genuinely balanced. One solution would be to provide participants with videotaped presentations, carefully prepared – and reviewed or audited – to ensure that all stakeholders are represented fairly. This might also have the advantage of substantially reducing the cost of such events. (The next chapter in this volume reports findings on just such a pilot scheme.)

There are other tensions between practicability and breadth of coverage. The participants in this event gave up a weekend – an impressive commitment, although it included the lure of participation in a major television programme. On a routine basis one would find it hard to persuade people to give up more than a half-day of their time. One possible development pathway for deliberative polls might involve much shorter events – covering a half-day, perhaps – with a sharper focus on a smaller number of specific issues. It may also make sense to have several small-scale events – which would be possible if there were standardised video presentations – rather than one large one.

The other advantage of a shorter event is that this would reduce the selectivity of the people participating. There is always the danger that the participants who attend may be the kind of individuals who are more 'evidence-based' in the way that they form, and change, their attitudes. If this is the case, then the attitude change found in this deliberative poll might exaggerate the extent to which the attitudes of the general public will change in response to information and/or discussion. An event of shorter duration may overcome this problem by attracting a less selective group of participants.

It seems to us that the debate about the utility of deliberative polls is an unfinished one. There is an obvious need to improve on the ways that opinion on complex topics is canvassed. Deliberative polls offer one way forward, but expense and doubts over the integrity of the 'factual' information fed to participants are important limiting features. If the latter problem can be overcome – through standardisation and rigorous auditing, for example – the cost might also be reduced.

In short, there is a need for some sort of variant of deliberative polling, and we think it might become routinely viable if there were a series of changes to the original design. These are:

1. To focus on a single issue, rather than a broad, complex social problem.

2. To use videotape of communications that permit external and independent review of balance and to allow for replication in subsequent administrations.

3. To conduct the 'deliberative' session in a single day or half-day.

4. To use a smaller number of deliberative poll participants in any single event.

5. To replicate each poll in different locations.

In this way, the deliberative poll methodology might become part of the landscape of public opinion research, rather than an isolated example as it is at present. Deliberative polling will never replace the standard, representative poll as a measure of public opinion. However, it may serve as a very useful adjunct and generate insight into community views that cannot be gleaned from the survey approach which carries so much weight with politicians.

Notes

1. For example, in the 2000 British Crime Survey, 80 per cent of respondents thought that judges were 'out of touch with what ordinary people think,' while 41 per cent thought they were 'very out of touch' (Mirrlees-Black, 2001).
2. The analysis was funded by the Esmée Fairbairn Foundation, to whom we would like to express our thanks.
3. Known at the time as Social and Community Planning Research (SCPR).
4. See Adair (1996). In the same edition of this journal there are other reviews of the deliberative poll methodology by Mitofsky, Newport, Bradburn and Converse, together with a response by Fishkin.
5. For example, all the main political parties put forward spokesmen at the deliberative poll. The Labour Party offered a better-known and arguably more charismatic speaker to the deliberative poll than the Conservatives or Liberal Democrats – the then shadow Home Secretary Tony Blair – who clearly made a big impact on the participants.
6. However, as Doble argues in this volume, the legitimacy of posing this forced choice is questionable.
7. A-level exams are those that qualify school leavers for a university place, and are generally taken by pupils aged 17.
8. For example, a prison governor spoke memorably and with impressive authority about the damage done to the young offenders passing through his institution.

References

Adair, J. G. (1996) 'The Hawthorne effect is a common artifact in social research', *Public Perspective*, December–January, pp. 14–16.

Doob A. N. and Roberts, J. (1988) 'Public punitiveness and public knowledge of the facts: some Canadian surveys', in N. Walker and M. Hough (eds), *Public Attitudes to Sentencing: Surveys from Five Countries*. Aldershot: Gower.

Fishkin, J. S. (1995) *The Voice of the People*. New York: Vail-Baillou Press.

Fishkin, J. S., Luskin, R. C. and Jowell, R. (2000) 'Deliberative polling and public consultation', *Parliamentary Affairs*, 53: 657–66.

Hough, M. and Roberts, J. (1999) 'Sentencing trends in Britain: public knowledge and public opinion', *Punishment and Society*, 1(1): 11–26.

Hough, M. and Roberts, J. (2002) 'Public knowledge and public opinion of sentencing', in N. Hutton and C. Tata (eds), *Sentencing and Society: International Perspectives*. Aldershot: Ashgate.

Mirrlees-Black, C. (2001) *Confidence in the Criminal Justice System: Findings from the 2000 British Crime Survey*, RDS Research Findings No. 137. London: Home Office.

Park, A. and Hough, M. (2002) *Public Attitudes towards Crime and Punishment*. London: National Centre for Social Research.

Roberts, J. and Stalans, L. (1997) *Public Opinion, Crime, and Criminal Justice*. Boulder, CO: Westview Press.

Chapter 10

Improving public knowledge about crime and punishment

Catriona Mirrlees-Black

This chapter presents findings from an experimental research study mounted by the British Home Office in 2000. The study contributed to a cross-departmental government strategy to promote public confidence in the criminal justice system (CJS) of England and Wales. It arose out of recognition of the low public ratings given to many aspects of the criminal justice system and the particularly low ratings commanded by sentencers. Research evidence suggested that public ignorance about the justice system would act as a considerable constraint on attempts to rebuild public confidence in it. Surveys in the UK and elsewhere had consistently shown how poor public awareness was in this area (Doob and Roberts, 1988; Indermaur, 1990; Tarling and Dowds, 1997; Hough and Roberts, 1998; Morgan and Russell, 2000; Mattinson and Mirrlees-Black, 2000). The public tends to overestimate crime rates and underestimate the severity of current sentencing practice. Moreover, these beliefs are correlated with negative attitudes towards the courts and sentencers in particular (Hough and Roberts, 1998). Those who have a more accurate understanding tend to be more positive in their attitudes, suggesting that education may be an effective method of promoting confidence in the system (Mirrlees-Black, 2001).

Providing the public with information was therefore identified as an important element of the strategy to promote public confidence. Little was known about how to go about the improvment of public knowledge, and there was very limited information about the kinds of effects that could be expected, if any. Most of the available evidence was from the US. For instance, the Public Agenda Foundation research in Alabama and Delaware measured the impact of a video and educational discussion on sentencing preferences, and found a marked shift in opinion towards alternatives to custody (see Doble, this volume; Doble, 1997; Doble and Immerwahr, 1997; Roberts, 1997). In the UK, Hough and Roberts (1998) had shown the impact of providing information on the range of disposals available on sentencing preferences. And as discussed in the previous chapter by Hough and Park, the British deliberative poll had demonstrated that it was possible to change attitudes to criminal justice. But there was no evidence that changes in public opinion could be directly attributed to improvements in knowledge, or indeed that measurable improvements in knowledge could be achieved for widely held negative beliefs about crime and sentencing. The decision was taken, therefore, to mount an experimental study to test the impact of different approaches to improving public knowledge.

A test of three modes of communication

The approach taken was to provide simple facts about crime and the CJS in three 'user-friendly' formats: a booklet, a seminar and a video, and to monitor the impact of these interventions on knowledge and attitudes using 'before' and 'after' interviews.

Just over 1,000 people were interviewed initially.[1] The main aim at this stage was to provide an overview of public opinion about the purposes of sentencing and the factors that should influence sentencing decisions, and to test people's reactions to various options that were being considered by a review of sentencing being conducted at the time.[2] Three subsets of respondents were then asked whether they would be prepared to read a booklet, attend a seminar or watch a video. The aim was to have 100 participants in each group. Although there were 109 in the booklet group, the actual samples fell short of this target for the video (n=74) and the seminar (n=37) groups, due mainly to different participation rates.[3] Given the small samples, these findings must be considered indicative rather than conclusive.

The booklet was designed to be simple and easy to understand, attractive and attention-grabbing. It was a square CD shape, with modern fonts, brightly coloured, with some charts and photographic images where appropriate. Many pages had 'call-outs' where short parts of the text were reproduced and enlarged.

Four seminars were held in London, Manchester, Cardiff and Birmingham respectively. Unlike deliberative polling, there was no initial debate of the issues among participants. A senior academic,[4] a local prison governor and probation officer presented the material covered by the booklet. This was followed by a question and answer session and general discussion.

The London seminar was filmed, and this formed the basis of the video. Footage of police cars, courts and prisons, and interviews with prisoners were incorporated to maintain viewer interest. A professional voice-over introduced the topic and linked elements together. To replicate the presentation of facts and statistics from the booklet, some screens were text and charts.

Although the content of each mode of communication was kept as similar as possible, there were inevitably a number of differences other than the mode of presentation. As has been mentioned, the video had some additional information to maintain viewers' interest. And although each of the four seminars used the same script, the discussions that followed each presentation inevitably raised different issues. There were also differences in the composition of the groups resulting from the different participation rates – a point returned to below.

Each format provided a brief description of the key stages of the criminal justice system together with some statistics on crime and sentencing. The language used was kept as simple as possible, erring on the side of over-simplification. For instance, from the booklet:

When an accused person appears in court he or she is asked whether they plead 'guilty' or 'not guilty' to the offence. Most people plead guilty and are then sentenced for the crime. If someone pleads guilty, it can reduce their sentence by up to a third. If they plead not guilty there has to be a trial. A trial is to decide whether or not they are guilty.

Statistical facts, all from government sources, included, for example, information about crime risks:

The chance of being a victim of crime varies according to where you live and how you spend your time. People living in inner-city areas, for instance, are far more likely to be victims than those in more rural areas. Also, young men are far more at risk than any other group of being attacked by a stranger. The elderly are at least risk.

And sentencing practices:

John, 25 years old, is a house burglar. He has quite a high chance of going to prison because 72 per cent of house burglars over the age of 21 are sentenced to immediate custody. He is likely to get a custodial sentence of about 2 years.

Virtually everyone who took part said that the information they were given was easy to understand, and all methods were generally rated as informative and helpful. The information on types of sentencing, levels of reconviction, and risks and trends in crime were said to be the most interesting.

Improvements in knowledge

Substantial proportions of all groups thought that they had learnt a lot from participating in the study. The seminar was rated most highly, with three-quarters saying that they had learnt a lot, followed by the video group. The extent to which participants had absorbed the facts covered in the three formats was assessed through eleven questions asked on both the 'before' and 'after' questionnaires: five covering CJS procedures and six covering CJS statistics.

Nine out of ten participants initially answered more than half of the questions incorrectly. The chance of getting a question correct was, of course, greater for those questions with fewer answer options, but even so, knowledge of sentence lengths, custody rates and crime trends was particularly poor. Each of the three methods used was effective at improving knowledge of the issues, with a significant increase observed in the proportion of correct answers for each of the three groups (Figure 10.1). Multivariate analysis confirmed that regardless of other factors related to improved scores (such as age, social class and levels

Figure 10.1 Change in mean knowledge score, by information source.

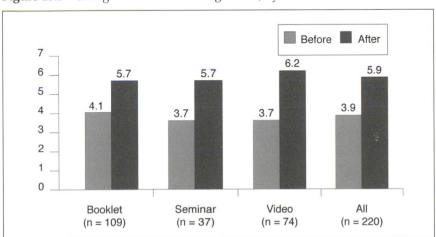

of educational attainment) those with the lowest initial scores improved the most.[5]

Some types of information had more impact (see Table 10.1). There were statistically significant increases in the proportion of people correctly answering questions about crime trends, prison place costs, sentence length and supervision of longer-term prisoners on release. Table 10.1 also compares the subgroup of 220 participants with the total population sample of 1,022 from which they were drawn. It can be seen that with the exception of two items (about supervision on release and the costs of imprisonment) participants were a little better informed about criminal justice than those who decided against participation.

There was some evidence that the more 'surprising' the information, the better it was remembered. The annual cost of a prison place was frequently mentioned as surprising, and this·was the question that showed the most dramatic improvement. Repetition of information also seemed to improve knowledge: the booklet group was more likely to identify the fine as the most common sentence, a fact that was repeated three times within the text of the booklet.

Did attitudes change?

Just under half of those participating admitted that they had changed their views about crime and sentencing in some way. Most of these were now more positive, with many participants saying that they now had more faith in the criminal justice system and, specifically, in alternatives to custody. Others said they felt more confident that there was an emphasis on crime reduction. Greater awareness of trends in crime, the risks of victimisation and an understanding of CJS procedures were most often cited as the reason for these changes. The small minority who were less positive mentioned the length of a custodial sentence served, a greater awareness of crime generally and a concern that they had been fed propaganda.

Aims of sentencing

The material did not explicitly cover the purposes of sentencing, although it was stated that the sentence given by the court depended largely on the seriousness of the crime. A crime reduction purpose may have been implied by the references to reconviction rates and programmes to tackle offending behaviour. It is perhaps not surprising, then, that there was little shift from the widest held view that the main

Table 10.1 Percentage of correct answers to the knowledge questions for the general population sample and for the project participants before and after receiving information

Question	Correct answer	Population Before n = 1,022	Participants Before n = 220	Participants After n = 220
In a magistrates' court a jury decides whether someone is guilty or not [2 options]	False	64	71	80
In the Crown Court it is the jury who decide the sentence for an offender [2 options]	False	47	53	58
What is the minimum sentence for an adult who has been convicted three times of house burglary? [4 options]	Three-year prison sentence	28	33	49
Which is the most common sentence given by the courts for all offences (except motoring)? [4 options]	Fine	50	54	62
Approximately how much of a prison sentence is spent in prison (not including life sentences)? [4 options]	A half	47	50	61
Prisoners serving a 12-month or longer sentence will be supervised on release [2 options]	True	44	42	65
An offender is least likely to get convicted again if he is given a prison sentence, a community penalty, or does it makes no difference? [3 options]	It makes no difference	45	48	50
Out of 100 convicted adult male burglars (21 and over) how many go to prison? [open response]	64 to 80	8	9	25
An adult male (21 and over) convicted of rape will get an average sentence length of? [open response]	8 to 9 years	6	8	37
Roughly how much does it cost to keep a prisoner in prison for a year? [open response]	£21k to £31k	11	10	60
What do you think has happened to the crime rate for the country as a whole over the past two years? [5 options]	Less crime	8	11	38

aim of sentencing should be 'changing the behaviour or attitudes of offenders to stop them reoffending'.[6] 'Punishment' followed with about a quarter giving this as their first choice.

Attitudes to prison

Not surprisingly, in light of previous research (see Roberts, this volume) and given its position within the justice system, prior to receiving the material, prison was judged to be the most effective method of meeting the aims of sentencing. This included issues such as changing offender attitudes, punishment and even making amends to victims. Having received the material there was an overall improvement in opinion regarding the effectiveness of prison, which is of course in line with the objective of promoting confidence in the CJS. For example, the proportion believing that 'offenders come out of prison worse than they go in' fell from 72 to 59 per cent.

These improved attitudes did not, however, manifest themselves in a widening of the kinds of cases for which custody was judged to be the most appropriate sentence. For example, in the sentencing task included in the questionnaires, there was a slight fall in the use of custody (from 9 to 3 per cent) for sentencing of a first time burglar. Even the use of custody for the repeat burglar – who attracted custodial sentences from over half of respondents – showed no statistically significant increase. This is not really surprising as there is plenty of evidence that the public are generally well disposed to the use of non-custodial sentences on a case-by-case basis (Hough and Roberts, 1998; Russell and Morgan, 2001).

Appropriateness of sentencing

A much used indicator of public opinion regarding sentencing is a variant on the question 'In general, would you say that sentences handed down by the courts, that is both the Crown Courts and Magistrates' Courts, are too tough, about right or too lenient?' In line with other UK surveys and with the responses to the main survey, most participants initially thought that sentences were too lenient.

The material included information on the proportionate use of custody and average sentence lengths for burglary, robbery and rape, and the proportion believing that sentences were 'about right' did improve from 21 to 31 per cent.[7] But two-thirds still thought sentencing was too lenient, and not all shifts in attitude were movements in the 'about right' direction (Figure 10.2). Indeed, 4 out of 10 of those who had initially thought sentences were about right subsequently decided they were too lenient.

Figure 10.2 Change in distance from attitude that sentences are 'about right', by initial opinion.

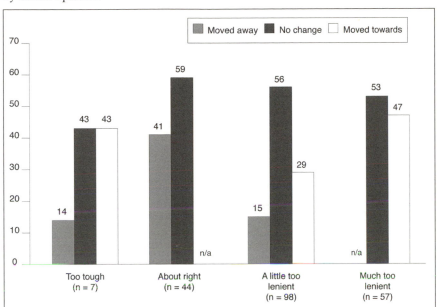

Confidence in the criminal justice system

Confidence in the criminal justice system was measured by four questions, and each showed some overall improvement among participants, although the confidence of some individuals fell (Figure 10.3). In the follow-up surveys, participants were asked why their level of confidence had changed, or not. Increased confidence was attributed by participants to, for instance, having 'read the booklet' or more specifically to an increased knowledge or understanding of the CJS.[8] Reasons for decreased confidence varied by individual with about a third referring to facts they had been given.[9] Those who continued to have low confidence referred mainly to personal experience or remaining concerns about lenient sentences, while continued confidence was most often attributed to trust in the system and falling crime rates.[10]

The relationship between knowledge and attitudes

Despite participants attributing their improved confidence to the information they had been given, there was little evidence of a direct

Figure 10.3 Change in confidence in the criminal justice system.

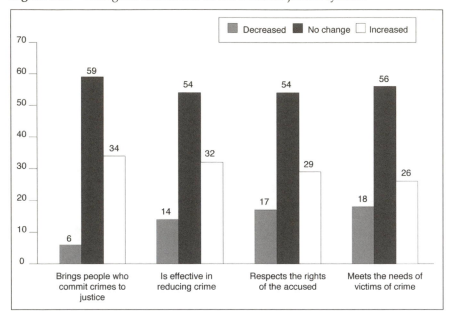

statistical link between improved knowledge and confidence. Those who had shown no improvement on the knowledge questions were as likely to have increased in confidence as those who had shown a large improvement. This may be because the recall of facts is a difficult task, and memory for facts may be (considerably) shorter term than the improved perceptions it brings about. The greater improvement in knowledge for the video group who were reinterviewed sooner, on average, may also reflect this. It may also be that the eleven knowledge questions did not cover the full range of material presented, so could have 'missed' real improvements in knowledge in other areas.

These findings also raise the possibility of a methodological artefact: that participants were aware of the hypothesis being tested, and consciously or unconsciously sought to confirm this by giving more positive responses on attitude measures in the follow-up survey. Delivering improved knowledge scores would have been somewhat more of a challenge! However, it is also possible that the experience of participating in the project was in itself sufficient to have a real impact on attitudes.

There was more encouraging evidence of a link between improved knowledge and attitudes to sentencing. Although improved percep-tions of the appropriateness of sentencing were proportionately as

Figure 10.4 Percentage saying sentencing 'about right', before and after receiving information, by change in knowledge.

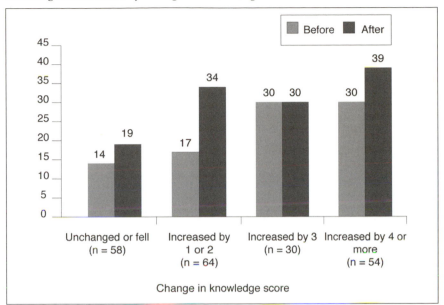

great for those who showed no improvement in knowledge as for those who did (Figure 10.4), multivariate analysis identified knowledge gain as a significant factor when other characteristics such as demographic differences, educational qualifications and the influence of initial belief were controlled for.

Is this a viable way of promoting positive attitudes?

Providing information about crime and the criminal justice system does appear to have a positive impact on knowledge and on attitudes, although whether the latter can be attributed to the former is less clear. However, the viability of using any of the three methods for promoting positive attitudes depends on a number of factors in addition to their effectiveness at changing attitudes. One of the most important of these is participation rates. Not everyone who was asked to read, watch or attend agreed to do so, and not all of those who initially agreed actually participated. Most importantly, there were identifiable differences between those who did and did not participate for each of the three groups. Although this undermines comparisons of the effects of the three information formats, and the extent to which findings can be generalised, it is probably fairly indicative of what might be expected in any larger-scale exercise.

The booklet had the highest participation rate, with 72 per cent of those asked agreeing to read it. In addition, all except four of the 80 per cent contacted for reinterview said that they had at least skimmed the document. It is, however, a very passive medium, and it is possible that people would be less motivated to read it if they did not know that they were going to be questioned later on its content. Those who read the booklet were relatively young, educated and typically had more liberal attitudes than those who chose not to.

The seminars were very well received and by encouraging discussion, they gave participants a chance to test or verify their understanding of some quite complex issues. However, it was extremely difficult to get people to attend. Only 36 per cent of those invited agreed to take part, and of these only 33 per cent turned up, despite a monetary incentive to participate.[11] Those who actually attended were more likely to be better educated, broadsheet readers, and/or from the higher social classes, and were far more likely to say they were very interested in law and order issues than those who did not attend.

A video has the potential to reach a larger audience, although it was hard to tell if it could achieve this because of a low reinterview contact rate in the study.[12] Seventy-four per cent of those offered the video agreed to watch it, but only 55 per cent of these were reinterviewed and 53 per cent had actually done so.

Cost and the extent to which the information spreads to a wider audience are also important considerations. Not surprisingly the seminar was by far the most expensive, partly due to the fixed costs of venues and refreshments but also the time contribution of organisers, presenters and participants. Also, these costs would be accrued anew at each event. The design costs of the booklet and video were a 'one-off', although each would have to be updated periodically. In the long term, there would be little difference between the booklet and the video in the unit cost of production, although dissemination costs would become more of an issue.

Of the three methods, the seminars were the most successful in prompting participants to go back and discuss the material with other people. The booklet was fairly successful in prompting discussion, mainly with family, but also friends. Nevertheless a substantial minority said they had not discussed it with anyone else. The information from the video was the least likely to have been shared. It was also far more criticised than the other two formats, attracting lower ratings on most criteria. No doubt this was because it lacked the polish to which people have become accustomed.

Considerable care was taken to ensure that the information provided was balanced and accurate. This paid off, in that only a very small minority of participants discounted the material as being government propaganda. Most people believed it was factual, although obviously it was hard for them to judge. But it is doubtful that the presentation of this kind of material can ever be entirely objective. Inevitably, the choice of 'facts' presented, the context within which they are framed, and the tone with which they are delivered will all have an impact on the way the messages are received. Furthermore there will be differential effects depending on the pre-existing belief systems and life experiences that each individual brings with them. This method of promoting confidence in the criminal justice system will only be effective to the extent that the material is widely regarded as factual and apolitical.

Finally there are questions about the durability of change. The follow-up interviews were all carried out within a few weeks of the initial exposure to information. The 1994 deliberative poll on crime and justice in Britain clearly had a long-term impact on attitudes (see Hough and Park, this volume). However, participants in that event spent an entire weekend corralled together in discussion about crime and punishment. In our experiment even the most interactive form of exposure to knowledge – the seminars – made quite limited demands on people's time, and may have correspondingly less impact in the long term. Clearly any future experiments should try to measure the persistence of change in knowledge and attitudes at least over the medium term.

Notes

1. The survey was commissioned by the Home Office. Interviews were conducted by RSGB with a quota sample of 1,022 people aged 16 and over living in private households in England and Wales in October 2000.
2. Appendix 5 of the report of the review (Halliday, 2001) covers the findings of this survey, together with those of a linked survey of most practitioner groups working within the criminal justice system.
3. A full report of the study is published in the Home Office Research series (Chapman, Mirrlees-Black and Brawn, 2002).
4. Professor Rod Morgan of Bristol University, who assisted with the design of the study.

5. All the multivariate analyses reported in this chapter involved logistic regression.
6. About a half of participants in each group opted for this as their most important purpose.
7. Among the 206 participants that responded to this question on both the before and after survey.
8. Total N = 85.
9. Total N = 15.
10. Total N = 156.
11. All three groups were given a payment on reinterview, but it was greatest for the seminar group.
12. There was a shorter period available for reinterviewing the video group, but respondents not having got around to watching it could also explain the low rate.

References

Chapman, B., Mirrlees-Black, C. and Brawn C. (2002) *Improving Public Attitudes to the Criminal Justice System: The Impact of Providing Information*, Home Office Research Study No. 245. London: Home Office.

Doble, J. (1997) 'Survey shows Alabamians support alternatives', in M. Tonry and K. Hatlestad (eds), *Sentencing Reform in Overcrowded Times: A Comparative Perspective*. Oxford: OUP.

Doble, J. and Immerwahr, S. (1997) 'Delawareans favor prison alternatives', in M. Tonry and K. Hatlestad (eds), *Sentencing Reform in Overcrowded Times: A Comparative Perspective*. Oxford: OUP.

Doob A. N. and Roberts, J. (1988) 'Public punitiveness and public knowledge of the facts: some Canadian surveys', in N. Walker and M. Hough (eds), *Public Attitudes to Sentencing: Surveys from Five Countries*. Aldershot: Gower.

Halliday, J. (2001) *Making Punishments Work: Report of a Review of the Sentencing Framework for England and Wales*. London: Home Office.

Hough, M. and Roberts, J. (1998) *Attitudes to Punishment: Findings from the British Crime Survey*, Home Office Research Study No. 179. London: Home Office Research and Statistics Directorate.

Indermaur, D. (1990) 'Perceptions of sentencing in Perth, Western Australia', *Australian and New Zealand Journal of Criminology*, 20: 163–83.

Mattinson, J. and Mirrlees-Black, C. (2000) *Attitudes to Crime and Criminal Justice: Findings from the 1998 British Crime Survey*, Home Office Research Study No. 200. London: Home Office.

Mirrlees-Black, C. (2001) *Confidence in the Criminal Justice System: Findings from the 2000 British Crime Survey*, RDS Research Findings No 137. London: Home Office.

Morgan, R. and Russell, N. (2000) *The Judiciary in the Magistrates' Courts*, RDS Occasional Paper No. 66. London: Home Office.

Roberts, J. V. (1997) 'American attitudes about punishment: myth and reality', in M. Tonry and K. Hatlestad (eds), *Sentencing Reform in Overcrowded Times: A Comparative Perspective*. Oxford: OUP.

Russell, N. and Morgan, R. (2001) *Sentencing of Domestic Burglary*, Sentencing Advisory Panel Research Report 1. London: SAP.

Tarling, R. and Dowds, L. (1997) 'Crime and punishment' in Jowell et al. (eds), *British Social Attitudes: the 14th Report.* Aldershot: Ashgate.

Chapter 11

Strategies for changing public attitudes to punishment[1]

David Indermaur and Mike Hough

The current state of public knowledge about crime and justice in industrialised countries poses serious challenges for those concerned with the quality of penal policy. Several chapters in this book have described the extent of public dissatisfaction with penal policy and practice; they have also revealed the complexity of attitudes that are layered, and different layers can be inconsistent. As John Doble (this volume) has demonstrated, people often want and expect contradictory and incompatible outcomes from their systems of justice. Above all, people are poorly informed about both crime and justice. This chapter sets out to explore the scope for strategies that improve public knowledge and public confidence in the administration of justice.

There are, of course, several other areas of social policy in which public opinion is equally multifaceted and equally ill-informed. Most of the population are unlikely to know a great deal about the operation of their country's welfare systems, for example; their understanding about public health systems may be equally patchy; they are likely to know even less about their immigration and asylum policy. Should governments simply accept that the delivery of public services is poorly understood, and that at least *some* of the cynicism and dissatisfaction with public services will be misplaced? We would argue against this view, at least with respect to criminal justice.

Criminal justice systems depend on public confidence for their effective operation. Without widespread belief in their fairness and effectiveness, they would eventually cease to function. They are not totally unique in this respect. For example, the educational system would collapse without a degree of parental support, and vaccination regimes work only if the majority of the population support and participate in them. But the capacity of most public services to operate effectively does not depend so directly on public confidence. The rule of law requires public consent, and governments ignore the crisis of confidence in justice at their peril. In this respect the criminal justice system occupies a unique place in the public sector, and public attitudes towards it demand a special response.

Second, when poorly informed, public opinion can drive policy towards ineffective or unfair responses to crime. In this respect, penal policy is little different from health, education or other areas of social policy. Often the process is a reactive one, in which politicians believe that they will be thrown out of office (or will fail to gain office) if they do not visibly respond to pubic opinion. But sometimes they can also be more proactive in exploiting public misunderstanding about any given issue in order to develop electoral support. Crime is a perennial source of public concern, and those politicians who promise tough and decisive action against it usually derive some electoral advantage. It is not surprising, therefore, that penal populism[2] has been part of the political landscape for many years. Penal populism thrives on public misunderstandings about crime and justice, and honest politicians are sometimes at a disadvantage if others are perceived as presenting 'solutions' to crime problems.

Whose responsibility?

This chapter is premised on the view that the problems posed by public misunderstanding and cynicism are problems of government, and ones which demand primarily a governmental response. There are other 'stakeholders', however. In the first place, the judiciary have – or should have – a central interest in ensuring that their decisions are properly understood. There are other groups as well. The growing voluntary sector in most of the jurisdictions covered in this book has a direct interest in the quality of penal policy. These professionals are involved either in the delivery of services relating to justice, or are involved in efforts to reform the system – or both.

Finally, there is the research community. Given that academic and government researchers provide the foundation of knowledge about crime and justice, it is disappointing that they have evinced so little enthusiasm for reaching a broader audience beyond their academic and policy colleagues. In so far as they have recognised problems that arise from misinformed public opinion, academics have largely been content to wring their hands in dismay. The prospect of entering the fray with 'spin doctors', public relations consultants and others involved in 'social marketing' strikes many as incompatible with academic standards. Equally, the function of 'public education' strikes many as too simplistic or even too paternalistic.

We believe that academics have an obligation to enhance the quality of public debates. Criminologists in particular should be interested in ensuring that information to which they have access is available to those who shape or constrain penal policy. We are not suggesting that criminologists should push an agenda or drive public opinion to a certain position; but they should be more concerned than they have been to improve the quality of public debate, and thus of public opinion. We realise that it would be easy to confuse a *higher* debate with a *preferred* debate; there are risks in being seen to move beyond the role of objective researcher to that of policy advocate, but we feel that the risks are worth taking.

Influencing public opinion on punishment requires first and foremost a good understanding of the nature of public opinion, and in particular the forces that can influence that opinion. Before attempting to influence public attitudes we should have a clear view of what is possible and how this can be achieved. The key concepts that may be a useful guide in this endeavour are realism and pragmatism. If we are to influence the nature of the politics of crime it will be through gradual steps that encourage greater scrutiny of crime policy, not through dramatic shifts or revelations.

The forces affecting the politics of crime are perennial and largely outside the influence of any one political party. Understanding the way crime policy is formed – what Rock (1986: 387) calls the 'grammar' of the process – means that we have to be pragmatic and understand well the few points in the process where we can exert some influence. The ways that we can influence public opinion depend firstly on understanding the development of public attitudes to punishment, secondly on understanding the key points of influence and thirdly on the interventions that may be effective in influencing public knowledge or attitudes. We will concentrate here on the latter two points but first we need to articulate what we see as the main problems with public attitudes to punishment.

Problems associated with public attitudes and knowledge

A brief recapitulation of the key problems in public opinion on punishment provides us with a guide as to what our objectives might be. The problems can be summarised under the following points:

- misunderstanding of the nature of crime and punishment;

- overestimating the utility of punishment and, in particular, the value of imprisonment;

- underestimating the value of alternative responses to crime.

These concerns have been criticised as capturing only the rational or knowledge-based aspect of opinion and ignoring the emotional and dispositional side. As Zaller (1992: 6) eloquently states: 'every opinion is a marriage of information and predisposition: information to form a mental picture and predisposition to motivate some conclusion about it.' Understanding the emotional or dispositional side of opinions is just as important as the informational side. This aspect of public opinion is vast and contains issues as broad as the symbolic meaning of crime and punishment in the face of rapid social transformation. Indeed it is these broad symbolic and emotional dynamics that have dominated most sociological discussion of public attitudes to punishment. This perspective is seen in the work of David Garland, Jonathan Simon and others.[3] Notwithstanding the volumes of literature looking at the role that punishment plays in the psychology of the community, the three principal issues may be crudely summarised as:

- the experience of insecurity and the implication that crime is its cause;

- the transformation, through political rhetoric, of popular fear, sense of threat and insecurity into emotions of frustration, anger and entitlement;

- the use of crime as a symbolic issue in response to which politicians can present themselves as determined, decisive and effective.

Broadly there are two types of problem that we are dealing with in regard to public attitudes. First, at the cognitive level is the level and quality of the information. Second, at the emotional level are the fears, frustrations and uncertainties experienced. To these two levels could be added a third – the political level – the 'hardening of attitudes', the retreat of liberalism and the exacerbation of popular fears by the media.[4] This third level really reflects the interplay of the former two. Politicians, doing what politicians do, will work with the available resources to maintain their electoral base. Few have qualms about exploiting public fears and uncertainties. Although we may be critical of politicians for using crime as a symbolic issue, it could be argued that this is a perennial aspect of political life and it is naive to expect otherwise.

It is important to stress that changing the way that penal policy is made, and changing the context within which policy is framed, cannot simply consist of marginalising or discounting public opinion. For durable change to occur, the public must be engaged. The level of public debate needs to be raised, and the quality of public scrutiny of penal policy has to be improved. Reform must, to some extent, be led but it also depends on cogent argument that is effectively conveyed in public debates. The problem of the influence and position of elites in the process of attitude formation and change has been the subject of much investigation by public opinion scholars (e.g. Zaller, 1992) and will be discussed further when we discuss strategies in more detail.

A model of influences

Public attitudes to punishment are clearly influenced by a range of factors. Some of these factors are fairly specific and have a direct impact; others are more amorphous and achieve their impact only indirectly. Some of the influences on public opinion have unintended political and penal consequences. Much of the press treatment of crime and justice falls into this category. Others form part of more deliberate political strategies.[5] However, the media are at the centre of all the influences. Not only do the broadcast and written media represent a central source of information upon which public knowledge of crime and justice is based; they also serve this function in a particular way, reflecting the commercial (or quasi-commercial)[6] pressures to retain their audiences and thus their revenue. The media also provide a major source of information not only to the public but also to policy-makers. Furthermore it appears that policy-makers get their ideas about what public opinion is from the media (Herbst, 1998; Beckett and Sasson, 2000).

Public opinion is clearly the product of a range of influences and most of those who have examined the formation of public opinion stress the highly interdependent nature of the various influences. This idea of a complex interweaving of influence and response is a common conclusion of those who have examined the relationship between media, crime and public policy.[7] Doppelt and Manikas (1990: 134) provide a succinct summary of this view when they point to '... a trisected chamber of reverberating effects among the media, the public and policy makers.' Into this trisected chamber come the efforts of lobby groups and various vested interests from left to right which try

Figure 11.1 A model of the interaction of media, public opinion, special interest groups and political decision-makers (adapted from Kennamer, 1992).

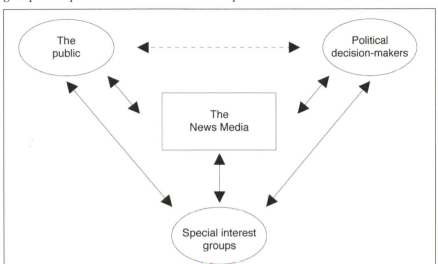

to influence the shape and direction of public debates. The best way to approach our field then is to acknowledge that public opinion exists within a dynamic framework dominated by political initiative, the media and special interest groups. A useful model that captures the interplay of these forces was proposed by Kennamer (1992 – see Figure 11.1). In this model the media occupy the heart of the interaction of the three forces involved in the generation of public policy: policy-makers, special interest groups and public(s). Each of these parties may only express themselves to other parties through the depiction of their position in the media. The media are the conduit for expression, for conveying positions and expressing postures. Media reaction to policy is often read by all three groups as being akin to, or at least somewhat in sympathy with, public opinion.[8]

It is often argued that the public absorbs material from the media in a critical, or even sceptical, way; the implication of this is that Figure 11.1 may overstate the power of the media. However, this ignores the influence of 'third person effects'. Third person effects refer to the belief held in varying degrees that although one(self) is not influenced by the media, others are. In this context the individual is apt to attribute a greater degree of importance to media content as it is believed to have a powerful conditioning effect. As Lasorsa (1992) points out, there is considerable evidence for this phenomenon. This effect may be at its most powerful in relation to politicians and policy elites. They regard themselves as distanced from the general public, and thus in need of windows into 'public opinion'.[9] For this group the media become both a source and an audience. The media can thus shape the accepted realities about crime and justice directly and indirectly.

Responding to, and influencing, public opinion

We now turn to examine some specific strategies that may have value in shaping public knowledge and attitudes. Such responses need to work with the forces outlined above. The existence and power of these influences is not likely to change. However, it may be possible to influence the ways in which these factors are constructed. It may also be possible to provide critical information and perspectives and questions at certain points in the dynamic process in order to influence the trajectory of the debate. Kennamer's (1992) model is useful in identifying the key players and the key connections. We shall use it to illustrate possible ways of responding to public opinion through the three main influences that shape and interpret that opinion.

If we hold the public to one side we see three main institutions or groupings which condition public attitude. These are: political decision-makers, the media and special interest groups. These three main institutions signal three main sites or forces that offer some prospect of leverage on the problem. Thinking strategically, it should be possible to work with two of these sites to counteract the negative influences of the third in misinforming or misleading the public.

There are several possible elements to any strategy intended to obstruct the perverse policy dynamics that can emerge when the general public is poorly informed, and we have identified the main ones elsewhere (Roberts et al., 2002). These include:

- setting up structural devices or institutions to serve as buffers between politicians and the judiciary;

- ensuring stricter political accountability for the costs of electorally attractive policies;

- mounting more effective challenge or rebuttal of policies whose surface plausibility is unsupported by research;

- achieving more effective promotion of policies that are supported by research evidence;

- providing a 'replacement discourse' – an alternative discussion that focuses on relevant goals such as the production of safety;

- providing the public with better information about crime and justice.

For the purposes of this chapter, however, we are concerned only with the final set of strategies – those intended to improve the quality of public knowledge and understanding about crime and penal policy.

Strategic provision of information

Providing information on crime and justice is obviously a more complex process than simply setting out 'the facts' and letting them speak for themselves. There is first the question of when and how information is presented. This concerns the context and the packaging. Then there is the question of the extent and nature of the information presented. There are usually more than two sides to every story, and any packaging of factual information involves a degree of selectivity. The media may be viewed as a central conveyer of public information. By virtue of this centrality, they can distort as much as they can inform – through the privileging of certain information and the depiction of crime and punishment in particular ways. The ways that the media depictions and selections can lead to distorted public perceptions of crime and punishment have been documented in detail in a number of works (e.g. Roberts and Doob, 1990; Iyengar, 1991; Roberts and Stalans, 1997; Surette, 1998; Oliver and Armstrong, 1998).[10] By ensuring relevant information is made accessible to the media, we may be able to generate a more informed debate on criminal justice policy. Zaller (1992), along with many other analysts of public opinion, is of little doubt that public opinion is indeed a product of '... elite-supplied information and leadership clues' (p. 311). Similarly Page and Shapiro (1992) argue for the underlying 'rationality' of public opinion but with the following important proviso:

To the extent that the public receives useful interpretations and correct and helpful information – information and interpretations that help it arrive at policy choices it would make if fully informed – the policy preferences it expresses can be considered 'authentic' ... Individuals or institutions that influence public opinion by providing correct, helpful political information can be said to educate the public.

Zaller notes that there are significant problems in determining what exactly is 'correct' and 'helpful', and it is fair to say the relationship between information, elite input and public opinion is highly vexed. What is clear, however, is that public attitudes towards penal issues are demonstrably malleable: people change their opinions in response to the level of factual information about the process that is available to them. Several chapters in this book have addressed this issue obliquely, and those by Hough and Park and by Mirrlees-Black have presented findings that offer direct confirmation: when people are given new information about crime and justice in experimental settings their attitudes shift demonstrably and durably. And in industrialised countries at least, it appears that when people are better informed about justice, their opinions tend to move towards the liberal pole of the continuum.

There is the potential for large-scale exercises to improve levels of information about crime and justice, and thus raise the quality of debate about penal policy. The findings reported by Hough and Park and by Mirrless-Black (this volume) provide some support for the value of such an exercise. There are two main ways in which this might be done: aiming to reach a broad audience indirectly – through the media – and directly targeting more narrowly defined audiences.

Indirect action: providing information to the media

To influence public opinion, the most fundamental strategy involves providing succinct, accessible information on crime to journalists. Encouraging journalists to access such information and explaining to them how such information can be useful to them is central to this strategy. Interest groups can also access this information for the promotion of alternative criminal justice responses. In providing information to the media it is crucial that such information is both timely and relevant. One systemic problem is that those with the ability and motivation to assemble properly evidenced information rarely work to the very tight time-lines of the media and politicians. One long-term strategy, therefore, may be to think in terms of building information resource centres, supported by international efforts, on matters to do with the efficacy of crime prevention and control efforts. Such information resource centres could also provide authoritative information on the nature and extent of our information on public opinion and knowledge on crime and punishment. Naturally such resource centres should provide information on-line and highly textured so that good information can be provided at the level and degree of detail required by the user.

There are other activities that may be initiated to counter media influences. These include actively critiquing assumptions and assertions in relation to public opinion. There is clearly inadequate knowledge of what precisely public opinion is, but media claims of representing public opinion can be powerful political forces if left unchallenged. The reason for this is the widespread belief that they reflect the public interest and the nature and extent of public opinion.[11] The media have the power to shape public opinion implicitly through the way crime is selected and depicted. What is depicted in the media reflects a decision on the part of editors that 'most people must be interested in this' or 'this will be relevant to the public'. The media, like politicians, have to make everyday decisions that are based on assessments of what will be popular. What is broadcast on the media therefore carries subtle suggestions regarding what the majority believes or supports. The media can therefore 'amplify' certain positions. Media and political uses of 'opinion polls' of doubtful validity further confound attempts to discern 'true' public opinion. Public opinion is largely forged and tested through a process of claim and counter-claim.

There is a range of specific actions that may reduce the distortions in public perceptions of crime and punishment. For example one of the most defensible of these would be to discourage police forces from providing video footage to television companies for the purpose of producing 'reality TV' programmes. Some authors have documented how access to this material tends to be at least implicitly conditional on portrayal of the police in a flattering light – regardless of the distortions done to public perceptions of crime (Doyle, 1998).

Some criminologists have advocated a more vigorous, informed and strategic approach in terms of getting relevant criminological knowledge into the media. For example, Barak (1994) calls for a 'newsmaking criminology' and Henry (1994) for efforts to provide the media with a 'replacement discourse'. Henry argues that 'A genuinely alternative, replacement discourse envelops not just crimes as popularly understood but harms that cause pain, regardless of whether these have been defined as criminal by the political process' (p. 314).

Henry (1994) also advocates many of the strategies outlined here, especially in disputing claims that appear in crime news. Reducing the legitimacy of news sources and questioning the validity of the data provide a major portal through which the stranglehold of media-based populism can be broken. Stories about crime and punishment can be reframed by criminologists prepared to do media work. Perspective and detail can be added along with pertinent comparative information. Occasionally the media themselves can be challenged. Public cynicism about the media is already quite high, as reflected in a spate of popular movies which reveal the way in which media coverage of events can be shallow, exploitative and self-serving.

Of course the media do not constitute a monolithic institution. There are systematic differences between the broadcast and print media, and within the latter, large differences exist between the tabloid and broadsheet press in most industrialised countries. Those that have an explicit obligation or self-defined mission to serve the 'public interest' will respond more warmly to attempts to raise the level of public debate than explicitly commercial ventures. At least regarding our countries (Australia and the United Kingdom) we remain highly pessimistic about the scope for persuading the tabloid press to place public interest above their news values, and cautiously optimistic about the room for progress in some other media constituencies.

Reaching subgroups of the public directly

As discussed, targeting the broadcast and print media is a potentially efficient way of reaching large numbers of people, but there are clear limits to what can be done. Important media sectors will have commercial or political reasons for withholding cooperation. So is there any scope for bypassing the media?

A few years ago, the only realistic conclusion would have been a negative one. Increasingly, however, *direct* access to significant groups of people is becoming a real possibility. The role of the Internet is critical here, of course, providing easy and free access to information to anyone with sufficient motivation or encouragement to seek it out.

The business of effectively communicating to the public clearly requires a much more sophisticated attempt than we have seen thus far to ensure that good quality information is effectively available. A strategy to achieve this is obviously a more complex undertaking than we would be able to overview here. However, this is likely to involve borrowing some private-sector marketing techniques that have already been used to good effect in other areas of social policy such as public health, safety and welfare. Any attempt to reach subgroups of the general population directly will involve several stages.

First some sort of analysis is needed to identify which are the key groups that need targeting – 'market segmentation' in marketing jargon. It is inevitable that some groups will be more *accessible* than others, that some groups will be more open to new sources of information than others, and that some groups will be more *important* to reach than others. For example, it might be a better investment to target teenagers who are cynical and misinformed about justice than their cynical and misinformed parents, and it is almost certainly better to do so than to target their grandparents. The reasons are that the teenage group are possibly more open to change, probably more accessible and certainly more significant 'consumers' of justice, both as victims and offenders, than their parents or grandparents. On the other hand this last group may have specific sorts of misperception about the nature of crime which also need addressing urgently.

Once key audiences have been identified and analysed, effective communication methods need to be specifically tailored for each group. While research, much of it described in this book, has identified the characteristics of those with least confidence in, and poorest knowledge about, justice, our knowledge about subgroups that are particularly open to change remains fairly patchy, as does knowledge about the most effective ways of securing this change. Clearly this is an area where further research investment is needed.

Modes of information provision

As much as the content of information the mode of information delivery may be relevant to the uptake of messages designed to influence public opinion on punishment. The new media provide great opportunity to propel forward strategic information to influence and inform the public and others on matters to do with crime and punishment. Information can be presented in an accessible and user-friendly way through the Internet while also allowing access to greater levels of detail if and when required. Websites allow the dissemination of information that would previously have been quite inaccessible to non-specialists. The Internet provides opportunities not only to make this information available but also prepares information in such a way that it is ready for uptake and active use by journalists, politicians and others. However, it is important to be realistic. Journalists will still prefer to rely on dialogue and interviews. The reliance on experts and the action of heated 'question and answer' sessions provides much of the staple fare of the journalists and for good reason.

Conveying the message persuasively

As penal policy has become increasingly politicised (cf. Roberts et al., 2002), it has become ever more important to attend not only to the substance of information about crime punishment but how this substance is conveyed. Those who wish to engender a better and more informed debate on the issues need to focus on the 'essential message' that they convey. This message is made up of an emotional component and an informational component. In constructing this message it becomes just as important how information is packaged and expressed as the actual informational content of the message. The appeal of simplified and tough-minded penal policy lies in its ability to resonate with public emotions such as fear and anger. Continuing to focus at the emotional level and venting moral indignation then directs attention away from the essential flaws of the policy. Those motivated to counter such tactics need to focus not simply on the information but how the essential message is constructed and communicated. The real battle is not over facts or details but over morals and emotions.

Freiberg (2000) emphasised this difference when he pointed out that we need to focus as much on 'affective' justice as 'effective' justice. Whether we like it or not it is often public emotions that define public debates and political initiative in the field of penal policy, not public information. Anyone who wants to improve public debate about crime needs to be attuned to this emotional dimension. For example, presenting information about crime will achieve little public uptake if it lacks a firm focus on a positive that is to be achieved (e.g. safety). It is in the business of posture and packaging that much of what academics potentially have to offer is lost. Rather than simply focusing at the informational level, something of the importance of the knowledge must also be conveyed. In other words, the benefits of rational, evidence-based penal policy have to be 'sold' to the public, not simply offered to them.

Sensing the emotional mood of the public is an essential skill for those groups – most obviously politicians, media editors and their journalists – whose livelihood depends directly upon public reactions. These actors know that their approach to crime must be emotionally 'correct' and resonate with the concern and urgency felt by the public. In the same way reformers speaking to the issue of crime and punishment must also convey a posture of active concern for the problem, followed by a plan for dealing with it. Such a posture communicates respect for the wishes and concerns of 'everyday' citizens. The plan for dealing with the problem should thus be 'action oriented' and ready for immediate implementation to reflect the urgency that this topic attracts.

Conclusion

In this chapter we have discussed some of the more direct ways that criminologists and others may act to enhance the quality of the debate around crime and punishment policy. This is obviously a large issue and highly related to our understanding of the problems with public knowledge and the ways in which such knowledge is distorted and shaped by the media. It is because of our understanding of how public attitudes can be influenced by the media, by special interest groups and by politicians themselves that we feel a need to advocate the creation of a 'circuit breaker'. Ultimately it is impossible to ensure that any institution remains free of political influence and ideology. We can, however, build in safeguards to ensure that the quality of the information provided on crime and punishment is adequate to guide public debate and policy properly. Creating a source of independent high-quality information and a capacity to evaluate the efficacy of crime policies, we believe, is the surest way to advance the quality of crime and justice policy.

Notes

1. We would like to thank Julian Roberts for helpful comments on an earlier draft.
2. The term penal populism has been adopted by a number of authors; we have defined and analysed the phenomenon in some detail in another book (Roberts et al., 2002).
3. This work has a long history dating back to the seminal work of Emile Durkheim whose perspective is reflected in many contemporary analyses (e.g. Tyler and Boeckmann, 1997). For a good collection see Schiengold (1997). Recently Scheingold articulated a new field of 'political criminology' (Scheingold, 1998) which is apposite to the present discussion as it approaches the politics of crime and punishment directly.
4. The particular role of the media in supporting penal populism has been documented in Roberts et al. (2002). Suffice to note here that the ways that the media can and do influence public opinion in favour of penal populism are many and varied. These include the exacerbation of public fears through the overuse of crime themes in TV news and TV drama.
5. Beckett (1997) and Beckett and Sasson (2000) provide examples of these.
6. Publicly funded broadcasting services are not at all protected from pressure to retain their audiences by virtue of their funding source.
7. Models such as the integrative conflict model of crime legislation and policy developed by Castellano and McGarrell (1991) examine the influence of factors from the distal to the proximal on crime policy. Between these two basic levels of influence is the dynamic and powerfully conditioning force of the media – framing not only reality to feed late modern anxieties but telling stories about how to think about the remedies to these anxieties and what political actors are doing or failing to do in 'making things better'.

8. Although 'old hands' at the game tend to see more clearly and quickly through media depictions to what may be real reflections of public sentiment and what may be various individuals, journalists or interest groups 'trying it on'.

9. Herbst (1998) in her study of US policy-makers argues that many policy-makers gain their views of public opinion from the media. Doppelt (1992) conducted a survey in the US which revealed that 30 per cent of the government officials surveyed said that news coverage had led to recent changes in the operations of their agencies (p. 125). Doppelt found that about a third of judges, court administrators, corrections officials and others in law enforcement believed that news coverage had led to substantive changes in the administration of justice.

10. It is fair to say that although there is some debate about whether it is the role of the media to provide information to the public on crime, the distorted knowledge and assumptions that the public has about crime and the efficacy of punishment is a function of media treatments of crime in greater or lesser degrees. This appears to be particularly the case at the tabloid/television end of the medium continuum and can be seen in dramatic form with the now documented effects of 'reality TV' (Oliver and Armstrong, 1998). This form of 'infotainment' which blurs the boundaries between news and entertainment still further has the potential to create serious deep-set mythologies about the nature of crime. This is because reality TV presents itself as providing a real and accurate portrayal of crime while in fact providing a highly selective set of images that reinforce the myth of action-oriented cops acting against 'bad' criminals.

11. Politicians are more sensitive to the selective power of the media to focus on certain issues and sometimes openly challenge media coverage as slanted towards a set agenda – be it from left-elitist journalists or a right-wing lobby group. This sensitisation appears to acknowledge the malleability of public opinion but also the limits of what can be achieved through media treatments. For example it would probably not matter how much focus was put on a certain crime problem to 'beat it up' if in the minds of most people it was a crime that was not relevant to them. Similarly stories on the inherent injustice of mandatory sentencing are unlikely to move the public if there is little underlying sympathy for the offenders affected.

References

Barak, G. (1994). 'Newsmaking criminology; reflections on the media, intellectuals and crime', in G. Barak (ed.), *Media, Process and the Social Construction of Crime: Studies in Newsmaking Criminology*. New York: Garland.

Beckett, K. (1997) *Making Crime Pay: Law and Order in Contemporary American Politics*. New York: Oxford University Press.

Beckett, K. and Sasson, T. (2000) *The Politics of Injustice: Crime and Punishment in America*. Thousand Oaks, CA: Pine Forge Press.

Castellano, T. and McGarell, E. (1991) 'Politics of law and order: case study evidence for a conflict model of the criminal law formation process', *Journal of Research in Crime and Delinquency*, 28: 304–29.

Doppelt, J. (1992) 'Marching to the police and court beats', in J. Kennamer (ed.), *Public Opinion, the Press and Public Policy*. Westport, CT: Praeger.

Doppelt, J. and Manikas, P. (1990) 'Mass media and criminal justice decision making', in J. R. Surrette (ed.), *Media and Criminal Justice Policy*. Springfield, IL: Charles C. Thomas.

Doyle, A. (1998) ' "Cops": television policing as policing reality', in M. Fishman and G. Cavender (eds), *Entertaining Crime – Television Reality Programs*. New York: Aldine De Gruyter.

Freiberg, A. (2001). 'Affective versus effective justice: instrumentalism and emotionalism in criminal justice', *Punishment and Society*, 3(2): 265–78.

Henry, S. (1994) 'Newsmaking criminology as replacement discourse', in G. Barak (ed.), *Media, Process and the Social Construction of Crime: Studies in Newsmaking Criminology*. New York: Garland.

Herbst, S. (1998) *Reading Public Oopinion*. Chicago: University of Chicago Press.

Hough, M. and Park, A. (2002) 'How malleable are attitudes to crime and punishment? Findings from a British deliberative poll' (chapter in this volume).

Iyengar, S. (1991) *Is Anyone Responsible? How Television Frames Political Issues*. Chicago: University of Chicago Press.

Kennamer, J. (1992) 'Public opinion, the press and public policy: an introduction', in J. Kennamer (Ed.), *Public Opinion, the Press and Public Policy*. Westport, CT: Praeger.

Lasorsa, D. (1992) 'Policy makers and the third person effect', in J. Kennamer (ed.), *Public Opinion, the Press and Public Policy*. Westport, CT: Praeger.

Mirrlees-Black, C. (2002) 'Improving public knowledge about crime and punishment'. (chapter in this volume).

Oliver, M. and Armstrong, G. (1998) 'The color of crime: perceptions of Caucasians' and African-Americans' involvement in crime', in M. Fishman and G. Cavender (eds), *Entertaining Crime – Television Reality Programs*. New York: Aldine De Gruyter.

Page, B. I. and Shapiro, R. Y. (1992) *The Rational Public*. Chicago: University of Chicago Press.

Roberts, J. and Doob, A. (1990) 'News media influences on public views on sentencing', *Law and Human Behaviour*, 14: 451–68.

Roberts, J. and Stalans, L. (1997) *Public Opinion, Crime, and Criminal Justice*. Boulder, CO: Westview Press.

Roberts, J., Stalans, L., Indermaur, D. and Hough, M. (2002) *Penal Populism and Public Opinion*. Oxford: Oxford University Press.

Rock, P. (1996) 'The opening stages of criminal justice policy making', *British Journal of Criminology*, 35: 1–16.

Scheingold, S. (ed.) (1997) *Politics, Crime Control and Culture*. Aldershot, VT: Ashgate.

Scheingold, S. (1998) 'Constructing the new political criminology: power, authority and the post liberal state', *Law and Social Inquiry*, 23: 857–95.

Surette, R. (1998) *Media, Crime and Criminal Justice: Images and Realities*, 2nd edn. Belmont, CA: Wadsworth.

Tyler, T. R. and Boeckmann, R. J. (1997) 'Three strikes and you are out, but why? The psychology of public support for punishing rule breakers', *Law and Society Review*, 31(2): 237–64.

Zaller, J. (1992) *The Nature and Origins of Mass Opinion*. Cambridge: Cambridge University Press.

Chapter 12

Privileging public attitudes to sentencing?

Rod Morgan

In response to international criticism of the treatment of Taliban and Al-Qaeda prisoners captured in Afghanistan and held at Guantanamo Bay, Cuba in January 2002, President Bush expressed the view that they were being treated no better than the American public thought they should be treated. We can set aside the question as to how precisely President Bush knew how the American public thought the prisoners should be treated: the point is that public opinion apparently legitimated the prisoners' conditions. The fact that the Guantanamo detainees had not yet been charged with, let alone convicted of, any criminal offence apparently counted for nothing. They were simply 'unlawful combatants'. The rights inscribed in the Geneva Conventions were said initially not to apply to them. The American people supported their President in his crusade against evil. The exercise being conducted at 'Camp X-ray' would extirpate the cancer of international terrorism, and the public approved. Period.

The Guantanamo scenario neatly conjures up one view of what the relationship is, or might be, between the severity of the state's response to crime and public opinion. Few commentators would argue that custodial conditions, or the nature of judicial punishment, should be determined by public opinion, not least on human rights grounds. Nevertheless, it is implicit in most discussions of criminal justice that a lack of confidence in and support for criminal justice arrangements and procedures, including the level of sanctions imposed by the courts, is a cause for concern. Congruence is desirable. If the public has confidence in the criminal justice system then at the various points where the system relies crucially on public co-operation, arrangements will work more smoothly and efficiently. Members of the public will be more likely to report crimes to the police, provide evidence against accused persons (thereby facilitating their prosecution), support the work of the courts and penal services as volunteers and act responsibly as jurors.

This desired conjunction begs a number of questions, however. Is the attainment of public confidence a paramount consideration? Or should the criminal justice system merely exhibit features that the public at large is likely to comprehend or support? Is public confidence in criminal justice policy determined by criminal justice policy? Or is it the product of more deep-seated features of contemporary life, over which criminal justice policy-makers and practitioners exert little or no control? Which institutions and processes mediate public opinion regarding criminal justice? Are the indices of public opinion on criminal justice issues sufficiently consensual, well informed and precise that one can base policies upon them? What scope, in other words, do criminal justice policy-makers have to enhance public confidence in criminal justice?

These are some of the questions addressed in this chapter and elsewhere in this volume. The issues are relatively universal. It may not be too parochial, therefore, if I illustrate some of the different ways in which they are capable of being dealt with by referring to two recent major English reports on criminal justice – the Halliday Report, *Making Punishments Work: A Review of the Sentencing Framework for England and Wales* (Home Office, 2001a) and the Auld Report on the *Review of the Criminal Courts of England and Wales* (Auld, 2001).

Halliday and Auld: two stances regarding public opinion

Both the Halliday and Auld reports are set against the backcloth of the British government's plan for criminal justice grounded on seven *aims*, two of which – 'Aim 2, Delivery of justice through effective and efficient investigation, prosecution, trial and sentencing, and through support for victims', and 'Aim 4, Effective execution of the sentences of the courts so as to reduce reoffending and protect the public' – are linked to an *objective*: to 'Increase public confidence in the criminal justice system' (Home Office, 2001b).

John Halliday regarded raising public confidence in criminal justice as one of the core aims of his review of sentencing. The introduction to his report states that the framework recommended should increase the contribution which sentencing makes to crime reduction *and* public confidence (Home Office, 2001a: 1). This is important because if the public have confidence in the outcome of sentencing then they can:

legitimately be expected to uphold and observe the law, and not take it into their own hands ... there must be confidence in the justice of the outcomes, as well as in their effectiveness. Achieving a satisfactory level of public confidence is therefore an important goal of sentencing, and the framework for sentencing needs to support that goal. (*Ibid.*: para. 1.3)

The Halliday report does not consider the raising of public confidence to be straightforward, however. The Review commissioned a survey of public opinion that showed that levels of public confidence in the adequacy of punishment and awareness of the actual levels of punishment are low (*ibid.*: para. 1.59). There is some evidence that 'fear of crime may promote desires for more punitive sentencing' (*ibid*: para. 1.60). It follows that efforts to raise public confidence in sentencing should not necessarily be focused only on sentencing practice and 'in any event, levels of punishment must be subject to some limits, based on principles of justice'. Further, there are wide differences of opinion about sentencing. The Halliday report therefore concludes that:

The available information does not suggest that the framework should be changed in order to produce different levels of punishment, in order to increase public confidence, as an end in itself. (*Ibid.*: para. 1.61)

So, for Halliday, public opinion is important both as an inspiration and an outcome. But it is not paramount. It is a factor to be taken into account. In relation to sentencing policy it is neither the straightforward product of what the courts do nor should it be allowed to determine future policy (see Roberts, 2002, for discussion).

Sir Robin Auld, a senior judge commissioned to undertake a broad review of the criminal courts, makes reference in his report to several of the same aspects of public opinion, but he draws rather different conclusions. He is generally impatient with government managerial statements of purpose, finding them to be either repetitive or banal. And he is magisterially dismissive about public opinion on the grounds that people are mostly ignorant or inconsistent in their views. Thus Auld notes that one of the current government's criminal justice *aims* is that the courts should dispense 'justice fairly and efficiently and promote confidence in the law'. He further notes that this *aim* is allegedly particularised – but in fact repeated – in the *objective* 'to promote confidence in the criminal justice system'. He is sceptical about the vogue for such generalised statements. He thinks that 'different priorities apply in different contexts and circumstances' (Foreword, para. 10).

Moreover, he doubts that 'we should ... expect too much of the criminal justice system, the courts in particular, as a medium for curing the ills of society' (*ibid.*: para. 9). Public opinion is 'elusive'. The 'community at large' is not consensual. Offenders are likely to feel hard done by, and victims are likely to feel that they have been treated indifferently or insensitively. Some people will feel that the system has been too lenient while others will believe that the rights of accused individuals have been trampled. Moreover, many people are ill-informed about criminal justice arrangements and decisions, not least because 'there is a tendency in much of the media to misunderstand and to misreport what happens in court' (*ibid.*: para. 31).

> Public confidence is thus, and is likely to remain, an imprecise tool for determining how well a criminal justice system is performing and what needs to be done to improve it. Public confidence is not so much an aim of a good criminal justice system; but a consequence of it. (*Ibid.*: para. 32)

Auld agrees that public confidence in the working of the criminal courts is desirable. But he does not consider that expressions of public opinion could be the foundation on which to build that confidence. It could not, nor should it be, a major determinant in shaping policy.

> Public confidence is not an end in itself; it is or should be an outcome of a fair and efficient system. The proper approach is to make the system fair and efficient and, if public ignorance stands in the way of public confidence, take steps adequately to demonstrate to the public that it is so. (*Ibid.*: chapter 4, para. 32)

Auld and Halliday: post mortem

As far as the practical policy implications are concerned, there may not be a huge gulf between the stances which Halliday and Auld take. We know very little about the basis of public confidence and the dynamics of changes in its level. It is foolhardy, therefore, to make unwarranted assumptions about what will change it. Thus, for example, there are no real grounds in the Halliday Report to support the statement in the foreword to the government's response to Halliday that:

Changes in direction and philosophy and layer upon layer of legislation [regarding the aims of sentencing] had left the aims and the practice of sentencing indistinct and confusing, resulting in a loss of public confidence in the entire criminal justice system. (Home Office, 2002: 2)

Indeed, it is precisely because the basis of public confidence is multifaceted and uncertain that the Halliday consultation document subsequently concludes that rebuilding public confidence is a complex issue 'likely to take a great deal of time and energy' (*ibid.*: 4). Even if it is true that 'The current climate of constant change is damaging to consistency of approach, transparency of process, and public confidence' (the view of the Council of Circuit Judges reported at *ibid.*: 6) this suggests that further extensive legislative changes of the sort recommended by Halliday to ensure that 'supervision in the community . . . [is a] demanding and challenging part of the total sentence' (*ibid.*: 2) is scarcely likely to have the desired outcome. Indeed, as one academic commentator cautioned the consultation team, there is 'no justification that sentencing reforms could affect public opinion' (*ibid.*: 7).

It may be true that 'much of the public's dissatisfaction arises from the way in which the criminal justice system actually does work' (CJCC, 2002) but the criminal justice system covers a good deal more than sentencing, including, arguably, features of the system (the prevalence of crime, visible police presence, police response, the crime clear-up rate, for example) of which the public are almost certainly more directly aware.

Nevertheless, it is dangerously arrogant to suggest, as Auld does (chapter 4), that because public opinion data are seldom so well drawn that they *could* be used to *determine* policy (he cites research by Morgan and Russell (2000) demonstrating that the majority of people are unaware of the different types of magistrates and of procedures in magistrates' courts), that the evidence should be ignored. Auld takes the view that commentators (he cites Morgan and Russell (2000) and Sanders (2001) who collected data demonstrating relatively high levels of public ignorance and confusion, and who then suggested that those data should *inform* the choices made), were being illogical or irrational. This is surely a philosophical error and a policy-making mistake.

There are a good many public policy issues about which most citizens have only a dim idea as to the facts – the likely implications of the UK adopting the Euro, the cost benefits of constructing a major dam, or the possible causes of and solutions to global warming, for example. But that does not mean that most people will not rapidly form a view of what is important or what should be done when matters are explained, or that their views should not be taken into account. Were public knowledge the necessary precondition for political participation, the case for democracy would be difficult to sustain. There is no reason why most people should be closely conversant with the facts of many public policy arrangements most of the time: but this is no reason for not consulting them about changes which, ultimately, are likely, in some degree, to affect every household.

It is the essence of participatory democratic theory that giving people the opportunity to participate in decision-making beyond the vote in periodic elections enhances their capacity for responsible citizenship (Pateman, 1970). The data collected by Morgan and Russell demonstrated widespread public ignorance and confusion about criminal procedure. It follows that their survey did not, as most surveys do not, provide clear, unambiguous indications of what policies will command public support. But their methodology and data revealed that the public, when matters are explained to them, do have views about which court procedures are appropriate for different categories of cases (Morgan and Russell, 2000: chapter 4). As a result, the authors drew attention to *some* of the values to which people subscribe and suggested that these indicated the possible *limits* of public support and tolerance to change. Good public surveys do exactly that.

To conclude, as Auld does, that a degree of public ignorance provides judges and politicians with a free hand to make policies that *they* deem to be fair and efficient, policies that can then be sold to the public, is to misunderstand what counts as *criminal justice*. Entry to the criminal justice *system*, it needs to be remembered, is an option, and most *potential* criminal justice transactions are dealt with, or not dealt with as the case may be, *outside* the system. It is vital, therefore, that the system be *informed* by what the public thinks.

Auld is nevertheless correct, however, that the system has an obligation to *inform* the public. It is sensible to think of confidence building in the criminal justice system across the board, as the Criminal Justice Consultative Council (CJCC) in England and Wales apparently is thinking. On the grounds that some of the existing lack of public confidence arises from 'poor knowledge and misperceptions' the CJCC is first pursuing initiatives designed to disseminate information. These include: distributing criminal justice system factsheets and booklets, opening up the system for public visits and Internet-based information (CJCC, 2002; see also Home Office, 2000, for a discussion as to how this might be done).

Some general propositions

The above conclusions are not dissimilar to those reached by several of the other contributors to this volume. They lead, I would suggest, to the following general propositions.

1. Public attitudes are complex and multidimensional in nature

First, although most policy-makers will despair at the suggestion that public knowledge and opinion regarding criminal justice be further researched, it remains the case that our knowledge of public attitude formation regarding criminal justice remains relatively superficial. As Loretta Stalans emphasises in her chapter, members of the public simultaneously hold attitudes that are selectively punitive *and* merciful. Attitudes are kaleidoscopic in nature and movement. People's views are shaped by both their personal experience (and the experiences of their close acquaintances) *and* the mass media. We are all 'creative story editors' regarding crime and justice. This insight should inform the media strategies developed by the criminal justice agencies. For the agencies also have stories to tell in a creative fashion if they are to succeed in persuading the public to support strategies whose appeal is not intuitively obvious. There is little evidence, for example, that the public particularly wants *tough* probation services: they want *effective* ones – services which deliver non-custodial interventions which effectively reduce the likelihood that the offenders subject to their ministrations will reoffend and revictimise.

Data collected by Russell and Morgan for the Home Office Sentencing Review (Russell and Morgan, 2001a), for example, showed that the most common responses by members of the public to the open-ended question: 'What should sentencing achieve?' do not include the words 'punish', 'deterrence' or 'rehabilitation', terms generally taken to summarise the objective of punishment. The most common responses are 'stop reoffending', 'reduce crime' or create a 'safer community', without any articulation as to how sentencing might achieve this outcome. People are generally not wedded to a particular philosophy of punishment, they just want something done which changes offenders' behaviour. This conclusion is confirmed when respondents are directly asked to choose between various sentencing objectives. The greatest number of people select the generalised 'Change the behaviour/attitudes of an offender to prevent them reoffending' in preference to 'punish', 'restrict opportunities to reoffend' or 'scare them so they will not do it again' (Russell and Morgan, 2001a: 29).

It is doubtful, therefore, whether simply attaching more punitive labels to court orders achieves very much – in England and Wales, for example, *community service orders* have recently been renamed (following the Criminal Justice and Court Services Act 2000) *community punishment* orders. Such marketing devices are more likely to confuse than convince (HMIP, 2002: pp. 6–7). If misinformation about criminal justice is to be corrected we need to know more about how members of the public *read* the *accounts* of criminal justice they receive. That is, we need to know more about people's underlying values and attitudes.

2. Don't assume that sentencers are aware of the nature of public attitudes

We should not assume that because judges are well educated and that other criminal justice practitioners, such as probation service staff, are mostly graduates with additional professional training, that they are therefore well informed about what we *do* know about public opinion and sentencing. They are susceptible to being influenced by the results of simplistic mass media *vox populi* surveys and sensationalist crime accounts. Even if they are not themselves persuaded by such accounts, they tend to believe there is a general lack of public confidence in the system and low public tolerance of alternative policies. This perception closes off the sentencing and policy options regarded as reasonable.

My experience since becoming the Chief Inspector of the Probation Service for England and Wales, for example, suggests that probation staff are generally *not* aware of the well-established findings, repeatedly confirmed by successive sweeps of the British Crime Survey and other research. My impression (and it is no more than that) is that whereas they perceive the majority of the public to be somewhat punitive in the sense that they believe sentencers to be too lenient – which is empirically well evidenced – they do not appreciate that most people: greatly underestimate the severity of sentences which the courts actually impose, and, when given specific sentencing scenarios to decide, favour decisions very similar to those actually made by the courts, with significant minorities favouring more lenient outcomes (Hough and Roberts, 1998; Mattinson and Mirrlees-Black, 2000).

Russell and Morgan (2001a) have recently confirmed these findings in a public opinion study on the sentencing of domestic burglary undertaken for the Sentencing Advisory Panel for England and Wales. In response to four sentencing scenarios, between one half and three-quarters of respondents favoured a less severe sentence than had actually been imposed by the courts. This occurred despite the fact that most respondents had earlier said that in their view the courts were too lenient, believing, mistakenly, that the courts impose more lenient sentences than is in fact the case. It is true that most respondents were more easily able to recognise factors aggravating the crime (e.g. the use of force, the infliction of injury, etc.) than factors in mitigation (e.g. absence of previous convictions, the presence of mental disorder). However, respondents' general views on sentencing also involved media-based assumptions of what *typical* burglaries involve – namely, damage and the loss of sentimentally important or valuable items. Thus, when faced with actual cases in which some or all of these features were absent, they were willing to depart from their tariff assumption that the offence of burglary should normally result in imprisonment. Moreover, they remained willing to consider non-custodial sanctions when mitigating factors were present in serious cases.

If I am correct that criminal justice practitioners are largely unaware of these detailed public opinion research findings, we should not be surprised. It would confirm what previous research on sentencer knowledge and perceptions has found (see Roberts, 1992). This suggests that there is as much need to educate criminal justice practitioners about public opinion as there is to educate the public about criminal justice practice.

3. Sentencers need educating about the range and complexity of community sentences

If it is true that the public want a more effective rather than a tougher penal system, then in addition to educating the judiciary to that effect, it is also vital that they be well informed about 'what works' – and I use that phrase in its general, evidence-based sense rather than in the narrow 'What Works' sense by which *particular* intervention programmes for offenders, generally cognitive-behavioural group programmes, have come to be known in the UK. In most jurisdictions, the number of non-custodial sanctions available to the courts is increasing. In addition to traditional financial, supervision and community service options, electronic monitoring or surveillance provisions are being added as well as conditional drug treatment and testing orders. Increasing the range and complexity of community-based penalties makes it imperative that sentencers understand their operational implications – what do they mean in practice relative to the domestic circumstances of the offenders for whom they are proposed and the risks of future offending, and how cost-effective are they relative to other penalties? The evidence suggests that sentencing options that work and are cost-effective command more public support than most sentencers appreciate. It follows that if, for example, the 'What Works' offending behaviour programmes are capable of delivering reduced risk of harm and reoffending outcomes, and the provisional evidence suggests that they are, then it is on sentencers that our educative firepower needs most to be concentrated.

A word of caution is necessary here, however. In England and Wales, the likely benefits of the 'What Works' accredited offending behaviour programmes have almost certainly been over-sold within those criminal justice agency circles in which they have been developed. It is one thing to measure outcomes for programmes precisely targeted at those offenders for whom they will optimally work, and which are delivered in ideal circumstances by well-trained, committed staff. It is quite another generally to roll out programmes where none of these conditions precisely apply. The benefits derived under these circumstances are likely to be much more marginal.

4. The relative cost of sanctions is an important consideration, but not a good selling point

For the same reasons as outlined above, some caution should also be exercised about the deployment of cost-based arguments regarding punishments. Sentencers and the public should certainly be informed about the direct costs of different penalties, not least because the evidence from the work carried out for the Halliday Review suggests that most people greatly underestimate the direct costs of imprisonment (Russell and Morgan, 2001a). But it is doubtful whether penalties should be *promoted* on cost grounds. Contrary to the rhetorical flourishes deployed by some commentators (see, for example, Mansfield and Wardle, 1993), a price always is and has to be put on justice (more elaborate and costly trial procedures are always reserved for offences for which imprisonment is the likely penalty, and 'law and order' services have to compete for government expenditure with other vital public services such as education and health), but arguments for penalties based on their lower direct costs run the risk of backfiring. Such arguments can easily be turned around and made to appear cynical regarding justice and public safety considerations, even if they are not.

5. Advancing community penalties requires a proactive media strategy

The criminal justice agencies and reform pressure groups need to develop proactive educational and media strategies. Julian Roberts et al. (2002) have usefully distinguished *disreputable* penal populism from mere penal populism (Bottoms, 1995). Human rights and utilitarian arguments need to be deployed against punitive posturing that is not popular and/or responsive. Of course such arguments also need to be deployed against those who hold *sincerely* held punitive views. But responsively popular policies at least enjoy democratic legitimacy and must therefore be challenged with that foundation in mind. However, those politicians and newspaper editors who promulgate punitive criminal justice views with wilful disregard of the evidence because, cynically, they hope to gain electoral or commercial advantage by so doing, have to be confronted and made to justify their postures. Such individuals, as David Indermaur and Mike Hough argue in their chapter here, need to be shamed and held accountable.

This battle for public hearts and minds will best be won if the alternatives to popularly punitive policies are capable of being seen to be credible and effective: that is, if they take appropriate symbolic form – the great merit of community service, for example, is that in Britain at least the evidence suggests the penalty is widely understood and its rationale appreciated (Tarling and Dowds, 1997) – and are independently evaluated so that the evidence of effectiveness comes from sources able to resist accusations of vested interest and special pleading. The endorsement of alternatives to custody by such prestigious bodies as independent sentencing commissions is an additional bonus.

6. Public ignorance of criminal justice is unsurprising and unlikely to change

We should not expect the public to be that well informed about criminal justice, a system with which most people have only occasional and partial contact – usually extending to little more than reporting an offence to the police. When the public do report being the victim of crime, the likelihood (for most high frequency crimes) of the crime being cleared up or, even if cleared up, their learning about what happened to 'their' offender is low. These realities are not likely to change in the foreseeable future. The introduction of victim informational and support schemes – victim statements at sentencing, for example – will increase public knowledge only marginally.

7. Increasing public knowledge may not always increase public confidence

We should be cautious in our expectations as to the likely confidence-raising benefits from generally disseminating information about the criminal justice system – although different degrees of optimism and pessimism are expressed on this issue by contributors to this volume.

It is true that those persons who currently know most about the criminal justice system also have the greatest confidence in it (Hough and Roberts, 1998; Russell and Morgan, 2001b). But it does not follow that improving the knowledge of those who currently know least will result in them having the same levels of confidence as those who currently know most.

Those who currently know the most about criminal justice tend to be the better-educated and more affluent respondents living in low-crime neighbourhoods and who have more positive attitudes regarding the benefits of authority. Were those sections of the population most at risk of crime better informed about such criminal justice system aspects as the low clear-up rate for recorded crime and the low likelihood of offenders being convicted, it is at least possible that they would be even more disenchanted with the criminal justice system than they already are. Further, to the extent that low confidence in the criminal justice system has very much to do with the performance of the criminal justice system at all, it seems likely that it is related to the general risk of victimisation and that that specific risk is reflective of the ontological uncertainties characteristic of the postmodern world (Bottoms, 1995). That is, the criminal justice system probably acts as a lightning rod for more general anxieties.

Conclusion

More than two decades of increasing party politicisation of law and order policies in the USA and UK (Beckett, 1997; Downes and Morgan, 1997, 2002) has damagingly induced a climate of some pessimism among criminal justice practitioners that penal populism has developed a competitively punitive momentum, self-sustaining, corrosive of human trust and extremely difficult to reverse. There are signs, however, that the trajectory of penal policy may now be changing. Judith Greene suggested, in her contribution to the conference that gave rise to this volume, that the dismal cycle so incisively analysed by Beckett of politicians 'strip mining' 'hot button' public criminal justice concerns, thereby heightening those anxieties, appears now to be waning. The 'public is starting to get it'. The penal fiscal crisis is beginning to bite. The proportion of the public calling for punitive policies is falling.

The germs of penal realism can be seen in the UK also. Since their emasculation in the 2002 General Election, the Conservative Party, who originally led the charge attributing rising crime to their political opponents (Downes and Morgan, 1997: 89–99) have shown signs of wishing to overtake the Labour government on the left. It was leading members of the Conservative Party who first opened up the debate that a uniformly prohibitionist drugs policy was not working and was possibly a mistake. This lead was subsequently followed by the incoming Home Secretary, David Blunkett, shortly after Labour's election victory. The Conservatives are also promulgating a more communitarian policing approach, with primary crime prevention overtones, than hitherto. And in response the Home Secretary has expressed anxiety about the dramatically rising prison population (at the time of writing, above 70,000 – a 70 per cent increase on what it was a little over ten years ago), a trend he wishes to arrest and ideally reverse (Downes and Morgan, 2002).

It is no rhetoric to suggest, therefore, that the reductionist programme which clearly underlies the various informational and educational proposals discussed by others in this volume possibly have a greater chance of being implemented and bearing fruit today than for many a year.

References

Auld Report (2001) *Report of the Review of the Criminal Courts of England and Wales*. London: Her Majesty's Stationery Office.

Beckett, K. (1997) *Making Crime Pay: Law and Order in Contemporary American Politics*. New York: Oxford University Press.

Bottoms, A. E. (1995) 'The philosophy and politics of punishment and sentencing', in C. Clarkson and R. Morgan (eds), *The Politics of Sentencing Reform*. Oxford: Oxford University Press.

Criminal Justice Consultative Council (2002) *Newsletter 26*. London: CJCC.

Downes D., and Morgan R. (1997) 'Dumping the "hostages to fortune"? The politics of law and order in post-war Britain', in M. Maguire, R. Morgan and R. Reiner (eds), *The Oxford Handbook of Criminology*. Oxford: Oxford University Press.

Downes, D. and Morgan, R. (2002) 'The skeletons in the cupboard: the politics of law and order at the turn of the millenium', in M. Maguire, R. Morgan and R. Reiner (eds), *The Oxford Handbook of Criminology*. Oxford: Oxford University Press.

HMIP (Her Majesty's Inspectorate of Probation for England and Wales) (2002) *Annual Report April 2001–March 2002*. London: Home Office.

Home Office (2000) *Promoting Confidence in the Criminal Justice System*. London: Home Office, Crime and Criminal Justice Unit.

Home Office (The Halliday Report) (2001a) *Making Punishments Work: A Review of the Sentencing Framework*. London: Home Office.

Home Office (2001b) *Annual Report 2001–2*, Cm 5106. London: Home Office.

Home Office (2002) *Making Punishments Work – Response to Consultation: Overview*, London: Home Office.

Hough, M. and Roberts, J. V. (1998) *Attitudes to Punishment: Findings from the British Crime Survey*, Home Office Research Study No. 179. London: Home Office.

Mansfield, M. and Wardle, T. (1993) *Presumed Guilty: the British Legal System Exposed*. London: Heinemann.

Mattinson, J. and Mirrlees-Black, C. (2000) *Attitudes to Crime and Criminal Justice. Findings from the 1998 British Crime Survey*. Home Office Research Study No. 200. London: Home Office.

Morgan, R. and Russell, N. (2000) *The Judiciary in the Magistrates' Courts*. London: Home Office/LCD.

Pateman, C. (1970) *Participation and Democratic Theory*. Cambridge: Cambridge University Press.

Roberts, J. V. (1992) 'Public opinion, crime and criminal justice', in M. Tonry (ed.), *Crime and Criminal Justice: A Review of Research*, Vol. 16. Chicago: Chicago University Press.

Roberts, J. V. (2002) *Public Opinion and Sentencing Policy'*, in S. Rex and M. Tonry (eds), *Reform and Punishment: The Future of Sentencing*. Cullompton: Willan Publishing.

Roberts, J. V., Stalans, L. S., Indermaur, D. and Hough, M. (2002) *Penal Populism and Public Opinion. Findings from Five Countries*. New York: Oxford University Press.

Russell, N. and Morgan, R. (2001a) *The Influence of Knowledge on Public Attitudes to the Criminal Justice System and Sentencing*, paper prepared for the Home Office Sentencing Review. London: Home Office.

Russell, N. and Morgan, R. (2001b) *Sentencing of Domestic Burglary: Research Report 1*. London: Sentencing Advisory Panel.

Sanders, A. (2001) *Community Justice*. London: Institute of Public Policy Research.

Tarling, R. and Dowds, L. (1997) 'Crime and punishment', in R. Jowell, J. Curtice, A. Park, L. Brook, K. Thomson and C. Bryson (eds), *British Social Attitudes: the 14th Report*. Aldershot: Ashgate.

Index